REBELS AND THEIR CAUSES

Rebels and Their Causes

ESSAYS IN HONOUR OF A. L. MORTON

edited by Maurice Cornforth

LAWRENCE AND WISHART
London

Lawrence and Wishart Ltd
39 Museum Street
London WC1A 1LQ

First published 1978
Copyright © Lawrence and Wishart, 1978

Printed and bound in Great Britain at
The Camelot Press Ltd, Southampton

CONTENTS

A. L. MORTON – PORTRAIT OF A MARXIST HISTORIAN

MAURICE CORNFORTH

This book of historical and literary essays has been prepared by colleagues, friends and admirers of Arthur Leslie Morton, Communist and Marxist historian, who celebrated his seventy-fifth birthday in the summer of 1978. Every colleague of A. L. Morton is a friend, and every friend of his an admirer. Some of those who have written here are associates from the pioneering times of the thirties, some are younger and have followed up since then. There is no British Marxist today, young or old, who does not owe a debt to Leslie Morton's work. For it was he who compiled that brilliant survey of the history of the British people from pre-Roman times to the present which provides a synthesis of background information for any Marxist study of social, economic and ideological developments in this country – *A People's History of England*. It was a contribution to British Marxism of a unique and immensely useful kind, whether in the ease, clarity and readability of its style, or in the sheer scope of its content combined with the thoroughness and penetration of its analysis.

Leslie Morton comes from farming stock. He was born at Stanchils Farm, Hengrave, near Bury St Edmunds, Suffolk, on American Independence Day, 4 July 1903. His father, Arthur Spence Morton, a Yorkshireman, had rented the farm a year previously, after his marriage to Mary Hannah Lampray. He was in a true sense a 'working' farmer – there was no job on the farm of which he was not master down to the last detail. Leslie was the elder of two sons; his brother, Max, later took over the farming business (on another farm by that time) when their father retired and Leslie himself disclaimed any ambitions to take on the management. Max Morton, like Leslie Morton, was to become an active member of the Communist Party. A sister, Kathleen, came between the two boys.

Leslie went to school at nine years of age, at the King Edward

VI Grammar School at Bury St Edmunds. Prior to that he had been under the tuition of a series of governesses – of whom his memories are not favourable. Released from their care, he cycled daily the four miles to Bury St Edmunds and then back again. He remained at the Grammar School until he was fifteen – at which age he was packed off to a minor public school, Eastbourne College. This establishment he liked even less than the governesses.

In 1921 he entered Cambridge University, an undergraduate at Peterhouse. Here for his first two years he took Part One of the History Tripos, and in his third year what was then called 'Part A', English. His left-wing political activities began when he joined the University Labour Club – along with two others who afterwards became prominent Communists, Allen Hutt and Ivor Montagu.

At that time, the immediate post-war years of the early twenties, intellectuals who felt concern about society and politics had to stand up and be counted as to whether they were for or against the Russian Revolution, for or against the strike demands, particularly of railwaymen and miners, and for or against taking industries into national ownership and starting up measures to relieve poverty and unemployment, and for a more equal distribution of wealth. Leslie found himself in the Labour Club among those who were 'for' – a very small minority in the University. At the same time, left-wing ideas were then associated and mixed up with protests against social conventions, respectabilities and inhibitions which the war (though as a farmer's son at Bury St Edmunds it had largely passed Leslie by) had done much to bring to a head, and which for free-thinking intellectuals were enshrined in new literary and artistic movements. In the twenties, the situation among the intellectual left, at Cambridge in particular, was different from, though the progenitor of, that which developed among the later generations of the thirties, after the great economic slump had set in and, still more, after the rise of fascism in Europe. For earnest discussion the left students of the thirties began to substitute direct action – student demonstrations and the like. The literary movements which had counted for so much seemed beside the point, if not outright reactionary.

It was, then, in the left intellectual climate of the twenties that Leslie began to take an interest in politics at Cambridge. With many there was always a distinct element of anti-parental revolt in all this. But such was not the case with Leslie, whose father, though conservative in his views, was far from being a rigid Tory. He recalls particularly his father once telling him that during Lloyd George's campaign against the House of Lords in 1910 he had looked up the history of that institution in J. R. Green's *Short History* and come to the conclusion that there was little to be said in its favour.

Leslie's career at Cambridge was fairly uneventful. On going down, he got a job as a teacher (not of any particular subject but of any subject required) at Steyning Grammar School in Sussex. A colleague there was Charlie Easton, who later was in charge of the Communist Party bookshop in Sheffield. Here, too, Leslie was in touch with a local poet, Victor Neuburg – who had an influence on the development of his ideas at that time. Neuburg was then running a little private printing press. Later, he was in charge of the 'poetry corner' of the *Sunday Referee* – and when, later, Leslie was unemployed in London he sometimes lent him a hand. He recalls that Neuburg had a vast pile of submitted manuscripts, including poems by Dylan Thomas, who said that he was dying and implored that they be published soon.

In 1926, as Leslie expresses it, 'the school had a shock'. For most of the staff declared themselves in favour of the General Strike and put theory into practice by consorting with the local railwaymen. The School Governors were far from pleased – and this led to Leslie's being out of work a year later. He was first advised to look for another job, and then his job was declared redundant.

In this emergency he took refuge with his parents, who had by then moved to Ipswich. And here he happened to see an advertisement in the *New Stateman and Nation* from A. S. Neill, who wanted a teacher at his progressive school, Summerhill, at Leiston near the Suffolk coast. Leslie applied and, living so near, was the first interviewed and got the job. Thus began a long though intermittent association with Summerhill. This private school was run on very 'free' principles – expounded by Neill in numerous books. That it was so successful was due not only to the principles, but to the personality of Neill. To a casual visitor (such as the author of this sketch, who later went there several times to see Leslie and others) it at first presented a scene of chaos; but one soon realised that under the system of pupils' 'self-government', with Neill as a kind of non-elected President, everything was in good order. Many of Neill's pupils attained distinction in various walks of life.

Leslie taught at Summerhill for one year, during which he married his first wife, Bronwen Jones, a fellow-teacher who had been with Neill for some time – Neill had begun in Austria, and Bronwen Jones had helped him establish Summerhill in England. Bronwen already had a son at that time (now a professor of Mathematics and Computer Science). At the end of the year she and Leslie moved to London, where they lived a rather unsettled existence. 'We bummed around,' as Leslie now describes it. At one time Bronwen worked for Arcos (the Soviet trade organisation, earlier the victim of the notorious 'Arcos Raid'), and Leslie kept a second-hand bookshop near Finsbury Park.

The chief point of the move to London emerges in the fact that Leslie immediately joined the Communist Party – something which it was then hardly possible to do in Leiston, a very small town centred around an agricultural machinery factory in the depths of the countryside. His first Party card was issued on 1 January 1929 – he had in fact joined shortly before but, for administrative reasons, waited until the New Year to get a membership card. He had been a regular reader of the *Sunday Worker* from its start in 1925, and was a regular reader of the *Daily Worker* from its first issue.

He joined the Communist Party 'local' in Islington – those were the days when Branches were called 'Locals', divided into 'Cells' and organised by the LPC (Local Party Committee) under the rather august DPC (District Party Committee). At that time, indeed, everything went by initials – for example, the LPC would seek guidance from the DPC on tactics in the LAI and WIR (League Against Imperialism and Workers' International Relief) and, of course, in the NUWM (National Unemployed Workers' Movement). The Local met in Bride Street, off Liverpool Road, in what Leslie now describes as 'a shed, hovel or slum'. The CP has made considerable progress since then.

In 1934 Leslie was taken onto the staff of the *Daily Worker*. He began by being made the Proprietor – a job of some risk, since the Proprietor was then the one who went to prison in event of trouble. This nearly happened to Leslie when William Joyce (later 'Lord Haw Haw') brought a case against the paper for 'incitement to violence' in connection with Mosley's fascist rally in Hyde Park. Leslie recollects William Gallacher telling him as he went into Court, 'Ye're not to let yoursel' to be bound over.' However, the *Worker* won the case, and Leslie was one of the few early proprietors not to land up in gaol. Besides being out on a limb as Proprietor, Leslie worked as a reporter, sub-editor, feature writer and, on occasion, as layout man and on helping to put the paper 'to bed'. The editor was then William Rust, in association with J. R. Campbell. Later, R. Palme Dutt and Idris Cox took their place (there were then always virtually a pair of editors, like the Roman Consuls or Spartan Kings). The editorial office was in Tabernacle Street, near Bunhill Fields, City Road, and the printing plant nearby in Worship Street. Little boys were busily employed rushing to and fro with copy and proofs. Among others on the staff were Allen Hutt and Walter Holmes and, slightly later, Claud Cockburn (Frank Pitcairn) and Ralph Fox. Of all the old *Daily Worker* staff, Leslie himself is now one of the very few survivors.

In 1934, too, Leslie had an opportunity to renew old associations with East Anglia. He went as *Daily Worker* correspondent on the Norwich and Norfolk contingent of the 1934 Hunger March. Though a grim business of the fight against semi-starvation, it gave those on the Norwich contingent, as Leslie puts it, 'the time of our lives'. For one thing, it was music all the way – and it was on this march that Leslie began to know the many East Anglian folk songs ('Bungay Roger' and many others) with which he was afterwards often to entertain his acquaintance (later, he helped with a BBC recording of some of the more polite of these songs). Besides, to encourage them on the march there was a comrade with a mouth-organ – who kept them in step as far as Ilford, but there was taken to hospital with a swollen face. The doctors could not make out what was the matter with him until they learned of his zestful employment (he made a quick recovery after a brief rest). On his first appearance on the streets of Norwich, before going to the March Preparations Committee at the Keir Hardie Hall (the ILP headquarters), Leslie was spotted by a suspicious character who hastened to the ILP with the news that '16 King Street' had sent 'an agent from London to take over the March'. In a back room at the Keir Hardie Hall Leslie was faced with this accusation, and had to explain that he was only the *Daily Worker* correspondent. It was then voted that he could accompany the March but should have no vote at the March Council. As it turned out – and this can be no surprise to those who know him – he was constantly consulted all the way. It was not, however, his first experience of a march of the unemployed; earlier, he had gone on a march to lobby the TUC at Brighton.

Leslie's work on the *Daily Worker* ended in 1937. This was partly due to his growing desire to write about history and literature on a scale that could not be catered for in the columns of a small newspaper, partly to his having been set to work at fund-raising – 'at which', as he correctly says, 'I am no good.' In 1934 he and his first wife, Bronwen, had parted – their son, Nicholas, accompanying her. And Leslie now settled down with his second and present wife, Vivien, the younger of the two daughters of the famous Communist speaker and writer T. A. (Tommy) Jackson. They found a place to live in Kentish Town, and here Leslie started work on the *People's History of England*.

By that time he had found that he had 'some talent for explaining things in a simple way'. Already, besides a few items on historical subjects in the *Daily Worker* (in which, as he says, it was very hard to find space), and one on A. E. Housman's poems (which some of the comrades considered 'unsuitable'), he had written a few articles for the *Criterion* and other slightly highbrow journals. T. S. Eliot, then editor of the *Criterion*, had been 'kind and encouraging'. He also wrote a piece on 'Communism and Morality' for the collection *Christianity and the Social Revolution*, edited by John Lewis and published by Victor Gollancz. This last proved important, since it established contact with Gollancz, who was to publish *A People's History* as a Left Book Club choice in 1938.

It was in this period, and also earlier, when he was teaching and afterwards 'bumming around' London, on occasion yearning for country scenes, that Leslie wrote a good deal of poetry – some of which was published in various journals, and a collection of which was published by Lawrence and Wishart in 1977. In his poetry, that same limpid style of expression was developed which afterwards was to make his books so easily understood and so persuasive, applied to the expression of personal thoughts and aspirations which did not and could not find outlet in the rough and tumble of day-to-day party work and left-wing journalism.

Finding himself at sufficient leisure in Kentish Town, Leslie embarked on writing the *People's History*. He decided to do it for the good and simple reason that there was no history of England written from a Marxist point of view, and he thought that such a history would be helpful.

A People's History of England is not a book of original research. The task Leslie set himself was, rather, to recount the known facts without embroidery, and explain their 'inner connections' – a job Marx had proposed in *Capital*, although Leslie has always been too modest to quote it. Indeed, he did not so much attempt to unearth these connections, as something buried deep to be dug out only by the tools of special research, as to make them manifest in the historical events as he recorded them. It is in this that the remarkable lucidity of the work resides. It contains a profound exercise in Marxist theory, but without any paraphernalia of abstract theoretical generalisation.

Before beginning to write, Leslie went on a solitary walking tour for several weeks, along the ancient Icknield Way, in winter, to gather local colour and think things out. Then he rather quickly wrote the opening chapters – whereupon he found himself 'stuck' and unable to write any more. The trouble, he decided, was living in London. The city no longer suited him, and there were too many distractions – particularly, demands of local party work. So he packed up a trunkful of books and other bare necessities of life and went to stay with his brother Max in the country. Their father had in the interim bought a large, mainly arable, farm – Paine's Manor, at Pentlow, a tiny straggling village on the Essex–Suffolk border, seven or eight miles from Sudbury in Suffolk. Max was now the farmer-in-chief, with the old man in part-time residence to give advice and help. So here Leslie enjoyed a spell of rural seclusion until the history was complete to the First World War. He had previously gained much stimulus from talks with his father-in-law, Tommy Jackson. And now his father, the Conservative farmer (retired), read every chapter as it was completed, and afforded much encouragement.

The book was finished at the end of 1937, and published by the Left Book Club in mid-1938. So it was written in a period of less than twelve months, including time spent on a walking tour, getting stuck at the start, and moving from London into the country – an amazing achievement of concentrated work by any standards. Leslie had, of course, been thinking about it for some time before he began it. This, he says, has always been his natural method of work. He spends a long time in cogitation, writing nothing, and then writes what he has to write very quickly.

A People's History of England has been more or less continuously in print, following the original Left Book Club edition, ever since its publication was taken on by Lawrence and Wishart immediately after the war, in 1945. That edition was reprinted in 1946. Then, following discussions in the Communist Party from which the Party's History Group was to emerge, a number of revisions were introduced into a new edition in 1948. This was reprinted three times in hardback, following which the paperback edition was issued in 1965. It has since been four times reprinted. All this makes twelve printings to date of the UK edition, with a total sale exceeding a hundred thousand copies. Additionally, there have been editions in the United States, and a total of thirteen translations.

The *People's History* finished, Leslie with Vivien moved back to Leiston, where they rented a cottage on Leiston Common. They have lived in Suffolk ever since. Vivien taught at Summerhill, and Leslie, though not on the staff, helped with the school and regularly gave lessons there. They used to take their meals at Summerhill.

By that time there was a flourishing branch of the Communist Party at Leiston, headed by the artist and illustrator Paxton Chadwick and his wife, Lee (who then also taught at Summerhill). The Chadwicks lived in a more modern residence on Leiston Common. The Communist activities at Leiston centred round the production of a duplicated monthly paper, the *Leiston Leader*, which was bought by nearly half the inhabitants. It specialised in reporting the doings of the Urban District Council, with cartoons drawn by Chadwick depicting the local Tories – everyone except the Tory councillors loved this. Paxton Chadwick was elected to the Council. After the war, Lee was elected to the East Suffolk County Council; and Paxton Chadwick, by virtue of seniority, became the UDC chairman.

The people of Leiston were both surprised and pleased to have a Communist Councillor at the head of the UDC.

Thus Leslie was once again up to his eyes in local party work. Besides activities in Leiston, he became a member of the Eastern Counties District Party Committee – which was centred at that period in Cambridge (the District Organiser was the writer of this record). Later, the centre was moved to Norwich, and back to Cambridge when the war began. The District was subsequently divided into two, but before then had covered a huge area from Lowestoft to Peterborough and King's Lynn to Welwyn Garden City. In 1940 Leslie was appointed the full-time organiser. He had a room he could use at a comrade's flat in Cambridge, and also the use of the Party's car, a diminutive Morris which he drove erratically though purposively.

But meantime, too, he had begun to think out the plan of his next book, *The English Utopia*, three chapters of which he wrote at Leiston by the time he was called up into the army in 1941.

Leslie's army career, if such it may be termed, was in the Royal Artillery, where he rose to the rank of Lance-Bombardier. He served entirely in England where, having been trained at Blandford, Dorset, he was mostly employed on navvying and construction work in the Isle of Sheppey.

An eye was continuously kept on him by Security – despite which he continued to send fairly regular contributions to the *Leiston Leader*. In one of these he argued for the Second Front and made some disparaging remarks about the then Minister of War. For this he was hauled up in 1944, confronted with the offending copy of the *Leiston Leader*, and told 'You'll hear more of this.' Two months later he was put under open arrest and sent to Court Martial – where, after prolonged study of King's Regulations and legalistic argument, he was acquitted on the grounds that the Minister of War was only a civilian whose activities army personnel might deprecate with impunity.

Afterwards, he put in for transfer to the Education Corps, for which he was recommended in view of his qualifications. The interviewing Board found a record of the Court Martial in his file, which the officer in charge indignantly waved in the air, exclaiming 'Disgraceful! This man was acquitted and the charge should not have been kept on record!' However, although recommended for educational work, Leslie was still navvying when demobilised.

While in the army, he wrote at odd moments of leisure studies in literature and history from which his book of essays, *Language of Men*, emerged – published by the Cobbett Press (a subsidiary of Lawrence and Wishart) in 1946. He also wrote some contributions to *British Ally*, the journal published by the British Embassy in Moscow.

Out of the army, Leslie returned to Leiston and resumed his activities there. In the first local election after the war he was elected, with other Communist Party candidates, to the Urban District Council – after which he became very heavily involved in local affairs. He also resumed the lending of a helping hand to Neill at Summerhill, and for several years wrote very little apart from items for the *Leiston Leader*.

Meanwhile, the project of *The English Utopia*, begun before his call-up and perforce abandoned, was working away at the back of his mind. And in 1950 he and Vivien uprooted themselves from Leiston and moved to Clare, in the Stour Valley in Suffolk, not far from Max Morton's farm at Pentlow. A small legacy had equipped him to buy a modest house – and this he found in the Old Chapel, at Clare. It is an ideal workplace for a historian – a small twelfth-century chapel which, after the Reformation, had been converted into a dwelling. The roof is tiled at the front and thatched at the back, and an old Norman arch provides the back door. For a long time Leslie refused to let the place be desecrated by such modern inventions as a kitchen water-heater, refrigerator or telephone – though he did have a bathroom built on.

Here, then, in 1952, as became usual with him after periods of gestation, he completed *The English Utopia* – that superb study of utopian ideas in England, starting from 'the Land of Cokaygne', and of their contrast with the 'anti-utopias' produced in our own time by prophets of doom.

Save for the interruption of wartime, Leslie remained a member of the East Anglia District Committee of the Communist Party (since 1941 centred in Ipswich) until he retired from it in 1974, then aged seventy-one. Year in year out he has taken on frequent speaking engagements in East Anglia, and played a leading part in Marxist educational work in the Party.

Many day-schools have been held, and the custom has continued up to now, at the Old Chapel at Clare, in the garden on fine Sundays in summertime. Besides this, he was elected by the Party's National Congress for a period to the national 'Appeals Committee' (a committee which, more impartially and benevolently than enemies would represent it, inquires into matters of party discipline). He was the British Communist Party's representative at the international conference on the history of the First International held in Berlin in 1964, and at another on the Paris Commune in Prague in 1970.

Leslie Morton has from its inception been a leading and very active member of the Communist Party's History Group – the subject of a separate essay in this volume, by E. J. Hobsbawm. He is still its chairman. And for years he has been a regular reviewer of books, mostly on history or literature, in the *Daily Worker* and, latterly, the *Morning Star*. He gave a one-term course of history lectures in 1967 at the University of Bratislava, in Czechoslovakia; and keeps up close contacts with historians and others at the University of Rostock in the German Democratic Republic (now the Wilhelm Pieck University at Rostock), where he was awarded an honorary doctorate in 1975.

Undeterred by these other activities, Leslie has continued steadily to produce books following the publication of *The English Utopia* in 1952. They have mostly followed one another at about two-yearly intervals.

In the fifties the Communist Party History Group proposed the preparation of a short history of the British Labour Movement up to the end of the First World War – the eve of the foundation of the Communist Party. This job was undertaken jointly by Leslie Morton and the late George Tate, Leslie writing the history from the late eighteenth century to the Chartist period, and George Tate carrying on from there. Several years were devoted to this task, and the book – *The British Labour Movement, 1770–1920* – was published by Lawrence and Wishart in 1956.

Leslie then turned his attention to an earlier period, to the formation and history of the numerous left-wing religious-political sects which had sprung up at the time of the English Revolution and had survived in odd corners of plebeian society and, despite persecution, for a century afterwards. The best known of these sects were the Ranters, but there were many other varieties – all violently opposed to the established order of society and its politics and morals, all engaging in very unconventional behaviour (nudism and 'free love' was a common variant), all looking forward to the 'New Jerusalem', and mostly believing themselves the sole elect of God. Leslie considered that the works of William Blake, at the eve of and during the industrial revolution in England, and especially his 'prophetic writings', showed the influence on the poet of surviving and submerged remnants of these sects. His initial study of them, and of their influence on Blake, was published in 1958 in a short book, *The Everlasting Gospel*.

This work tied up with his interest as a Suffolk man in local history. He had become associated with the Suffolk Institute of Archaeology, and he and Vivien were both stalwarts of the Workers' Educational Association at Clare – he has for long been its local chairman. He found evidence of the activities of the radical sects of the seventeenth century in Suffolk, and contributed two articles on them to the *Proceedings* of the Suffolk Institute. He continued research into this line of country for some years, whence emerged a bigger book, *The World of the Ranters*, in 1970.

Leslie was (and still is) engaged in a variety of special studies in particular episodes and personalities in English history and literature, and in the course of time began to turn out a series of essays. Enough had accumulated by 1966 to be published together by Lawrence and Wishart under the title *The Matter of Britain*. This book contains studies as various as the Arthurian Cycle (whence derives the traditional expression 'The Matter of Britain') and the development of feudal society, Shakespeare's historical outlook, the Levellers, the Brontë sisters, John Ruskin and E. M. Forster. *The Everlasting Gospel* (by then out of print) was republished as one of the items. Meantime, in 1963, he had written, also, for Lawrence and Wishart, a short paperback, *Socialism in Britain*.

His remaining work to date has been concerned with editing four collections of writings by English revolutionaries – first, *The Life and Ideas of Robert Owen*, in 1962; then, in 1968 and 1973, two volumes of William Morris – the first containing *A Dream of John Ball* and *News from Nowhere*, together with Morris's narrative poem about the Paris Commune, *The Pilgrims of Hope*, the second a selection from the political writings of William Morris; finally (that is, finally to the date of this present record), *Freedom in Arms*, a collection of Leveller writings. For each of these books he contributed an introduction of singular lucidity, breadth and conciseness.

His latest published work was the *Collected Poems* (1977) – songs, but not yet, one suspects, those of the swan.

Leslie Morton stands out, throughout his career as writer and as Party worker, as a model type of Communist intellectual. When he started to write as a committed Marxist, there were very few 'intellectuals' in the British Communist Party. Now there are many; and British Marxism has won a lasting and ever more influential place in national life, and an international reputation. Leslie is one of those, and perhaps more than he realised a chief one of those, who have contributed to this outcome, singularly untrammelled by whatever political and ideological stereotypes might have been from time to time in currency. Whether on the staff of the *Daily Worker*, writing for and distributing the *Leiston Leader*, serving as an Urban District Councillor, a member of the District Party Committee, or as lecturer and writer, he has always been a Party worker, down to earth whether in political agitation or in writing on history and literature – working with people and for people, and writing for people in a way to be understood, to encourage and to teach.

THE HISTORIANS' GROUP OF THE COMMUNIST PARTY

ERIC HOBSBAWM

The present record, based on memory, on consultation with several old friends* and on a substantial collection of materials, does not claim to be an actual 'history' of the Historians' Group of the Communist Party, and it covers only the years between 1946 and 1956. Nevertheless it may be of some interest even to those who do not happen to have belonged or who still belong to it. For the Historians' Group played a major part in the development of Marxist historiography in this country, and – for reasons which are even now difficult to understand, the bulk of British Marxist theoretical effort was directed into historical work.[1]† It played some part in the development of British historiography in general. Finally, members of the group also had a significant role in the discussions which rent the Communist Party after the Twentieth Congress of the CPSU in 1956–7, and in the genesis of the various New Lefts which followed.

The present paper therefore attempts to rediscover not merely what the Group did, but also to ask and answer some questions about its rather unusual role in the ten years after the Second World War. It was not formally set up as a group until after the war. If I remember correctly, it grew out of a conference organized to discuss a planned new edition of A. L. Morton's *A People's History of England* in which both the author and the Party wished to embody the results of discussions among Marxist historians since the date of first publication (1938). These less formal discussions had begun as Christopher Hill recalls, with meetings in Marx House and Balliol in 1938–9 which led to the production of Hill's essay on the English Revolution in 1940. They were, it appears, organized by Robin Page Arnot – the oldest Marxist historian alive in Britain and

---

* Particularly with Christopher Hill, John Saville and Victor Kiernan, who commented on an earlier draft, but are not responsible for what I have written.

† See notes at end of each article.

fortunately, at the time of writing, still very much on the active
list. A number of people contributed to Hill's text, and several –
the late Dona Torr and Douglas Garman and (pseudonymously)
the still active J. Kuczynski debated the booklet after publication
in *Labour Monthly*. The actual Historians' Group, formally
established after the war, is still in existence. However, the years
between its foundation and the crisis of 1956–7 form a self-
contained period, and this is the subject of my memoir.

I

There was no tradition of Marxist history in Britain, though
there was a powerful tradition of radical and labour-oriented
history, of which Cole and Postgate's *The Common People* (1938,
new edition 1946) was then the most recent example. (In fact,
one of the earliest tasks of the Group in 1946 was a critical
discussion of this then influential work.) For practical purposes
little Marxist history written in English before the 1930s was
available, and the shortage of such work even in the 1930s is
indicated by the fact that P. C. Gordon Walker's article on the
Reformation in the *Economic History Review* was widely referred
to as Marxist. Foreign Marxist work in translation was also not
widely known or available, with the exception of some Russian
work (M. N. Pokrovsky, Theodore Rothstein), among which
Hessen's 1931 paper on 'The Social Roots of Newton's *Principia*
ought to be singled out, because of its influence not only on
potential Marxist historians but also on potential Marxist
natural scientists. There were also some works from the heyday
of pre-1914 German social-democracy (Kautsky on Thomas
More, Bernstein's *Cromwell and Communism*). However, the basic
texts on which we based our attempts at a materialist
interpretation of history were the writings of Marx, Engels and
Lenin themselves. Many of these had been far from readily
accessible before the wave of publications in the mid-1930s,
which produced Dona Torr's edition of the *Selected
Correspondence of Marx and Engels* and other works.[2]
    When the student generation of the 1930s, who provided the
main stock of the Group, began to produce Marxist historians, a
few relatively senior intellectuals were already Marxist, or
beginning to draw closer to Marxism. Though none of them
were actually historians by profession, like all Marxists they

were drawn to history and contributed to it. The most eminent, the archaeologist and pre-historian V. Gordon Childe, does not seem to have influenced us greatly to start with, perhaps because he was not associated with the Communist Party. The most flourishing group, the Marxist classicists (e.g. Benjamin Farrington, George Thomson) were rather remote from the interests of most of us, though Thomson's *Aeschylus and Athens* (1940) was much admired and discussed. (The Group organized a critical discussion of this work and its successor, probably in the early 1950s, with contributions from social anthropologists – including a now famous name in the field – archaeologists and philologists.) However, the major historical work which was to influence us crucially was Maurice Dobb's *Studies in the Development of Capitalism* which formulated our main and central problem. This crucial work was not published until 1946. A. L. Morton's *People's History* has already been mentioned. Thus little work by senior Marxists was available, and some of it (e.g. Roy Pascal's neglected study of the German Reformation of 1932) was not widely known.

Since CP members then segregated themselves strictly from schismatics and heretics, the writings of living non-Party Marxists made little impact, though C. L. R. James' *Black Jacobins* was read, in spite of the author's known Trotskyism, and some of us could not but notice that such books as Arthur Rosenberg's *Birth of the German Republic* (London-Oxford, 1931) were Marxist in their interpretation of imperial Germany. Actually, we would have probably suffered anyway from the extraordinary provincialism of the British in the 1930s who, communist and non-communist alike, paid next to no attention to most of the brilliant minds present among them as refugees from Nazism. Karl Korsch, Karl Polanyi and Frederick Antal, to name merely a few who were Marxist or Marxist-influenced, made virtually no impact here in that decade. If anything, membership of the CP drew our attention to some foreigners who would otherwise have been entirely overlooked (e.g., for those who could read German, Georg Lukács), and to foreign communists who took an active part in British discussions during their emigration (e.g. Jürgen Kuczynski).

The main pillars of the Group thus consisted initially of people who had graduated sufficiently early in the 1930s to have done some research, to have begun to publish and, in very exceptional cases, to have begun to teach. Among these Christopher Hill already occupied a special position as the author of a major interpretation of the English Revolution and a link with Soviet economic historians. Others who had published before 1946 or were just about to publish included Brian Pearce, then a Tudor historian, V. G. Kiernan, whose encyclopedic knowledge had already produced a book on the diplomacy of imperialism in China, James B. Jefferys, already a post-doctoral nineteenth-century economic historian whose wartime industrial experience had made him, among other things, the author of what is still one of the best trade union histories (*The Story of the Engineers*, 1945) and F. D. Klingender the art-historian, whose contacts with the group were not to be close. One or two of the most prominent pre-war Marxist historians of this degree of seniority had already by 1946 moved away from association with communist groups and will not be mentioned as they are entitled to retrospective privacy.

The older products of the 1930s were soon joined by a group of students who were slightly junior in professional terms, though after six years of war comparatively mature. No very sharp line separated those who had actually begun some research before 1939 from those who had merely graduated, and this intermediate stratum – R. H. Hilton, Max Morris (later eminent in the National Union of Teachers), John Saville, E. J. Hobsbawm – contained some who immediately established themselves as active and leading members of the Group. The minds of several had been broadened by work or war-service abroad, notably in India (Kiernan, Saville, Pearce) and this, as Kiernan recalls, safeguarded us against excessive provincialism and concentration on contemporary history. The sixteenth and seventeenth centuries, for instance, or even medieval agrarian history, were by no means purely academic for those who had experience of and an interest in pre-capitalist or incompletely capitalist societies.

A modest, but for practical purposes unnoticed, generation gap separated this group from the intake of post-war students, which diminished over the years of the Cold War, though recruitment (especially from Balliol) never quite ceased. Most of these new members reached the group as post-graduates, but the last and youngest of the pre-1956 recruits, Raphael Samuel (now of Ruskin College and 'History Workshop') actually began to attend meetings as a schoolboy. However, this was not yet a time when all people with a serious interest in history automatically envisaged a university career, since openings were few, except in university-linked adult education departments into which a number of the ablest went, e.g. the late Henry Collins, Lionel Munby (both ex-Oxford), E. P. Thompson and – no longer in the CP after the war – Raymond Williams (both ex-Cambridge). An even larger number became schoolteachers, at least for a time. For those not already in academic posts before the cold-war blacklisting began in the late spring of 1948, the chances of university teaching were to be virtually zero for the next ten years. Nevertheless, a core of Marxist historians with university and adult education jobs existed, and this, as John Saville rightly suggests, probably helped the group to maintain a solid continuity over the difficult years which followed.

With all these students and ex-students were joined a miscellaneous group of (generally older) people who had little in common except Party membership and a devotion to Marxism and history. Some of these took part in the work of the group with unshakeable loyalty and assiduity, e.g. Alfred Jenkin, its long-time treasurer, now retired to his native Cornwall from the British Museum. Others were constantly available, e.g. Jack Lindsay, whose encyclopedic erudition and constantly simmering kettle of ideas let off steam in discussions ranging from classical antiquity to the twentieth century. For some the Group was, if not exactly a way of life, then at least a small cause, as well as a minor way of structuring leisure. For most it was also friendship.

These were the people who would make their way, normally at weekends, through what memory recalls mainly as the dank, cold and slightly foggy morning streets of Clerkenwell to Marx House or to the upper room of the Garibaldi Restaurant, Laystall Street, armed with cyclostyled agendas, sheets of 'theses' or summary arguments, for the debates of the moment. Saffron Hill, Farringdon Road and Clerkenwell Green in the first ten post-war years, were not a sybaritic or even a very welcoming environment. Physical austerity, intellectual excitement, political passion and friendship are probably what the survivors of those years remember best – but also a sense of equality. Some of us knew more about some subject or period than others, but all of us were equally explorers of largely unknown territory. Few of us hesitated to speak in discussion, even fewer to criticize, none to accept criticism.

History, like love, is something about which all of us think we know something once we are old enough. Moreover, history is a valued component of the labour movement, since its ideological tradition and continuity largely rest on the collective memory of old struggles. History is the core of Marxism, though some recent schools of Marxists appear to think otherwise. For us and for the Party, history – the development of capitalism to its present stage, especially in our own country, which Marx himself had studied – had put our struggles on its agenda and guaranteed our final victory. Some of us even felt that it had recruited us as individuals. Where would we, as intellectuals, have been, what would have become of us, but for the experiences of war, revolution and depression, fascism and anti-fascism, which surrounded us in our youth? Our work as historians was therefore embedded in our work as Marxists, which we believed to imply membership of the Communist Party. It was inseparable from our political commitment and activity. Eventually this very sense of unity between our work as historians and communists led to the crisis of 1956–7, for it was among the historians that the dissatisfaction with the Party's reactions to the Khrushchev speech at the Twentieth Congress of the CPSU first came into the open. In the event many of the most active and prominent members of the Group left or were expelled from the Party, though fortunately the personal relationships between those who went and those who stayed were not, on the whole, disrupted. Though the Group continued – and in recent years has undergone a revival – 1956 undoubtedly marked the end of an epoch.

II

This break was particularly dramatic, precisely because in the years 1946–56 the relations between the group and the Party had been almost entirely unclouded. We were as loyal, active and committed a group of Communists as any, if only because we felt that Marxism implied membership of the Party. To criticise Marxism was to criticize the Party, and the other way round. Thus one of our ablest members, Edmund Dell, announced his disagreements with the Party by means of a number of theses about dialectics, which the Group discussed at a special conference on 6–8 January 1950. He did not think that a belief in dialectics 'assists the practising historian and the practising politician, and may confuse them'. He did not think 'dialectics' actually described 'the nature of change'. However, the sting of these theoretical observations lay in the tail:

> The testing of a social theory in practice is rendered difficult by the complexity of the evidence. It might, however, be of value to review the political decisions of the Communist Party at crucial moments during the last ten years. Whether one felt that the size and variety of the errors made in this period are the result of too slight an understanding of Marxism or of too dogmatic an adherence to it will no doubt depend on one's view of the upshot of this discussion.

Dell left the CP soon afterwards – he had not convinced the rest of us – and entered upon what has since proved to be a distinguished but non-historical career. During this period he was exceptional, though later other ex-members of the Group, notably the medievalist Gordon Leff, were to combine criticism of the CP with that of Marxism. However, the bulk of the Group members who left in 1956–7 continued to regard themselves as Marxist.

From the Party's point of view we were almost certainly the most flourishing and satisfactory of the numerous professional and cultural groups which operated under the National Cultural Committee. Organizationally, though not a basic unit (branch) of the Party, we were virtually self-sufficient. We had a chairman, secretary and committee (15 strong in 1952; later divided into a smaller working and a larger 'Full' committee); we raised such subscriptions and donations as were necessary to finance our activities, organized fares-pools for our meetings and more or less ran our own affairs. The core of the group consisted of the 'period sections', ancient, medieval, 16–17th century and 19th century, and the Teachers' Section, numerically strong but fluctuating in its activity. During the early 1950s local branches of the group were set up – in Manchester, Nottingham and Sheffield – largely on the initiative of one dynamic member who campaigned tirelessly for local history and launched the Group's *Local History Bulletin* in October 1951. This eventually turned into *Our History*, the cyclostyled bulletin of the Group published, with varying degrees of regularity, from October 1953 and in a more elaborate form since 1956. (At the time of writing it has reached issue 67.) The branches of the History Group, backed by local Party and union organizers with an interest in history and, as so often, active as amateur historians themselves,[3] were to 'popularize our history, especially in the labour movement, including of course our Party', i.e. to study

> the facts of their own local history, particularly the record of the local Labour and other progressive movements, and seeing that these facts are used in every possible way to illustrate the nature of the class struggle and to revive the old militant tradition (*Local History Bulletin* 12 January 1952).

The regional branches did not spread widely, though at one time there appears to have been a tendency – of which I have no recollection myself – to transfer most of the Group's work to such local units. In fact, their activities fluctuated and faded. The Group remained London-centred, though its members, local and imported, took their message throughout the country, particularly on such historically significant occasions as the anniversary of 1649, which led to a good deal of public activity. However, at least two conferences were held in the provinces: one in Nottingham (1952) on 'The History of the British People's Opposition to War' at which the present writer vaguely recalls giving the introductory talk, another in Birmingham (1953) on 'Nineteenth-Century Radicalism'.

We were or tried to be good communists, though probably only E. P. Thompson (who was less closely associated with the Group than Dorothy Thompson) was politically important enough to be elected to his District Party Committee. The Party seemed quite satisfied with our work. For reasons considered below, we felt little constraint. The one field in which we did, was admittedly central for a group such as ours: the history of the British labour movement itself. To investigate and popularise this was, naturally, a major task for those of us with modern interests. Apart from personal work, we soon set out (inspired by Dona Torr) to produce an ambitious collection of documents, of which four volumes appeared in 1948–49: *The Good Old Cause 1640–1660* (ed. C. Hill and E. Dell), *From Cobbett to the Chartists* (ed. Max Morris), *Labour's Formative Years* (ed. J. B. Jefferys), and *Labour's Turning Point* (ed. E. J. Hobsbawm). That the series was not continued was partly due to a lack of suitable authors, partly to the relative lack of success of the last two of these volumes. They were designed for a public of trade union and adult education readers, which did not take them up, and for a public of students which did not yet exist. But it was also due in part to the difficulty of dealing with the history of the movement since the foundation of the Party in 1920 which, as we all knew, raised some notoriously tricky problems.

In fact, the Group, with the full support of the Party, set about the preparation of a Marxist history of the movement. We even organized a weekend school in 1952 (or 1953) at the Netherwood guest house near Hastings, haunted by the ghosts of progressive reunions of the past, as well as, some claimed, by more orthodox parapsychological phenomena. There historians and party functionaries united to discuss this history, as expounded by old cadres like John Mahon (1918–1926), Jack Cohen (the General Strike), Idris Cox (1926–1945) and John Gollan (post-1945) under the chairmanship of James Klugmann. Since the British CP is a family-sized organization, we knew several of them, though as officials and sometimes friends, rather than as remembrancers and analysts of past struggles. Others some of us met for the first time: Horace Green (of the Northeast), Bert Williams (of the Midlands), Mick Jenkins (of the East Midlands). Some stick in the mind more than others: Marian Ramelson, a marvellous person who later wrote a fine book on women's struggles, Frank Jackson, an ancient, stubborn, droopy-moustached building worker whose loyalties and – sometimes sectarian – memories went back to the days of the SDF, George Hardy, whose career as a craftsman had taken him from the North Sea coast through Canada to the USA, and through the IWW to Comintern organizing in the Pacific. For us as historians it was a memorable and instructive experience.

But it did not allow us to write the planned book. The gap between what historians thought it necessary to write and what was regarded as officially possible and desirable to write at this stage – or even much later – proved too large. The history eventually written by A. L. Morton and George Tate (historian of the London Trades Council) merely covered the period from 1770 to 1920 (1956). The same problem was to prove insoluble in 1956 when, following the Twentieth Congress of the

Communist Party of the Soviet Union and under some pressure from its historians, the Party prepared to write its own official history, which is still in progress. There was a sharp division of opinion in the Commission which discussed this project under the chairmanship of Harry Pollitt. (The Group was represented on it by E. J. Hobsbawm and Brian Pearce.) The view of the historians was clear, though Pearce, soon to join a Trotskyist group, was much more critical of the CP's past record. Given that anti-communists were giving publicity to their version of Communist Party history and that the facts, however inconvenient, were perfectly well known to anyone interested in the subject, it was mere ostrich-policy to conceal them. They had to be discussed frankly from our point of view; and in any case the only useful kind of history was a serious, and if necessary critical or self-critical assessment of the Party's past policies, successes and failures. The point was accepted, at least in theory, by R. Palme Dutt, who later attempted such an assessment of the policy of the International himself,[4] though in a rather cursory manner. On the other hand Pollitt and some others, for reasons which are quite comprehensible, seemed unenthusiastic about any history other than what might be called the regimental variety, which maintained the spirit of the militants, especially in difficult times, by the memory of past sacrifices, heroism and glory. The Group was not to be associated with the actual history of the CP which has, at the time of writing, reached 1929. However, it and the present phase of the historiography of labour movements in the communist period, which permits of a great deal more elbow-room for critical discussion, lies well beyond the years with which this memoir deals.

Yet the problem of party-history was quite exceptional. On the whole we did not feel any sense of constraint, of certain matters being off limits, nor did we feel that the Party tried to interfere with or distort our work as communist historians. This may appear surprising, for during those years of ultra-rigid Stalinism and Cold War, the Party line (wherever it originated from) was only too likely to extend deeply into matters which at first sight had no evident relation to politics such as (in the Lysenko period) genetic theory; and history, even in its remoter periods, was much more directly linked with politics. Politics then often insisted *a priori* on the 'correct' interpretation, which it was the business of Marxist theory to 'prove', i.e. to confirm. There is no doubt that we ourselves were apt to fall into the stern and wooden style of the disciplined bolshevik cadres, since we regarded ourselves as such.[5] Our arguments were sometimes designed *a posteriori* to confirm what we already knew to be necessarily 'correct', especially in our discussions on Absolutism and the English Revolution. I do not know how many old members will now be satisfied, on rereading the Group's 'State and Revolution in Tudor and Stuart England' (*Communist Review*, July 1948) with the results of these discussions. Some had mental reservations even then, and recall the arguments stimulated by our chief doubter, V. G. Kiernan, with greater satisfaction than the agreed conclusions. Yet the net result of our debates and activities was enormously to widen rather than to narrow or distort our understanding of history. What is more, we did not feel the constraints of the orthodoxy so signally tightened in the Stalin–Zhdanov–Lysenko years as much as some others, though perhaps our political leaders were more aware of it.[6]

There are a number of reasons why, by and large, our work as historians did not suffer more from the contemporary dogmatism. First, it must always be remembered, that even during the most dogmatic Stalinist period, the authorized versions of Marxist history were concerned with genuine historical problems, and arguable as serious history, except where the political authority of the Bolshevik Party and similar matters were involved. While this patently made it a waste of time to debate, say, the history of the Soviet Union – except to discover new citations with which to embellish official truth – it left substantial scope for genuine analysis over the greater part of the human past. Indeed, the debates of Soviet historians could be reasonably integrated into such a discussion, and the work of some of them which survived from earlier periods (such as that of E. A. Kosminsky on feudal England) or was published during these years (such as B. F. Porshnev's study of popular risings in France) was respected and influential outside Marxist circles, even when not accepted. Moreover, communist intellectuals were encouraged (if they needed any encouragement) to study the texts of Marx and Engels as well as of Lenin and Stalin; nor was there (according to Stalin himself) an obligation to accept all of them as literal truth. In brief, the received orthodoxy both of historical materialism and of historical interpretation, was not – except for some specific topics mainly concerning the twentieth century – incompatible with genuine historical work.

Second, there was no 'party line' on most of British history, and what there was in the USSR was largely unknown to us, except for the complex discussions on 'merchant capital' which accompanied the criticism of M. N. Pokrovsky there. Thus we were hardly aware that the 'Asiatic Mode of Production' had been actively discouraged in the USSR since the early 1930s, though we noted its absence from Stalin's *Short History*.[7] Such accepted interpretations as existed came mainly from ourselves – Hill's 1940 essay, Dobb's *Studies*, etc. – and were therefore much more open to free debate than if they had carried the by-line of Stalin or Zhdanov.

Third, the major task we and the Party set ourselves was to criticise non-Marxist history and its reactionary implications, where possible contrasting it with older, politically more radical interpretations. This widened rather than narrowed our horizons. Both we and the Party saw ourselves not as a sect of true believers, holding up the light amid the surrounding darkness, but ideally as leaders of a broad progressive movement such as we had experienced in the 1930s.[8] We knew that the small group of Marxist academics was isolated. This very isolation enforced a certain unsectarianism on us, since many of our colleagues would have been only too ready to dismiss our work as dogmatic oversimplification and propagandist jargon, had we not proved our competence as historians in ways they recognized and in language they could understand. Outside the Party there was then no intellectual public which took Marxism seriously, or even accepted or understood our technical terminology. Yet we also knew that the isolation of the cold war was artificial and temporary. As one of us wrote during this period in an article attempting to sum up our attitude:

> Marxists . . . believe that their method alone enables us to provide a successor to the old 'Liberal-Radical' view of British history which will be adequate in science and scholarship, while giving the citizens of this country a coherent picture of our national development and answering their questions. Non-Marxists would probably agree that such a new view must be influenced by and indebted to Marxism.[9]

In a sense we saw ourselves as continuing the major national tradition of history, and many non-Marxists as prepared to join in this task with us.

Therefore communist historians – in this instance deliberately *not* acting as a Party group – consistently attempted to build bridges between Marxists and non-Marxists with whom they shared some common interests and sympathies. The first major effort of this kind was perhaps the 'Past and Present' series of Studies in the History of Civilization, which lasted – flourished is perhaps too strong a word – for some years after the war under the editorship of Benjamin Farrington (with the assistance of Gordon Childe, Bernard J. Stern of the American Marxist journal *Science and Society*, and Sydney Herbert of Aberystwyth.) It published an exceptionally interesting and neglected series of small volumes by both Marxist and non-Marxist authors.[10] I cannot recall any involvement of the Group as such in this project. A few years later, in the totally unpropitious climate of 1952, the late John Morris nagged and bulldozed some members of the Group to launch the review *Past & Present* as a deliberately constructed common forum for Marxists and non-Marxists, specialist and non-specialist historians. Gordon Childe, Dobb, Hill, Hilton, Hobsbawm and Morris, together with two eminent non-Marxist scholars, the late Professors A. H. M. Jones and R. R. Betts, formed the nucleus of the team which started what has since become one of the leading historical journals in the world, and had already laid the basis of its later reputation by 1956. The non-Marxists resisted considerable pressures to withdraw from its Board (to which at least one eminent non-Marxist succumbed), and a special word of thanks is due to those non-Marxist historians who, knowing the views of the majority of the editors, were nevertheless willing to brave the cold-war boycott by contributing to its early issues.[11] *Past & Present* was never the responsibility of the Group or under Party authority, and considerable efforts were made to maintain its independent status, which was never once challenged or even queried by the Party. In short, we were as unsectarian as it was possible to be in those years.

Fourth, the official leadership of the Party concerned with 'culture' was very well disposed to us, partly no doubt because our loyalty and militancy were not in any doubt prior to 1956,

partly because the Group flourished, but also because the
functionaries concerned, notably Emile Burns, James
Klugmann, Douglas Garman and Sam Aaronovitch were
genuinely interested in our work and gave it their active support.
Finally, it is worth mentioning a certain old-fashioned realism,
which never left the British Communist Party. Thus, like other
communists during this period, we discussed the theory of the
increasing pauperization of the working class (6 June 1948).
'Absolute pauperization' was then strongly maintained by
Jürgen Kuczynski (whose *History of Labour Conditions* in its first
version had been published in Britain during the war), but was
publicly doubted by Maurice Dobb. Though hesitant to criticize
a view which appeared to many to have Marx's own authority, it
seems clear that most of us found it impossible – unlike the
French CP in those years – to maintain that the workers were
worse off than in 1850, and therefore saw no necessity to do so as
Marxists. I can recall no objection to our view from the Party.
This did not, incidentally, prevent us from strongly criticizing
the 'optimistic' views about the impact of the Industrial
Revolution in the early nineteenth century which were then
gaining ground. In fact the 'standard-of-living debate', now
well-known to historians everywhere, grew out of the Group's
decision to reopen this question. The present author and John
Saville were asked to draft a suitable article, though in the end
Saville's part was limited to critical comments on the draft for
which Hobsbawm bears responsibility, and which was
published in the *Economic History Review* in 1957.

III

The 1930s and 1940s were a period which attracted able
intellectuals to Marxism, and the Communist Party was
therefore fortunate to possess a pool of promising historians.
When, in 1954, Lawrence and Wishart published a volume of
essays in honour of Dona Torr (*Democracy and the Labour
Movement*, ed. John Saville, with the advice of George Thomson,
Maurice Dobb and Christopher Hill),[12] which was also designed
as a sort of shop-window for the work done by members of the
Group, the results were by no means discreditable. If, to the
work there published by Hill, S. F. Mason, Ronald Meek, Henry
Collins, John Saville, Daphne Simon, E. J. Hobsbawm and

Victor Kiernan, we add the work of others published elsewhere – E. P. Thompson, Rodney Hilton, A. L. Morton, George Rudé, not to mention our seniors, the balance-sheet of British Marxist history was even more satisfactory. The Bibliography issued by the Group (1956?) did not distinguish between Marxist and 'near-Marxist' work, but a brief analysis of its 18 pages yields results which speak for themselves:

Work by historians associated with the Group 1946–1956*

	1945 and before	*1946–1956*
Books	9	34
Articles		
in CP journals	4	59
in other journals	4	61

This calculation is evidently not intended to measure the work of the Group as such. Several of its most active members were teachers, who did not write much or at all, while others were engaged in local research and activities directly linked to the labour movement. It simply indicates that the Group contained a vigorous nucleus of people who tried to translate its Marxist discussions into historical research and publication. This lends some interest to the debates in which the Group engaged, and which are, for most of the members of that period, what they chiefly remember about it.

Given the academic and educational interests of the bulk of its members, it was natural that the group should initially organize its discussions around particular books or projects for books – Morton's own history and Cole and Postgate have already been mentioned. Significant academic works which seemed to require specific discussion, continued to mobilize us. Thus Powicke's *King Henry and the Lord Edward* appears to have been discussed by the Medieval Section among other matters on 21–22 July 1947 – in the rooms of the St Pancras CP in Camden Town – while the appearance of H. R. Trevor-Roper's *The Gentry*

* For various reasons, the figures have a slight margin of error. CP journals are: *Communist Review, Modern Quarterly, Marxist Quarterly.* Pamphlets have not been included. Contributions to volumes are counted as 'articles'. British Marxist historians not associated with the Group but listed in the Bibliography published 5 books before 1945, 13 between 1946 and 1956. Their contribution to the articles after 1946 was very much smaller. Reviews are not counted.

and Pennington and Brunton's *Members of the Long Parliament*
moved the 16–17th Century Section to organize a special
meeting on these works on 3–4 April 1954. However, in the
nature of things, the Group and its Sections tended to discuss
large and general themes.

The incompleteness of the Group's records, and the
unfortunate habit of not dating all its documents, makes it
impossible to reconstruct its various debates chronologically. It
seems that the classicists and medievalists united early to
consider the decline of antiquity and the transition to feudalism
(January 1947, and again 24–6 September 1948), while the
nature and breakdown of feudalism produced conferences based
initially on Dobb's *Studies* (21–22 July 1947) and later (March
1952, July 1952) stimulated by the well-known Dobb-Sweezy
controversy of 1950 (published by Jack Lindsay in 1954, with a
further exchange and additions by Takahashi, Hill and Hilton).
However, the major debates were those which primarily focused
on the 16th–17th century. There were two major sessions on the
problem of Absolutism, accompanied by theses and counter-
theses, translations of relevant Soviet debates and elaborate
minutes (1947–January 1948), which resulted in a formal statement of the Group's views in the *Communist Review*. Another conference dealt with agrarian problems in 16th- and 17th-century
England (September 1948) with papers by Hilton, E. Kerridge,
M. E. James, Allan Merson and K. R. Andrews. The debate on
the English bourgeois revolution and ideology – a subject close
to Hill's heart then as later – led to a series of discussions which
began in September 1949 (with papers by Dobb, Hill and S.
Mason), continued in March 1950 in the direction of science and
the comparative analysis of Protestantism. This in turn
produced a conference on the Reformation (September 1950).
In later years the activities of this section seem to have been less
intensive or less well recorded.

The other major group, the 19th Century Section, was
consistently less international and comparative in outlook. For
practical purposes it confined itself to Britain, and largely to a
number of well-polished questions which amounted to
variations on the theme of the nature and roots of reformism in
the British labour movement. The problem of 'absolute
pauperisation', as already mentioned, was discussed quite early
(1948), settled to our satisfaction and ceased to preoccupy us.

On the other hand some years later the Section returned to the problem of the 'labour aristocracy' which had also been discussed in 1948, this time in the context of various debates on Reformism and Empire, which also took it into the field of labour ideology, 1875–1918, and to the Birmingham conference on nineteenth-century Radicalism. The other theme which seems to have preoccupied the section was that of the development of the modern state apparatus, both central (1950) and local. As for the no-man's land between the Group's two most flourishing sections, we simply had nobody who knew much about it, until George Rudé, a lone explorer, ventured into the period of John Wilkes. (He may have taken the initiative in getting us to organize our only conference on eighteenth-century Britain.) Hill sometimes ventured forward from the seventeenth century, Henry Collins was pressed to venture backwards from the Corresponding Societies of the 1790s; but the gap remained.

Yet the most ambitious effort of the group mobilized members of all sections except the classicists. This was a project on the entire history of British capitalist development, long prepared and discussed in a week of intensive sessions at Netherwood in July 1954. It was, it seems, suggested by Dona Torr, who watched over it like a benevolent abbess. Something like thirty of us took part in the discussions of seventeen papers at one time or another, including at least two outside contributors invited along for their expertise, Raymond Williams and Basil Davidson. (As we concluded from this as from other experiences, we were particularly weak on the history of the empire and colonial exploitation, Scottish, Welsh and Irish history, and 'the role of women in economic life'.) To judge by the papers, which are in my possession, we took enormous pains over this conference.[13] In a sense it was a systematic attempt to see where we had got in eight years of work, and where Marxist history ought to go next.

Almost a quarter of a century has passed since this attempt to draw the map of capitalist development – including the white spaces – and both history and Marxist history have been transformed in the period since 1954. It is therefore not surprising that the debates of the time have long been overtaken. When A. L. Morton gave his pioneer paper on 'The Role of the Common People in the History of British

Capitalism' – it was much admired – we could hardly suspect that 'history from below' would, some twenty years later, be one of the most flourishing fields of study.

Our knowledge has become far greater: thus we then discussed the Industrial Revolution essentially on the basis of inter-war or even pre-1914 research, since the topic then attracted surprisingly little attention. Entire new historical fields have since been opened up – urban history, historic demography, not to mention the great fashionable catch-all of 'social history'. Labour history was only just beginning – thanks largely to the work of communist historians of our generation – to advance beyond the point reached before 1939 by Cole. And so on.

Yet, looking back over these now ancient papers and minutes, what is striking is how many of our questions remain at the core of Marxist, or indeed general, historical debate. This is partly because Marx's basic questions remain central to any historical analysis of capitalist development: in the early 1950s anti-Marxist historians would have preferred to eliminate the Industrial Revolution from history, but it simply couldn't be. It is also partly because we avoided cutting ourselves off as Marxists from the rest of historical science: Dobb's *Studies*, which gave us our framework, were novel precisely because they did not just restate or reconstruct the views of 'the Marxist classics', but because they embodied the findings of post-Marx economic history in a Marxist analysis.[14] In some ways, therefore, the historians who were then isolated and provincial were some (though not all) of those whose work was taken up in Britain for anti-Marxist purposes, whereas we were – in spite of disagreements – part of a general movement against 'old-fashioned' politico-constitutional or narrative history. 'Namierism', against which we polemised, had enormous prestige among our British academic colleagues, but the present writer can recall being taken aside by Fernand Braudel in Paris, on our first meeting in the 1950s, and asked: 'Do tell me, who exactly is this Namier that my English visitors keep talking about?' A third advantage of our Marxism – we owe it largely to Hill and to the very marked interest of several of our members, not least A. L. Morton himself, in literature – was never to reduce history to a simple economic or 'class interest' determinism, or to devalue politics and ideology.[15]

Nevertheless, it would be absurd to suggest that our 1954 debates are today more than an interesting document in the intellectual history of British Marxism. Their suggestions have been embodied in (and perhaps through the influence of) the subsequent work of some of those who took part in them – and some of the later themes and views of several who have since published works they had not then even thought of can be traced back to the Netherwood school.

Two of our conclusions have since borne evident fruit: 'There were some contested questions on which we could contribute, e.g. . . . the Hayek view on early industrial revolution', and 'We are in a position to throw new light and to suggest new syntheses on certain problems, e.g. the common people.' Others have not. 1956 intervened before we could get much further with our project to produce a volume of essays under the suggested title 'Some Marxist Contributions to the Study of British Capitalist Society', and the revision of the Marxist view on the English bourgeois revolution in the form of a larger work has not been carried out collectively, though a large number of books by Hill now supplement the relatively slim production of 1954. The plan to hold a general school for Marxist historians 'every few years' did not survive 1956. On the other hand the other perspective outlined in 1954, to 'carry discussions beyond the Party' and to draw non-Marxist historians into discussions with Marxist ones, has undoubtedly been realised, if in ways unpredicted by us then. It is probably impossible today for any non-Marxist historian not to discuss either Marx or the work of some Marxist historian in the course of his or her normal business as a historian, and, given the increase in the number of Marxists, it is much harder today to avoid discussing history with them than it was when Churchill and Eisenhower presided over the English-speaking world. To some extent this is certainly due to the work of the Group: of the thirty or so historians who took part in the discussions at Netherwood, probably at least twenty-five wrote or at least edited books in due course.

IV

Then came 1956. The Group survived the storms of that traumatic year and the loss of many – perhaps most – of its most devoted and publicly known members (e.g. the great majority of the contributors to *Democracy and the Labour Movement*), but its later history cannot really be compared to that of the years 1946–56, especially since it was to be many years before a new generation of Marxist historians were once again to be attracted to the Communist Party in any numbers. This is not the place for an account of the crises and conflicts which shook the British CP in 1956–7, but one question must nevertheless be faced: why were communist historians, whether or not they subsequently left the party, so prominent among the critics of the official party attitude at the time? For there can be no doubt that they were. The Group's Full Committee (which met on 8 April 1956, a few days after the British Party's Congress had concluded without any public discussion of the Stalin issue) rebelled against the official spokesman sent to address them and passed some sharply worded critical resolutions.[16] So far as I can recall, after this the Group itself did not express any further collective views, and was indeed increasingly split, but the fact that many of the most vocal critics came from among its members is a matter of record. The three most dramatic episodes of 'opposition' – the *Reasoner*, the publication of a letter by a number of intellectuals in the *New Statesman* and *Tribune*, and the Minority Report on Party Democracy at the Twenty-fifth Congress of the CPGB, were all associated with communist historians (Saville, Thompson, Hilton, Hill, Hobsbawm, among others), who were therefore also publicly attacked as a body by various loyalists. These disputes are now themselves part of history, and need not be revived here.

It was no doubt natural that the historians, as probably the most consistently active and flourishing group of communist intellectuals – unlike the scientists, it had not been shaken by the Lysenko affair, unlike the literary intellectuals, only marginally affected by the debates over Christopher Caudwell – should enter the debate. It felt itself to be a major target of the attack on unstable and doubting intellectuals which some official spokesmen and loyalists launched immediately after the Twentieth Congress; and unjustly so, since it consisted overwhelmingly of people who had survived the exodus of temporary communists after 1939 and the erosion of the years after 1945. This sense of resentment is reflected in the meeting of 8 April 1956, but does not explain why criticism seems to have been even more widespread among the historians than in other groups.[17]

The fact is that historians were inevitably forced to confront the situation not only as private persons and communist militants but, as it were, in their professional capacity, since the crucial issue of Stalin was literally one of history: what had happened and why it had been concealed. Moreover, as the discussions immediately made clear, the suppression of Soviet history could not be divorced from the question why other parts of contemporary history had not been confronted – not least such hotly disputed episodes in the history of the British CP as the 'Third Period' and 1939–41. (Both of these were raised at the meeting of 8 April.) Indeed, and even more fundamentally, such failures raised the general question of how Marxists ought to confront contemporary history and contemporary reality. As one critic put it at the same meeting: 'We have accepted Soviet articles on contemporary history in a way we did not for earlier centuries. We stopped being historians as regards the history of the CPSU or current affairs, or became cynical like (. . .). Must become historians in respect of present too.' Moreover, the failure to be historical was not merely retrospective. As another critic argued, it was not enough simply to welcome what the CPSU had done at the Twentieth Congress: 'We do not know, we can only endorse policy – but historians go by evidence.' And, as the principal critic put it, Khrushchev's attack on the 'cult of personality' was not really an analysis of the phenomenon. We did not even know whether what was said about Stalin was correct or not, so long as we only took it on authority.

These were not, of course, merely matters of professional conscience, though naturally this was important to historians. They were drawn into the centre of the debate because historical analysis was at the core of Marxist politics. It may be suggested that they found themselves so largely among the critics because the – probably inevitable – reaction of the Party leadership appeared to deny this. It was natural that Party leaders – not only in Britain – were tempted to minimise the disruption their parties faced by playing down the significance of the crisis. Business must go on as usual, or as near to usual as could be expected. Nothing had fundamentally changed, the Khrushchev revelations must be 'kept in perspective', and if the party only

managed to keep its head and surmount this latest among the
many shocks it had undergone and absorbed over the years, it
would continue to progress.[18]

Yet even if historians could appreciate the motives of the party
leadership and perhaps sometimes even recognize the short-
term legitimacy of their tactic, it was difficult to approve it.
Surely, as the chief critic pointed out at that initial meeting –
more than six months before the *Daily Worker* recognized the
existence of a crisis in the Party – this was 'the most serious and
critical situation the Party was in since its foundation'? Surely,
we were at a turning-point in the history of the communist
movement? Surely, whatever the short-term prospects, the
long-term prospects of the movement required the very frank
and self-critical analysis of what had gone wrong – including
our mistakes as British communists – which the official tactic
once again seemed to avoid, but which was now actually
possible, perhaps only for a short moment? Surely what was at
issue was not simply what happened in Eastern Europe, but the
future of the Communist Party and of socialism in Britain?

Whether these views were right or wrong, and to what extent,
are no longer questions of burning interest – indeed time has
answered some of them. In any case this is not the place to
conduct a general inquest into that traumatic year in the history
of the British Communist Party. At all events when it ended the
Historians' Group had been decimated. However, as already
noted, the great bulk of those who left the Communist Party
(and therefore the Group) during that period have continued to
work as Marxist historians, unlike most of the brilliant, and now
immensely distinguished and influential young historians who
left the Communist Party of France during the equivalent
period. And, fortunately, the friendship and comradeship of the
years before 1956 survived the tensions and disputes of the time
and the more permanent divergences of political allegiance.
1956 disrupted the history of the Historians' Group as an
organized unit within the Communist Party, but not the
development of Marxist history in Britain or the relations
between those who, whatever has since happened to them, look
back without regret on their years in the Group.

V

What did the Group achieve during the first ten years of its existence? Many of its routine internal activities are no longer of any interest, except to specialists in the history of one phase of the British Communist Party: the committee meetings, reports and other organizational labours which fill so much of the time of political activists, but are justified only by the results achieved by organization. Nevertheless, these labours should not go unrecorded, if only in justice to those who, like Daphne May and others, bore the brunt of them. The work of the Group depended on them. Again, much of what we did was absorbed into the texture of Party life and activity, and cannot realistically be separated from both: pamphlets, articles in the Party press, propaganda, talks to meetings and conferences and the like. Much of the historians' work was of this kind – a pamphlet on press freedom by E. P. Thompson, a lecture and leaflet on Robin Hood by Rodney Hilton, material for a Tees-side school on labour history by the editor of the *Local History Bulletin*. Such things may or may not have had some measurable effects – on a local campaign, on the development of individual activists – but to trace them, even if this were possible, is as pointless as to try to identify the effect of one man's spade or one day's watering on a vegetable patch. Still, something may have been achieved. Thus Hill writes retrospectively:

> I think that the celebration of 1640 – and especially of 1649 – did something for the Party in giving it confidence in a non-gradualist tradition to an extent that it is difficult for the younger generation perhaps to realise.

There remain the results of the Group's work which can be identified, though obviously in most cases not measured: its effects both on its members and, through their individual and collective work, on the interpretation and teaching of history. The individual and collective aspects cannot be separated, for the Historians' Group of 1946–56 was that rare, possibly unique, phenomenon in British historiography, a genuinely co-operative group, whose members developed their often highly individual work through a constant interchange among equals. It was not a 'school' built round an influential teacher or book. Even those most respected in the Group neither claimed to be authoritative nor were treated as such, at least by the numerically dominant nucleus of the Marxists of the 1930s or earlier vintages. None of us enjoyed the authority or prestige which comes from outside professional recognition, not even Dobb whose position in the academic world was isolated. Fortunately the Party invested none of us with ideological or political authority. We were united neither by common subject-matter, style nor set of mind – other than a desire to be Marxists. And yet it is certain that each of us as an individual historian, amateur or professional, as teacher or writer, bears the mark of our ten years' 'seminar' and none would be quite the same as a historian today without it.

Before trying to summarize our achievements, it may be useful to suggest some things we failed to do. For obvious reasons we failed to make much of a contribution to twentieth-century history at the time, though the positive side of this abstention[19] was that the Marxist historians of 1946–56, unlike the newly radicalized generations of the late 1960s, did not concentrate excessively on the nineteenth and twentieth century labour movement. We never doubted that the study of ancient philosophy (Farrington, Thomson), of early Christianity (Morris), of Attila (Professor E. Thompson) or medieval peasants (Hilton) was as 'relevant' as that of the Social Democratic Federation or the General Strike. Again, in our work on general capitalist development we were probably too reluctant to query such orthodoxies as had been established (e.g. in the USSR during the attacks on Pokrovsky). Curiously enough we were not, on the whole, very strong on the economic side of economic history, and our work probably did not advance as far as it might have done for this reason. It would be wrong to look back upon our work with other than rather qualified self-satisfaction.

On the other hand, our achievements were not insignificant. First, there is little doubt that the rise of 'social history' in Britain as a field of study, and especially of 'history from below' or the 'history of the common people', owes a great deal to the work of the members of the group (e.g. Hilton, Hill, Rudé, E. P. Thompson, Hobsbawm, Raphael Samuel). In particular the serious concern with plebeian ideology – the theory underlying the actions of social movements – is still largely identified with historians of this provenance, for the social history of *ideas* was always (thanks largely to Hill) one of our main preoccupations.

Second, the members of the group contributed very substantially to the development of labour history.[20] Third, the study of the English Revolution of the seventeenth century was largely transformed by us; and though this is largely due to Hill's 'dominant position in the field of Revolutionary studies today',[21] Hill himself would be the first to agree that the debates among Marxist historians on the Revolution and on his work, from 1940 onwards, played a part in the development of his views. The historiography of the English Revolution today is by no means predominantly Marxist; on the other hand, but for the Marxists it would certainly be very different. Fourth, members of the group have influenced the general teaching of history through the often very popular general textbooks which they have written, as well as through other works. In this respect A. L. Morton pioneered the way with his *People's History*, which still remains the only Marxist attempt to write the entire history of Britain (or rather England).[22] Fifth, the journal founded in the worst days of the Cold War by a group of Marxist historians, *Past & Present*, has become one of the leading historical journals in the world. Though it was never Marxist in the literal sense, and even dropped its sub-title 'a journal of scientific history' in 1958, the initiative, and to some extent the general stance of the journal, originally came from the Marxists, and their contribution to it was therefore crucial, at least in the early years when it established its standing.[23]

These are not negligible achievements. They justify recalling the ten fruitful years which began with Leslie Morton's desire to consult other Marxist historians for the second edition of his *People's History*. At all events, if no one else reads this memoir with interest or profit, one thing is certain: it will recall a part of their past to the middle-aged and ageing survivors of the Historians' Group of 1946–56, wherever their paths have since taken them.

NOTES

1 This in spite of the prominence – and the intellectual distinction – of Marxist economists in the 1930s, such as Maurice Dobb, the early Eric Roll, H. W. Dickinson and John Strachey, and the strikingly impressive group of Marxist natural scientists of the period, headed by J. D. Bernal

and J. B. S. Haldane. Incidentally both Dobb and Bernal themselves also produced historical work of very great importance.

2 John Saville would perhaps lay more stress on the historical writings produced by British communists during the 1930s than the present author.

3 Among them may be mentioned Mick Jenkins, Horace Green and Bill Moore of Sheffield, whose 'Sheffield Shop Stewards in the First World War' has since been reprinted in a selection of *Our History* studies, Lionel Munby (ed.), *The Luddites and Other Essays* (London, 1971).

4 R. P. Dutt, *The Internationale* (London, 1964).

5 See, for example, Daphne May, 'Work of the Historians' Group', *Communist Review*, May 1949, which is taken from a report to the Group. Any one of us would, as officials of the Group – Daphne May was its Secretary – have written in the same manner.

6 On looking through the files of the *Communist Review* it is notable that the numerous contributions by members of the group in 1948 and especially 1949 cease in and after 1950, though not in the more intellectual *Modern Quarterly* and its successor, the *Marxist Quarterly*.

7 A leading member of the Indian CP still used this Marxian concept in a book as late as 1952 (cf. E. M. S. Namboodripad, *The National Question in Kerala*); certainly without heterodox intentions.

8 As the Party's National Cultural Committee put it in November 1947: 'Direction of attack against our real enemies "to kill our enemies, not cure our friends".' And again: 'Must learn to discriminate between the leaders of certain reactionary trends and those misled by them, so that our attack is in the right direction.'

9 E. J. Hobsbawm, 'Where are British Historians Going?', *Marxist Quarterly*, II/1, 1955, p. 25.

10 *History* by Gordon Childe, *From Savagery to Civilization* by Grahame Clarke, *The Growth of Modern Germany* by Roy Pascal, *Feudal Order* by Marion (Molly) Gibbs, *Plough and Pasture* by E. Cecil Curwen, *Writing and the Alphabet* by A. C. Moorhouse, *The Decline of the Roman Empire in the West* by F. W. Walbank and *Men, Machines and History* by Sam Lilley. Two of the authors were active in the Group.

11 I would mention the late Max Gluckman, W. G. Hoskins, R. S. Lopez, G. C. Homans, Jean Seznec and Asa (Lord) Briggs. In return the Marxists were particularly careful not only to dissociate the journal from exclusive Marxism (cf. Preface to the Group's 'Bibliography of Marxist and Near-Marxist Historical Work Available in English' (first edition duplicated, *c.* 1956), but also to give the non-communist Board members an individual veto over the choice of articles. In 1958 the membership of the Board was broadened, as we had always intended it should be, and Marxists (some of whom had by then left the CP) were no longer in the majority.

12 Dona Torr was a powerful influence on several of the young Marxist historians, though not equally close to all. She was the editor of the *Selected Correspondence of Marx and Engels* (1934). Her published work does not do justice to her impressive erudition, and she never completed what was to have been her major book, *Tom Mann and His Times* (vol. I, 1956; fragments from vol. II, edited by E. P. Thompson, were published as 'Tom Mann and His Times 1890–1892' in *Our History*, 26–7, 1962).

13 Elaborate minutes of the thirteen sessions were kept (by Alf Jenkin, Edwin Payne, Louis Marks and Victor Kiernan) and compressed, with the help of the speakers, into a 30-page report which was subsequently distributed. The main organizational burden fell on Diana St John.

14 At least two active members of the group were in contact with the French 'Annales' school, as well as with some French Communist historians.

15 Hill's paper on ideas and literature, 1660–1760, was particularly admired.

16 The Minutes of this Meeting, attended by 19 out of the 34 possible members of the 'Full Committee', are in my possession.

17 Cf. John Saville, 'The Twentieth Congress and the British Communist Party' in *The Socialist Register*, 1976, p. 7.

18 The official speaker, as summarized in the Minutes of 8 April: 'Some jolted and may leave us, but ultimately situation will be more favourable – Soviet Union's corrections and perspective – new possibilities. Need for discussion of doubts and problems, but positively and in balanced way and historical perspective. Everything likely to settle down again in six months.'

19 However, the Group contained people who pursued private researches into the history of the British communist movement and public ones into that of the USSR, but at the time this work remained in the shadows.

20 I think the majority of the contributors to the *Essays in Labour History*, ed. Asa Briggs and J. Saville (1960), were or had been associated with the Group.

21 R. C. Richardson, *The Debate on the English Revolution*, 1977, p. 98.

22 An earlier Cambridge attempt, recalled in T. E. B. Howarth, *Cambridge between the Wars* (London, 1978), came to nothing. It was to have been edited by Roy Pascal. In addition to the contributors mentioned by Howarth – H. J. (now Sir John) Habbakuk, Vice-Chancellor of Oxford and Edward Miller, now Master of Fitzwilliam College, Cambridge – V. G. Kiernan and Michael Greenberg were involved. E. J. Hobsbawm, though mentioned in Howarth, was not. Oxford Marxist historians knew nothing of this project, which proves that there was no national coordination of Marxist historians at this date (probably 1937–8). Why the plan foundered – at least two chapters were drafted – is unclear.

23 Three members of the original editorial board are still associated with it, as well as some later arrivals also associated with the Group in 1946–56.

FROM LOLLARDS TO
LEVELLERS

CHRISTOPHER HILL

In the 1640s, when the censorship broke down and church courts ceased to function, a whole host of radical ideas popped up and were freely expressed. The question I want to ask is how far these ideas had had an underground existence before 1640, so that the novelty is only in the freedom to express them: or were they novel ideas, the product of novel circumstances? In the space at my disposal I cannot do more than throw out a few suggestions, and that is fortunate, for I have no completed thesis to put forward, only a few working hypotheses, a list of questions I am asking myself.

My point of departure was a book that I wrote called *The World Turned Upside Down*, in which I tried to analyse some of the more extreme ideas of the radical minority of the 1640s and 1650s. I sent a copy of this book to G. R. Elton, with an apologetic remark that I knew it was not his sort of book, but it was what I had written. Professor Elton replied, courteously but trenchantly: 'the ideas you find put forward are awfully old hat – commonplaces of radical and heretical thinking since well before the Reformation'. I had already noticed some parallels for myself between late Lollard ideas, as described by J. A. F. Thomson and A. G. Dickens, and my seventeenth century radicals.[1] What began to interest me was the possibility of continuity, and its mechanisms.

Now of course there are very special problems in attempting to trace continuities of underground ideas. By definition those who held them were anxious to leave no traces. Before the nineteenth century we can very rarely hear the lower orders speaking for themselves in a natural tone of voice. We hear instead what JPs in Quarter Sessions, judges in ecclesiastical courts, heresy-hunting pamphleteers, thought their inferiors were thinking, with all the dangers of distortion from such sources. ('Who writ the history of the Anabaptists but their enemies?' asked the Leveller Richard Overton; and the Leveller

William Walwyn spoke of 'that lying story of that injured people, . . . the Anabaptists of Münster').[2] Alternatively, we have to rely on inference, from the survival of particular doctrines in particular areas. In putting together scraps of evidence, which have survived by chance, we are unlikely to arrive at decisive conclusions. The problems are perennial whenever we try to reconstruct the history of the common man, still more of the common woman. Nearly all our history is upper-class and male. One of the delights of the English Revolution is the exceptional nature of the surviving evidence, thanks to the exceptional political liberty and the relative cheapness of printing.

Let us remind ourselves how very radical some of the ideas were which surfaced in the 1640s and 1650s. Levellers advocated political democracy, a republic with a widely extended franchise, abolition of the House of Lords, election of magistrates and judges, drastic legal and economic reforms. The Diggers and others carried the Leveller emphasis on natural rights to advocacy of a communist society. Sectaries and Milton extended the Puritan attack on bishops to rejection of the whole idea of a state church – its courts, its tithes, its fees, its control of education and the censorship, the very distinction between clergy and laity. They carried anti-sacramentalism to the point of regarding worship as discussion. Spiritual equality and the doctrine of the inner light were extended to rejection of the idea of 'sin', to a belief in human perfectibility on earth. Many denied the divinity of Christ, the immortality of the soul. Some ceased to believe in a local heaven or hell; the gospel story was treated as an allegory. Winstanley found the word Reason preferable to God. The protestant ethic, the dignity of labour, monogamous marriage, all came under attack.

Many of the proponents of these ideas looked back to Lollards and Marian martyrs as their ancestors. Foxe had of course accustomed Englishmen to this pedigree, to this answer to the question 'Where was your church before Luther?' But Foxe, we know, often played down the radicalism of his heretics.[3] Many of the views of Lollards and Marian martyrs would have been punishable under Elizabeth – which did not stop her making political capital out of Foxe's book. In the seventeenth century Levellers like Lilburne, Overton, Walwyn, a reformer like William Dell, emphasized the more radical elements in the heretical heritage. The point was regularly made from the other side. John Cleveland spoke of 'Presbyter Wyclif' and 'Tyler's toleration': the sneer was repeated by other poets, Abraham Cowley and John Collop. Charles I, in his answer of 18 June 1642 to Parliament's 19 Propositions, warned that, if opposition to him continued, 'at last the common people . . . [will] set up for themselves, call parity and independence liberty, . . . destroy all rights and properties, all distinctions of families and merit, and by this means this splendid and excellently distinguished form of government end in a dark, equal chaos of confusion, . . . in a Jack Cade or a Wat Tyler'.[4]

Continuities certainly existed between fifteenth century and seventeenth century radicals. Some are geographical: Lollardy and later heresy are found especially in clothing counties, in pastoral and woodland areas. Certain doctrines persist. I shall try to look at both types of continuity.

The Weald of Kent and Sussex was an area of forests, with few gentlemen and few manors. Parishes were large, and many families rarely attended church. It was a heavily populated and industrialized area (clothing and iron); the population was mobile and wayfaring, with 'multitudes of rogues and beggars', since there were many opportunities for casual labour.[5] Masterless men abounded who were fodder for conscription in time of war. The Weald had been a Lollard area; it remained very radical in religion, producing a group of 'free-willers' under Edward VI, and what Collinson calls 'rustic Pelagianism' under Elizabeth. There were many Marian martyrs. Rye was especially Puritan, or worse. Its poorer townsmen, their pastor said in 1537, 'reeked of Lollardy and ribaldry'.[6] The Weald produced radical heretics; there were food riots in Kent in 1630: and in the sixteen-thirties the largest single contingent of emigrants to Massachusetts came from there. Both John Taylor the Water-Poet, a man of conservative sympathies, and the radical George Wither thought it necessary to differentiate between Christendom and Kent. In the sixteen-twenties and sixteen-forties there was much support for political radicalism from the Weald and other traditional heretical areas.[7] It was John Trendall, stone-mason of Dover, on whose behalf Archbishop Neile in 1639 wished to revive the practice of burning heretics. Next year ten labourers from the old Lollard centre of Tenterden were up before the church court for refusing to pay

tithe on wages: 'what care we for his Majesty's laws and statutes?'
the churchwardens of Little Horsted in the Sussex Weald were
asking.[8] A host of sectaries appeared in the forties, at Tenterden
among other centres. Kent was one of the earliest counties to
have women preachers.[9] Kentish radicalism produced a strong
Leveller movement, and culminated in a Digger colony and a
near-Digger pamphlet. It was a Muggletonian centre of some
significance. Samuel Fisher, who evolved from a Baptist into a
Quaker, and who argued in a scholarly folio that the Bible was
not the Word of God, operated around Ashford.[10]

Essex is my next county, another woodland area, especially in
the North, the traditional radical region. Itinerants and
squatters abounded. The cottage clothing industry of this area
was described as a breeding ground for Lollardy. John Ball had
preached in Colchester. Essex participated in the Lollard revolt
of 1414, and heresy survived into the sixteenth century.[11] There
were major disturbances in the county in 1549, the year of Ket's
rebellion. There were more Marian martyrs from Essex than
from any other county except Kent (and London). In 1566 there
was an abortive rising in the clothing towns in the north-east of
the county. Under Edward VI there were groups of 'free-
willers', under Mary lower-class conventicles, and under
Elizabeth Familists, in Essex as in Kent. In 1581 there was a
preaching place in the woods at Ramsey, with straw and moss
for seating, 'and the ground trodden bare with much
treading'.[12] (Essex was also a county in which there was an
unusually large number of indictments for witchcraft in the
sixteenth and seventeenth centuries.[13] Here I can only hint at
the possible connections which caused Lollards, Anabaptists
and early Quakers to be denounced as witches). When the
famous Puritan William Ames was expelled from Christ's
College, Cambridge in 1610, he was promptly offered a city
lectureship at Colchester. But the bishop ensured that he was
not allowed to accept it.[14]

'What can rich men do against poor men if poor men rise and
hold together?' artisans were asking in Essex in 1594. Next year
they were threatening to hang sellers of victuals – a simple
remedy against inflationary price increases. In 1629 there were
two riots at Maldon (also Essex) led by Anne Carter, a butcher's
wife. She was hanged, with two others.[15] The Familist John
Everard held an Essex living. After 1638 Essex was the scene of

violent anti-clericalism. The common people pulled down communion rails and images. At the county elections in 1640 'rude vulgar people', 'fellows without shirts' (the English equivalent of sans-culottes?) threatened to 'tear the gentlemen to pieces' if the popular candidate were not elected.[16] 'Many thousands' turned out to sack the papist Countess of Rivers's house, and then transferred their attention to non-papists. When manorial documents and evidences were destroyed at Colchester in 1641 the jury gave an ignoramus verdict against the plunderers. They were indicted again at the assizes, but the sheriff could not get a jury to convict. At Milford, Essex, 'no man appeared like a gentleman but was made a prey to that ravenous crew'. 'The rude people are come to such a head,' said a Colchester gentleman, 'that we know not how to quiet them.' They 'must take advantage of these times lest they never have the like again', said an Essex enclosure rioter in 1642; 'there was no law settled at this time that he knew', said a poacher in the same county in the same year.[17]

In January 1642 6,000 Essex freeholders signed a petition against bishops: the county was described (by a Puritan) as the 'place of most life of religion in the land'. Thousands from Essex marched on London after the arrest of the Five Members.[18] Bruno Ryves's account of the principles held by the lower classes of Chelmsford around 1643 is prophetic of much that was to be developed later: but it also recalls much that had gone before. Kings are burdens. The relation of master and servant has no ground in the New Testament; in Christ there is neither bond nor free. Ranks such as those of the peerage and gentry are 'ethnical and heathenish distinctions'. There is no ground in nature or Scripture why one man should have £1000 *per annum*, another not £1. The common people have long been kept under blindness and ignorance, and have remained servants and slaves to the nobility and gentry. 'But God hath now opened their eyes and discovered unto them their Christian liberty.' Gentlemen should be made to work for their living, or else should not eat. Learning has always been an enemy to the Gospel; it would be better if there were no universities, and all books except the Bible were burned. Any gifted man may be chosen by a congregation as its minister. Baptists, Ranters and Muggletonians were all to be found in Essex in the forties and fifties.[19]

The Chiltern hills of Buckinghamshire formed another Lollard area, where there was a revolt in 1413–14. Again heresy survived into the sixteenth century. In 1521 more were persecuted for heresy in Buckinghamshire than in all the rest of England. A century later Isaac Penington, the Long Parliament's Lord Mayor of London, later a regicide, came of a family resident in Buckinghamshire since the 1550s. In 1640 the elections at High Wycombe and Great Marlow provided classic examples of class conflict. County freeholders elected John Hampden, and rode up to London in their thousands to defend the Five Members against Charles I's attempt to impeach them in January 1642. Buckinghamshire Levellers sponsored anti-enclosure riots, and produced two pamphlets – *Light Shining in Buckinghamshire* and *More Light Shining in Buckinghamshire* – which are close to the Diggers in sentiment, though both were published before digging started at St George's Hill. Winstanley's colony was endorsed by a third pamphlet from the Chiltern Hundreds, *A Declaration of the Well-Affected in the County of Buckinghamshire* (May 1649). Like Kent, Buckinghamshire had a Digger colony, at the old Lollard centre of Iver, with its own pamphlet (May 1650).[20] Quakers found an early welcome in the county of Penington and Penn: High Wycombe was one of the centres of the near-Ranter Story-Wilkinson separation.

Readers of Dickens's admirable *Lollards and Protestants in the Diocese of York* will remember that many of the most savoury Lollard remarks came from the moorland and clothing areas of the West Riding of Yorkshire, another remote region of huge and uncontrolled parishes. In the sixteen-twenties this area produced Grindletonians, who put the spirit before the letter of the Bible, and thought that heaven was attainable in this life; in the sixteen-forties the lower classes in the West Riding forced the gentry to take up arms for Parliament. John Webster, religious radical and would-be reformer of the universities came from the Grindleton area; George Fox found his first congregations there, including James Nayler and many other Quaker leaders. Drunken Barnaby found Familists in Bradford in the sixteen-thirties. There were Ranters later. From another Lollard area, Gloucestershire, the reformer William Tyndale came in the sixteenth century, the anti-Trinitarians John Bidle and John Knowles a century later. Levellers and Quakers found their greatest support in the south of England in Bristol. There were antinomians, Brownists and enclosure riots in Gloucestershire in the sixteen-thirties, forties and fifties. There was a Digger colony; later there were Ranters. Or we might take Wiltshire or Somerset, East Anglia, Coventry or London, where the parish of St Stephens, Coleman Street, seems to have harboured extreme heretics for a century and more. In seventeenth-century Scotland the main strength of radicalism came from Ayrshire, an old Lollard area.[21]

I do not want to impose too much organizational coherence upon those who transmitted the ideas I have been discussing: that is one of the dangers of historical hindsight. In the fifteenth and early sixteenth centuries the orthodox spoke of 'Lollards'; under Elizabeth of 'Anabaptists' or 'Familists'. There were indeed Lollard and Anabaptist groups, and the Family of Love also had some sort of organization. We do not know very much about any of them yet: more research is needed. But I suspect that clerical inquisitors imposed classifications, 'isms', for their own convenience. They started with some idea of what 'Lollards', 'Anabaptists' or 'Familists' ought to believe, just as they started with assumptions about what 'witches' believed. Leading questions would then encourage suspects to conform to the expected type.

So though there were 'Lollard', 'Anabaptist' and 'Familist' trends in popular thought, we should not necessarily postulate the existence of an organized underground. But there are tantalizing hints. Elizabethan Familists are said to have been linked by itinerant weavers, basket-makers, musicians, bottlemakers, joiners. In 1622 Thomas Shepard in Essex knew about the Grindletonian Familists, lurking in the obscurity of a Yorkshire Pennine valley.[22] The clothing industry linked Essex and the West Riding. The Grindletonians were to be associated retrospectively with Coppinger (who had Kentish connections) and the Yorkshire gentleman Arthington, disciples of William Hacket who in the fifteen-nineties believed he was the Messiah. There were Quakers in the sixteen-fifties in parts of Cambridgeshire where there had been Familists 80 years earlier.[23]

Familists – like Lollards before them – tended when challenged to recant, but to remain of the same opinion still. This unheroic attitude was related to their dislike of all established churches, whether protestant or catholic. Their refusal of martyrdom no doubt helped their beliefs to survive, but it increases the historian's difficulty in identifying heretical groups with confidence. Only after the excitement of the reign of Edward VI were lower-class heretics for a brief period prepared to court martyrdom: after 1660 one suspects that many former Ranters and Baptists reverted to the ways of their Familist predecessors and returned formally and unbelievingly to the national church. The Ranters 'would have said as we said and done as we commanded, and yet have kept their own principle still', said Durant Hotham, stressing this Lollard and Familist way of acting as the main difference between Ranters and Quakers.[24]

Before 1640 the traditions I have been describing circulated verbally. Historians, themselves the products of a literary culture, relying so much on written or printed evidence, are always in danger of underestimating verbal transmission of ideas. Men did not need to read books to become acquainted with heresy: indeed censored books were the last place in which they would expect to find it. Again and again the great heresiarchs deny being influenced by their predecessors. Luther was astonished to find that he was reproducing Hus's heresies: Milton was astonished and delighted to find that many protestant divines had anticipated his views on divorce.

With all these reservations, let me now suggest some continuing lower-class traditions which burst into the open in the 1640s. There is no need to produce further evidence of the point I have already stressed, class hatred, since this has recently been fully documented in Mr Brian Manning's magnificent *The English People and the English Revolution*. More generalized illustrations of hostility to social subordination are refusal to remove the hat in the presence of magistrates or social superiors, and addressing them as 'thou' in symbolic assertion of equality. The Quakers inherited a long-standing lower-class tradition here. The fifteenth century Lollard William Thorpe kept his hat on in the presence of authority. Refusal to bow to superiors was noted in the fifteenth century York Mystery Plays. Some Marian martyrs kept their hats on. So did Essex heretics in 1584, William Hacket in 1591, an oatmeal-maker up before the High Commission in 1630, the future Leveller John Lilburne in 1638, John Saltmarsh in 1647, and very many others.[25] John Lewis, burnt at Norwich in 1583 for anti-Trinitarianism, 'did thou each wight'; so did Essex heretics under Elizabeth. Refusal to take an oath is also a rejection of political authority: we find it among Norwich and Essex Lollards, some Anabaptists, Barrowists, Lilburne. Again this was inherited by the Quakers. The myth of the Norman Yoke enshrines a similar anti-authoritarian and anti-aristocratic attitude, rejection of the ruling class and its law. So does 'When Adam delved and Eve span/Who was then the gentleman?' quoted in the reign of Edward VI, in 1593 and often after 1640 – 'this levelling lewd text', Cleveland called it. Sneers about Jack Straw, Wat Tyler and Jack Cade were frequent. Fuller said the rebels of 1381 were 'pure Levellers'. Sir Thomas Aston referred in 1641 to 'the old seditious argument, that we are all the sons of Adam, born free; some of them say, the Gospel hath made them free. . . . They will plead Scripture for it, that we should all live by the sweat of our brows.'[26]

The Digger community at St George's Hill, we now know, was only one of ten or more such experiments; communist ideas are to be found in many writers not directly associated with the Diggers, such as the Ranter Abiezer Coppe and the author of *Tyranipocrit Discovered*; they were attributed to the Leveller Walwyn. John Ball and Essex Lollards were alleged to have said that property should be common. Similar charges were made against participants in Cade's rebellion in 1450.[27] Such accusations may be the product of the alarmed imaginations of the rich; but since community of property is commended in the New Testament it is unlikely that no lower-class Bible-reader would take the point. An Essex man did, late in Henry VIII's reign: Chelmsford radicals a century later were said to have done so. Tyndale came dangerously near to justifying community of property, and such ideas occurred in the mid-sixteenth century often enough for one of the 42 Articles of 1552 and of the 39 Articles of 1562 to be directed against them.[28]

Turning to divergences from the norm in more specifically religious matters, Essex Lollards said that priests should marry and work, and attacked non-preachers. Pluralism was as bad as bigamy, said an Essex Lollard burnt in 1440. Another in the same county 17 years later said that the best man was the best priest, and that confession should be made only to God – anticipating the lay initiative in Puritanism and the sects. John Ball thought tithes should be paid only by men richer than the

priest. Ministers should not be paid, said Augustine Draper, of
Essex, in 1587: he also denied the immortality of the soul.
Opposition to tithes became standard among the radicals of the
revolutionary decades. Wyclif had thought that the exercise of
civil jurisdiction by ecclesiastics, and in particular the use of
force, was antichristian. So did many seventeenth century
radicals, including John Milton.[29]

The seventeenth century view that a layman is as good as a
parson, that the whole ecclesiastical hierarchy is antichristian,
that tithes and a state church should be abolished, together with
universities as training centres for the clergy; advocacy of
'mechanic preachers' who enjoy the spirit of God, so much
more important than academic education: all these ideas are so
familiar from Wyclif and the Lollards through Anabaptists and
Familists to Levellers and sectaries in the sixteen-forties and
fifties that full documentation would be superfluous. Familist
ministers were itinerant craftsmen, and indeed the conditions of
underground sectarianism forced the emergence of mechanic
preachers. Anti-sacerdotalism was a necessity as well as an
ideology. Some Lollards, and a reformer like William Tyndale,
even thought that women might preach.[30]

Secondly comes a strong emphasis on study of the Bible, and
use of its texts – as interpreted by the individual conscience – to
criticize the ceremonies and sacraments of the church. Worship
of images, for instance, was denounced as idolatry. Sacredness
was denied to church buildings: worship and prayer could take
place anywhere. Some Essex Lollards advocated adult baptism,
which looks forward to Samuel Oates, weaver and button-
maker, dipping in Essex in 1645–6 as well as begetting Titus.
Millenarianism, familiar in lower-class underground
movements, was found among the later Lollards; it reappeared
in England in the 1590s and 1640s.[31]

Arminianism, the doctrine that men may save themselves by
their own efforts, does not seem a particularly dangerous heresy
to us today. But it did to orthodox sixteenth and seventeenth
century Puritans. (We must distinguish between radical
Arminianism, rejecting the sacraments of the church as aids
to salvation, and Laudian Arminianism). Many English
heretics in the sixteenth century rejected predestination,
attached greater value to works than to faith, and emphasized
human freedom and effort – a sort of pre-Arminianism, which

can be found among Familists, as well as among continental
Anabaptists, from whom it was taken over by the English
General Baptists. A Kentish heretic, Henry Hart, 'a froward
freewill man', who wrote a treatise against predestination in
1554, anticipated Milton in saying that human freedom to
choose between good and evil was essential if God was to be
absolved of responsibility for evil. An Essex heretic in 1592
thought that 'all the world shall be saved'; Thomas Edwards in
1646 attributed the idea of universal salvation to Familists and
other radicals. Thomas Shepard's interest in the Yorkshire
Grindletonians in 1622 led him to ask 'whether that glorious
state of perfection might not be the truth?' The belief that
perfection could be attained in this life had been held by
London tradesmen in 1549 and 1631, and by many Familists in
between. In the sixteen-forties Mrs Attaway and William Jenny
believed that it could not stand with the goodness of God to
damn his creatures eternally: Walwyn was to say that eternal
punishment was too great for 'a little sinning'.[32]

Another recurrent heresy is anti-Trinitarianism. Some
Lollards denied the divinity of Christ and the Holy Spirit. The
rapid spread of anti-Trinitarianism both in the liberty of
Edward's reign and in prisons under Mary gave rise to great
alarm among orthodox protestants – so much so that the godly
John Philpot had to apologize for 'spitting upon an Arian'.[33] In
1555 denial of the divinity of Christ by an itinerant joiner, later a
well-known Familist, was the subject of discussions in an illegal
meeting in a Colchester tavern, to which servants and
husbandmen travelled long distances from outside the county.
Some of the Marian martyrs were probably anti-Trinitarians,
and between 1548 and 1612 at least eight persons were burnt in
England for heresies concerning the Trinity. Among them was
Marlowe's friend Francis Kett, grandson of the leader of the
Norfolk rebels in 1549, who was a mortalist and rejected the
authority of ministers to excommunicate. Marlowe, himself
from Kent, was said to have called Christ a bastard; in 1560 a
Kentish man had said that those who believed Christ sat on the
right hand of the Father were fools.[34] The three Legate brothers
from Essex, one of whom was burnt in 1612, were anti-
Trinitarians: so was Wightman, the last Englishman to be burnt
for heresy, also in 1612. The heresy was associated especially
with Familists, who rejected the whole theology of the

Atonement, Christ's vicarious sacrifice; some abandoned belief
in the historical existence of Christ. For them the word Christ was
a metaphor for the divine spark which exists in every man.
William Pynchon of Essex carried anti-Trinitarianism to
Massachusetts in the 1630s; John Bidle of Gloucestershire, John
Milton and very many others proclaimed it in England in the
forties and fifties.[35] The humanity of Christ enhanced the dignity
of man.

Another heresy which recurs among underground groups
was mortalism, the doctrine that the soul either sleeps from
death until the general resurrection or dies with the body.
Professor N. T. Burns has so thoroughly demonstrated the
continuous existence of *Christian Mortalism from Tyndale to Milton*
that I refer to him for evidence, though with a caution that
mortalism existed in England well before the Reformation –
among Essex Lollards, e.g. Tyndale was a mortalist.[36] The
42 Articles of 1552 condemned mortalism, though the
condemnation was omitted in the 39 Articles of 1562.
Elizabethan Familists were alleged to be mortalists, believing
that the resurrection occurred in this life. Some held that the
soul was annihilated at death. Among mortalists were Augustine
Draper of Essex, who also thought the clergy should not be
paid; and the anti-Trinitarians Francis Kett and Edward
Wightman, burnt respectively in 1589 and 1612. Mortalism too
travelled to New England where Mrs Anne Hutchinson and
Samuel Gorton were accused in the 1630s of being mortalists as
well as Familists. In the forties and fifties Richard Overton,
Clement Writer, Lodowick Muggleton and John Milton were
only some of a large number of adherents to the belief.[37]

Mortalism was often accompanied by, or led to, a species of
materialism. In 1428 the Lollard Margery Backster anticipated
Milton in a crude reference to the ultimate physical fate of bread
eaten in the eucharist, in order to show that it could hardly be
the body of Christ. Dickens quotes many similar remarks. A
man from north-west Kent in 1538 denied that God had created
him, and many early heretics believed – like the Ranters of the
1650s – that 'all comes by nature', and that matter is good in
itself.[38] Such doctrines can by a natural progression lead to anti-
asceticism, glorification of the body, a belief that life is to be
enjoyed here and now. This may be expressed as an antinomian
libertinism: the elect are exempt from the moral law since God

is in them; they partake of God's nature. Such doctrines in England were denounced by Thomas Rogers in 1607.[39] They surfaced in the sixteen-forties, some in *Paradise Lost*.

If at death the body returns into its elements, as a drop of water taken out of the ocean returns to it again, mortalism can also lead to scepticism about heaven and hell, which become states of mind rather than geographical locations. Some Lollards denied the existence of heaven and hell, and placed Purgatory in this world. The devil too was internalized. This could combine with allegorical interpretations of the Bible to make the whole Christian myth describe conflicts which take place only within the believer. Familists were said to hold that Christ and Antichrist were not real persons, heaven and hell not real places: all were states of mind. In the sixteen-twenties the Grindletonians, like Thomas Münzer before them and Gerrard Winstanley after them, emphasized the spirit as against the letter of Scripture, a doctrine not unknown to Milton. A Norfolk anti-Trinitarian in 1579 anticipated the Ranters by saying that the New Testament was 'a mere fable'.[40]

The poet Gower in the fifteenth century described labourers who were not satisfied with the bread and water on which they had been brought up but demanded good food and drink – and did not believe in God. There were 'libertines' in Essex in 1551, and later men who rejected 'sin' and were critical of the Bible in a way that looks forward to Clement Writer and Samuel Fisher in the sixteen-fifties. One described himself as an atheist.[41] This led on to sexual heresies. 'A lewd fellow out of Essex' in 1457 objected to church marriage: it should be a civil ceremony, as Buckinghamshire heretics taught in the first decades of Henry VIII's reign, and as the Barebones Parliament enacted in 1653. 'Marriage is superfluous', the Venetian Ambassador reported heretics as saying in 1499. Sixteenth-century Familists married and divorced by simple declaration before the congregation. The Yorkshire custom of 'handfast marriages' was taken up by Ranters and Quakers. Some Lollards may have advocated polygamy, though the evidence is doubtful. It was defended in 1548, in Kent in 1572, by Milton in the sixteen-fifties.[42]

We isolate heresies for the purpose of analysis, but they normally came in combination. Sir Thomas More linked anti-Trinitarianism with advocacy of common ownership of property.[43] Edmund Leach has suggested that anti-

Trinitarianism, millenarianism and social revolt go together, among the early Christians and in seventeenth-century England. Radical Arminianism, rejection of infant baptism, antinomianism, mortalism and materialism were frequently linked with Leach's heresies in England, as Thomas Edwards noted in *Gangraena* in 1646. In the same year the respectable inhabitants of Great Burstead, Essex, saw similar connections. They petitioned against 'a dangerous sect' which had arisen in their parish, admitting and rebaptizing all comers, 'setting up mechanics for their preachers, denouncing the order and ministry of the Church of England as antichristian'. They taught 'unsound opinions' like universal grace, the abrogation of the law, the sinfulness of repentance.[44] Their name was legion, and they had a long pedigree.

Looking back to Lollards and Familists helps to emphasize that, if there was a continuing underground, it was essentially composed of laymen. This fits in with what we are coming to know about the initiative in Puritanism of lay members of congregations in refusing to allow their minister to wear the surplice or to conform to other ceremonies. The Puritan clergy were moderate reformers, safely educated at Oxford or Cambridge. They naturally had not much use for lay mechanic preaching. There were initially some Lollard hedge priests, but they counted for less and less with time. Familist ministers seem normally to have been craftsmen.

The church was the official parish meeting place; and it belonged to the official clergy. The meeting place of the unorthodox was the tavern or ale-house, from Lollards to Familists and on to Baptists, Levellers and Ranters. The only other popular meeting place was the open air; Quakers preached there. Lawrence Clarkson said that a tavern was the house of God.[45] The popularity of the ale-house, apart from the obvious reason, was partly due to the evolution of a new itinerant clothing working-class, which sought social intercourse and information about jobs in taverns. JPs deeply resented any attempt to remove control of ale-houses from their hands, whether by Buckingham's protégés Mitchell and Mompesson or by Oliver Cromwell's Major-Generals.

So I suggest as a hypothesis for further investigation that there may have been a continuing underground tradition — not necessarily organization — in which we can identify certain heretical and seditious beliefs. Professor Elton's famous statement that there was no connection between Lollardy and the Reformation is true only if we interpret the Reformation in the narrowest sense as Henry VIII's act of state. But if we ask why England became a protestant country we cannot leave Lollardy out of account, though it was the more radical protestants who looked back to the Lollards. Bruce McFarlane was right to call his book *John Wycliffe and English Nonconformity*. I think we can trace direct links in ideas from Lollards through Familists and Anabaptists to the radical sectaries, the Levellers, Diggers, Ranters and Quakers of the mid-seventeenth century.

This leads on to a final question. What happened after 1660? It took some time to realize that defeat was final, that the above-ground decades had been a mere interlude. In 1678–81 something surfaced again in London. But the defeat of the radicals in 1685 facilitated the coup of 1688, when Whigs and Tories united against the radicals no less than against James II. Some emigrated, to the West Indies, New England and the continent. Some no doubt lapsed into silent bloody-mindedness. Some became sectaries; the Quakers cast off their radical wing and became pacifists. All sects were purged by the fierce persecution of the three decades after 1660. They had to recognize that Christ's kingdom was not to be built on earth now, but was to be expected in heaven in the sweet bye and bye. But the Levellers were never wholly forgotten. Goldsmith praised them. Jefferson quoted William Rumbold. There had been men who called themselves Levellers in revolt in Worcestershire in 1670, in anti-enclosure riots in 1724, in Ledbury in 1735, in the Lowlands of Scotland in the seventeen-twenties, in the Hudson valley in 1760, other American rebels under William Prendergast in 1765.[46] The Leveller sea-green colours reappeared in the streets of London in 1681, and the Whig Green Ribbon Club took its name from them. London weavers in 1675 had rioted in green aprons, and green aprons soon came to be 'almost regarded as a badge of Quakerism'.[47] The fact that the Chartist flag was green is usually attributed to Irish influence; but why did Irish protestants adopt the colour in the first place? In 1690 William III's troops in Ireland wore green, and some are said to have chosen the Leveller sea-green, so there may be continuity from Levellers through Whigs to United Irishmen and Chartists. At all events the Levellers were still remembered in the Chartist movement.[48] Was it only because of Robespierre's complexion that Carlyle labelled him 'sea-green'?

Nor is it only a matter of politics. A. L. Morton showed that Blake was aware of the Ranter past, and Burns may have been.[49] How the ideas were transmitted is more difficult to document. A lay clerk of Norwich cathedral about 1700 was alleged to think that 'there is no heaven but a quiet mind and no hell but the grave' – almost a literal quotation from many Ranters. Wesley in the seventeen-forties met antinomian preachers in the Black Country – an old Lollard/Ranter area – who believed in community of property and did not believe in monogamy.[50] The linked doctrines of mortalism, millenarianism and the perfectibility of man on earth were still being discussed in a Kentish General Baptist congregation in the middle of the eighteenth century.[51] In 1756 the Robin Hood Society met every Monday night at a pub in Butchers' Row, London. Here Deists, Arians, Socinians, Papists and Jews aired their doubts about the resurrection, the incarnation, the Trinity ('their everlasting butt'), the authenticity of the Scriptures, of the Gospel miracles. They were a set of mechanics – tailors, barbers, butchers and shoemakers.[52] Where did the millenarian revivalism come from which accompanied the American as it had accompanied the English Revolution? What about the New England antinomians of the eighteen-twenties and thirties, whose belief that perfection was attainable on earth led to sexual eccentricities and experiments as it had done in old England nearly two centuries earlier? If we look for them, I think we can find other traces, before 1640 and after 1660. One of the objects of this paper is to encourage others to look.

NOTES

1 Cf. G. F. Nuttall, 'The Lollard Movement after 1384, its characteristics and continuity', *Transactions of the Congregational Historical Society*, XII (1935), pp. 243–50.

2 C. Hill, *The World Turned Upside Down* (Penguin edn), p. 120.

3 I. B. Horst, *The Radical Brethren* (Nieuwkoop, 1972), pp. 146–8.

4 J. Cleveland, *The Rustic Rampant*, in *Works* (1687), p. 506; A. Cowley, *The Civil War* (ed. A. Pritchard, Toronto U.P., 1973), pp. 88, 103; J. Collop,

Poems (ed. C. Hilberry, Wisconsin U.P., 1962), p. 48; J. Rushworth, *Historical Collections (1659–1701)*, V, p. 732.

5 A. Fletcher, *A County Community in Peace and War: Sussex, 1600–1660* (1975), pp. 3, 21, 61, 165–6, 193, 200.

6 J. Foxe, *Acts and Monuments* (ed. J. Pratt, n.d.), IV, pp. 123, 181, 619; V, pp. 16, 647–52, 841; VII, pp. 287–321, 329–41, 383, 604, 750–2; VIII, pp. 130–1, 151–6, 243–7, 253–5, 300–3, 320–77, 394, 430–3, 504–6, 549–50, 566–8, 576, 695, 729–30, Appendix VI; P. Collinson, *The Elizabethan Puritan Movement* (1967), p. 37; cf. pp. 96–7; Horst, op. cit., pp. 122–40; Fletcher, op. cit., pp. 62, 91, 124; J. W. Martin, 'English Protestant Separatism at its Beginnings: Henry Hart and the Free-Will Men', *Sixteenth Century Journal*, VII (1976), pp. 58, 66–7; Claire Cross, *Church and People, 1450–1660* (1976), pp. 25, 28, 37–9, 73–4, 98–9, 112, 114, 170; P. Clark, *English Provincial Society from the Reformation to the Revolution: Religion, Politics and Society in Kent, 1500–1640* (1977), pp. 23, 30–1, 56, 60, 63, 67, 77, 101, 156, 399, 401–2, 441, and *passim*.

7 J. Walter and K. Wrightson, 'Dearth and the Social Order in Early Modern England', *Past and Present*, No. 71, p. 27; P. Clark, 'Popular Protest and Disturbance in Kent, 1558–1640', *Economic History Review*, XXIX (1976), pp. 365–82; *English Provincial Society*, pp. 335, 381, 389, 393; J. Taylor, *All the Works* (1973 reprint), II, p. 114 (rightly 124); G. Wither, *Fragmenta Prophetica* (1669), p. 130, in *Miscellaneous Works* (Spenser Soc., sixth collection, 1878).

8 Fletcher, op. cit., p. 22.

9 *Calendar of State Papers, Domestic, 1639*, pp. 455–6; B. Manning, *The English People and the English Revolution* (1976), p. 41; C. Hill, *Society and Puritanism in Pre-Revolutionary England* (Panther edn. 1969), p. 298. Mr Peter Clark helped me with Tenterden.

10 Hill, *The World Turned Upside Down*, pp. 46–7, 124–7, 259.

11 Foxe, op. cit., IV, pp. 214–17, 584–6, 695, 706–7; V, pp. 29–34, 38–42, 251; VI, pp. 729–40, 782; VII, pp. 86–90, 97–123, 139–42, 329, 370, 605, 718–30; VIII, pp. 107–21, 138–41, 303–10, 381–94, 420–3, 433–6, 467–8, 525–6, Appendix VI; Horst, op. cit., pp. 122–3; Collinson, op. cit., p. 223; Collinson, 'The Godly: Aspects of Popular Protestantism in Elizabethan England', *Papers Presented to the Past and Present Conference on Popular Religion* (1966), p. 16; Martin, op. cit., p. 66; Claire Cross, op. cit., pp. 25, 37–9, 73–4, 77, 98–9, 112.

12 A. G. Dickens, 'Heresy and the Origins of English Protestantism', in *Britain and the Netherlands*, II (ed. J. S. Bromley and E. H. Kossman, Groningen, 1964), pp. 53–5, 60.

13 C. L'E. Ewen, *Witch Hunting and Witch Trials* (1929), p. 100; A. Macfarlane, *Witchcraft in Tudor and Stuart England* (1970), *passim*.

14 K. L. Sprunger, *The Learned Doctor William Ames* (Illinois University Press, 1972), pp. 24–5.

15 Walter and Wrightson, op. cit., p. 36.

16 J. Gruenfeld, 'The Election for Knights of the Shire for Essex, Spring 1640', *Essex Archaeological Soc. Trans.*, II (3rd Series, 1967), pp. 145–6; J. A. Sharpe, 'Crime and Delinquency in an Essex Parish, 1600–1640', in *Crime in England, 1550–1800* (ed. J. S. Cockburn, 1977), pp. 90–109.

17 C. Holmes, *The Eastern Association in the English Civil War* (C.U.P. 1974), pp. 35–6, 43–4.

18 Manning, op. cit., pp. 32–3, 104.

19 Hill, *The World Turned Upside Down*, pp. 37, 263.

20 Foxe, op. cit., IV, pp. 123–6, 211–43, 580–6; V, p. 434; K. V. Thomas, 'Another Digger Broadside', *Past and Present*, No. 42 (1969), pp. 57–68; Hill, *The World Turned Upside Down*, pp. 21, 117, 126; A. G. Dickens, 'Heresy and the Origins of English Protestantism', pp. 53–6; Claire Cross, op. cit., pp. 28–32, 35, 42, 73, 98; T. Edwards, *Gangraena* (1646), I, p. 64.

21 Hill, *The World Turned Upside Down*, pp. 83, 121, 124–5, 218, 226–8, 234, 239; Manning, op. cit., pp. 210–16; A. Hassell Smith, *County and Court: Government and Politics in Norfolk, 1558–1603* (Oxford U.P., 1974), p. 203; Foxe, op. cit., IV, pp. 133–5, 243, 557–8; VI, p. 612; VII, pp. 384–402, 799 sqq.; VIII, pp. 163–202, 256, 401–5, Appendix VI; Claire Cross, op. cit., pp. 27–8, 35–7, 73, 75, 112; Imogen Laxton, 'The Reformation and Popular Culture', in *Church and Society in England, Henry VIII to James I* (ed. F. Heal and R. O'Day, 1977), pp. 66–7.

22 M. Spufford, *Contrasting Communities* (Cambridge U.P., 1974), p. 247; Hill, *The World Turned Upside Down*, pp. 26–7, 45, 83–4.

23 K. V. Thomas, *Religion and the Decline of Magic* (1971), pp. 134–6; Spufford, op. cit., p. 351. I owe the information about Coppinger to Mr Peter Clark.

24 Hill, *The World Turned Upside Down*, p. 257.

25 Foxe, op. cit., VIII, p. 314; J. Strype, *Annals of the Reformation* (Oxford U.P., 1824), IV, p. 97; F. G. Emmison, *Elizabethan Life: Morals and Church Courts* (Chelmsford, 1973), pp. 309–10; Hill, *The World Turned Upside Down*, p. 29.

26 Ed. H. E. Rollins, *Old English Ballads, 1553–1625* (Cambridge U.P., 1920), p. 56; Emmison, op. cit., p. 126; Cleveland, *Works*, p. 402; T. Fuller, *Church History* (1842), I, p. 451; Sir T. Aston, *A Remonstrance Against Presbytery* (1641), Sig. I 4v; O. Lutaud, *Winstanley* (Paris, 1976), p. 60. For the Norman Yoke see my *Puritanism and Revolution* (Panther edn, 1968), pp. 58–125.

27 I owe this point to Mr Robin Jeffs.

28 L. B. Smith, *Henry VIII* (Panther edn, 1973), pp. 144, 149; W. Tyndale, *Doctrinal Treatises* (Parker Soc., 1848), pp. 97–9; Horst, op. cit., p. 147.

29 Emmison, op. cit., p. 110; cf. Hill, *Economic Problems of the Church* (Panther edn, 1971), pp. 121, 133; Foxe, op. cit., IV, p. 178.

30 Foxe, op. cit., IV, pp. 213, 234, 580.

31 Ed. H. E. Rollins, *Cavalier and Puritan* (New York, 1923), pp. 171–8; J. A. F. Thomson, *The Later Lollards, 1414–1520* (O.U.P., 1965), pp. 240–1; Thomas, op. cit., p. 144.

32 Martin, op. cit., pp. 55–74 *passim*; Horst, op. cit., pp. 122–40; Emmison, op. cit., p. 101; Hill, *The World Turned Upside Down*, pp. 83–4, 147–8, 184; Thomas, op. cit., pp. 133–4; Claire Cross, op. cit., pp. 98–9, 114, 170. I am indebted to discussions with Professors Joseph Martin and Jean Moss about sixteenth-century Familism.

33 I am grateful to Professor Martin for drawing my attention to this. Cf. Clark, *English Provincial Society*, p. 101.

34 Thomson, op. cit., pp. 36, 82, 106, 196, 248; J. Jewell, *An Apology for the Church of England* (Parker Soc., 1848–50), II, p. 1241; Spufford, op. cit., p.

247; Dewey D. Wallace, 'From Eschatology to Arian Heresy: the Case of Francis Kett', *Harvard Theological Review*, 67 (1974), pp. 461–2. The last point I owe to Mr Peter Clark.

35 H. J. McLachlan, *Socinianism in Seventeenth Century England* (O.U.P., 1951), p. 234.

36 N. T. Burns, *Christian Mortalism from Tyndale to Milton* (Harvard U.P., 1972), *passim*; cf. Claire Cross, op. cit., p. 95.

37 Burns, op. cit., pp. 57–8, 69–72.

38 Foxe, op. cit., III, pp. 594–5. I owe the last point to Mr Peter Clark. Cf. Thomas, op. cit., p. 170.

39 T. Rogers, *The Faith, Doctrine and Religion Professed and Protected in . . . England* (C.U.P., 1681), p. 39. First published 1607.

40 Hill, *Antichrist in Seventeenth Century England* (O.U.P., 1971), pp. 142–3; *The World Turned Upside Down*, p. 66; Thomson, op. cit., pp. 36, 184; Thomas, op. cit., p. 169; Wallace, op. cit., p. 465; Clark, *English Provincial Society*, pp. 56, 156, 178, 199. Cf. my *Change and Continuity in 17th century England* (1974), p. 15.

41 R. H. Hilton, *The English Peasantry in the Later Middle Ages* (Oxford U.P., 1975), p. 24; Horst, op. cit., p. 134.

42 Ed. G. L. and M. A. Harriss, *John Benet's Chronicle for the Years 1450 to 1462* (Camden Miscellany, XXIV), p. 166; Foxe, op. cit., IV, p. 243; D. M. Loades, *Politics and the Nation, 1450–1660* (1974), p. 147; A. G. Dickens, op. cit., p. 19; Thomson, op. cit., pp. 64–6, 78, 127, 130, 159, 177.

43 More, *Refutation of Tyndale* (1532), quoted by G. R. Elton, *Reform and Reformation* (1977), p. 44.

44 E. Leach, 'Melchisedech and the Emperor: Icons of Subversion and Orthodoxy', *Proceedings of the Royal Anthropological Institute*, 1972, pp. 5–14; A. C. Edwards, *English History from Essex Sources* (Chelmsford, 1957), pp. 77–8.

45 M. H. Keen, *England in the Later Middle Ages* (1973), p. 243; L. B. Smith, *Henry VIII*, p. 150; Hill, *The World Turned Upside Down*, p. 200; Claire Cross, op. cit., pp. 21, 73, 79; Clark, *English Provincial Society*, pp. 63, 156, 181, 405.

46 D. M. Wolfe, *The Image of Man in America* (Dallas, 1957), p. 19; *Victoria County History of Worcestershire*, IV, p. 192; G. P. Gooch, *The History of English Democratic Ideas in the Seventeenth Century* (Cambridge U.P., 1898), p. 359; E. P. Thompson, *Whigs and Hunters* (1975), p. 256; W. A. Speck, *Stability and Strife: England 1714–1760* (1977), p. 131; J. H. Lawson, 'Parrington and the Search for Tradition', *Mainstream* (Winter 1947), p. 39.

47 R. M. Dunn, 'The London Weavers' Riot of 1675', *Guildhall Studies*, I, p. 17; ed. N. Penney, *The Short Journal and Itinerary Journals of George Fox* (Cambridge U.P., 1925), pp. 350–1, where many examples are given.

48 T. A. Jackson, *Ireland Her Own* (1946), p. 63.

49 A. L. Morton, 'The Everlasting Gospel', in *The Matter of Britain* (1966), pp. 83–121; cf. *The World Turned Upside Down*, p. 382.

50 Hill, *The World Turned Upside Down*, pp. 380–1.

51 Burns, op. cit., p. 121.

52 Richard Lewis, *The Robin Hood Society. A Satire by Peter Pounce* (1756), pp. v–vi, 19, 79. I owe this reference to the kindness of Dr Vincent Carretta.

POPULAR DRAMA AND LEVELLER STYLE – RICHARD OVERTON and JOHN HARRIS

MARGOT HEINEMANN

I

They [the Levellers] wrote effectively not merely because they were exceptionally gifted or technically well equipped, though this can fairly be claimed at least for Overton and Walwyn, but because they wrote with a purpose clearly understood and deeply felt, and for an audience which they knew to be close and immediately responsive. . . . They stand near the head of one of the great streams of English prose, the stream which later was to include such mighty figures as Bunyan, Defoe, Paine, Cobbett and Shaw (A. L. Morton, 'The Leveller Style', in *The Matter of Britain*, 1966, p. 82).

Leveller rhetoric intensifies the strengths of common speech. Like the prose of Shakespeare's characters, it is packed with proverbs and colloquial sayings, using concrete and sometimes coarse images from everyday life for vividness and wit. It is rhythmic, energetic, irreverent, as well as weighty and dignified when the occasion requires.

One of the main influences on Leveller style was of course the Bible – the only book many of the rank and file will have known well – and the plain preaching based on it. I want to suggest that some of the most effective writers were also inspired by the other great source of instruction and culture open to ordinary Londoners, the theatres and the published texts of their plays. This seems pretty clear from the evidence of style alone; but it can also be shown that these men had personal links with the theatre which must have helped to form them and their writings.

That Parliamentary Puritans of every shade were united in hatred of the theatre – or at least its popular forms – is now recognized by most seventeenth-century historians to be a myth, though it still survives in many literary discussions. Prynne, who really was a committed opponent of plays, was typical not of Parliamentary Puritanism as a whole, but of the most rigid and dogmatic Presbyterian section within it, with which both Cromwellian Independents and Levellers later came into collision. Certainly he cannot be taken as a typical representative of the Puritan outlook in the 1630s among the masses of ordinary Londoners who later formed the basis of support for Lilburne.[1] While a considerable section of Puritan clergy (and of non-Puritan clergy for that matter)[2] and many Puritan merchants and businessmen opposed the theatre as a moral snare and a waste of precious time, Parliamentary-Puritan groups among the aristocracy included some of the best-known patrons of the drama, and among the more plebeian supporters of Parliament there must have been many, especially of the apprentices, who went to the popular playhouses.

Indeed many influential people with Puritan views in the twenty years before the civil war used or wished to use the theatre as a medium to influence wider opinion. Middleton's *Game at Chess* (1624), favoured by the Pembroke circle, is the most famous example. But even when the censorship tightened up further, and the companies were increasingly becoming 'royal slaves', many of the leading opposition peers, like the Earls of Essex, Warwick, Holland, Manchester and Pembroke, all interested in the drama, seem to have patronised the authors of plays with an obvious political reference (for instance Arthur Wilson, Massinger and Glapthorne).

Meanwhile the popular playhouses, such as the Red Bull and Fortune, from time to time put on plays which dramatised the criticisms and grievances of Londoners against the prerogative government. Most of these play-texts have disappeared, either destroyed by the censor or considered too 'low' and dangerous for printing; and we know of many only by the scattered records of their suppression. But enough remains to show that there was a large and profitable audience for 'opposition' drama: otherwise the companies would hardly have risked staging it. Thus there were anti-Spanish plays about foreign affairs, rousing sympathy for intervention on the Protestant side in Europe;[3] plays praising Magna Carta;[4] satirising bishops who went in for altars and ceremonies; libelling the ecclesiastical courts and their officers, and the rich citizens who ran the wine monopoly; criticising kings who raise taxes at their pleasure; and dealing (this in 1640) with Charles's unpopular Scottish expedition. It is a comprehensive list.[5]

When Parliament closed the theatres after the outbreak of war (September 1642) this did indeed gratify the anti-theatre lobby; but it was also an obvious security measure to prevent riotous assemblies and forestall possible Royalist propaganda (and, for that matter, the dramatising of popular grievances). Entertainment was held to be unsuitable anyway in a time of civil war, which called rather for discipline and prayer. Those dependent on the theatres as actors, musicians, theatre staff and dramatists faced disaster, and some of the best regular playwrights, we are told a year or so later, were 'for mere necessity compelled to get a living by writing contemptible penny pamphlets' (*The Actor's Remonstrance*, January 1643–4).

Judging by the number of anti-Laudian, anti-Strafford satires in semi-dramatic form printed around 1642, some of these hard-up dramatists were aiming at a Parliamentary-Puritan city audience rather than a Royalist one. These lively tracts return again and again to the same grievances, against the bishops and their Courts, against the persecution of Puritan ministers and the harrying of Puritan laymen, against rich Churchmen greedy for tithes and monopolists who squeeze money out of the poor. What made them saleable was the variety of forms, incidents, satirical images and semi-dramatic burlesques through which the same argument was presented so as to seem new and entertaining. Among these pamphlets are a number attributed to the most humorous and inventive of later Leveller pamphleteers, Richard Overton.[6]

II

The suggestion that Overton was at one time involved in the drama is supported by a good deal of varied evidence, none of it decisive in isolation, but convincing if one looks at it as a whole.

Little has hitherto been known about Overton's early life, but it has now been effectively shown that he was younger than earlier biographers supposed.[7] There is strong reason to believe that he was that Richard Overton who matriculated at Queens' College, Cambridge in 1631. His known work contains plenty of evidence that he was an educated man (if not necessarily University-educated), and Cambridge in the 1630s was a centre of Puritan scholarship and preaching. Nor was it only the gentry who went there. The town grammar schools, mostly non-fee-

paying and often under strong Puritan influence, were sending
boys in growing numbers in the early seventeenth century, who
might come from families of farmers, craftsmen or small
traders.[8] If we assume Overton *cannot* have had a University
education, we then have to explain how he came by the Latin
quotations and other signs of learning in his work. It seems
more likely on the face of it that he did.[9]

In the same year that he matriculated (1631–32) Overton acted
in a Latin comedy called *Versipellis* (meaning *The Turncoat*), the
whole cast being Queens' men. One would dearly like to know
more about this play. Unfortunately the text has disappeared;
we know only that it was set in Antwerp, and that the author was
probably Thomas Pestell (among whose papers it was found),
who was a Leicestershire clergyman and chaplain to the Earl of
Essex, and whose son, another Thomas Pestell, was one of the
student actors.[10]

The elder Pestell was patronised by (and wrote flattering
poems to or about) many of the Puritan peers who opposed the
Laudian regime, notably Essex, Holland, Manchester, Warwick
and Mandeville. He was summoned and fined by Laud's Court
of High Commission in 1633 for scandalous behaviour, and
especially for making insulting remarks and puns about Laud's
Commissary Sir John Lambe:[11] so it seems not unlikely that
Versipellis had a satirical irreverent tone like that of many of
Pestell's surviving poems.[12]

Cambridge in the 1630s was indeed a centre of religious
conflict; for Laud was set on forcing the University, by tradition
much more Puritan than Oxford, to conform to his rulings on
doctrine, preaching and ceremonies. In 1636 he finally
succeeded in establishing his own supremacy and right of
visitation there, against strong opposition led by the Chancellor
Lord Holland.[13] The leaders of the Laudians in Cambridge were
Matthew (afterwards Bishop) Wren and John (later Bishop)
Cosin, successively Masters of Peterhouse (next door to
Overton's college of Queens'). Both figure much later in
satirical pamphlets ascribed to Overton,[14] who seems to have
kept an interest in Cambridge politics. His deep commitment to
liberty of speech and discussion and religious toleration could
well have been formed in the bigot-ridden University of that
time.

The small world of college drama reflected these tensions.

Though college plays were traditionally partly exercises in classical translation or imitation, partly slapstick, bawdy and schoolboy jokes, they might have topical local or social satire thrown in. The most gifted and popular Cambridge playwright of the time, Thomas Randolph, a young Fellow of Trinity somewhat over-inclined to drink and debt, was a protégé of Holland and patronised by the Puritan and anti-Laudian gentry.[15] His less gifted rival, Peter Hausted of Queens', after preaching over-zealously at the University Church in 1634 against nonconformity, was dragged from the pulpit, arrested and mobbed by the Puritan townsfolk. Randolph's most popular play, *Aristippus* (shown both at Cambridge and later in London), included anti-Spanish and pro-Parliament satirical references, which had to be cut out when it was printed and several times reprinted from 1630 to 1635 (the year in which Randolph died).[16]

Randolph's general line is to balance mockery of 'Spanish' Arminians and high-flyers with mockery of narrow Puritan sectaries. This was about as far as one could hope to go with safety in the 1630s, and perhaps as far as he or his Puritan-Anglican Court patrons wanted to go. But it's noticeable, even so, that the anti-Puritan satire is much less sharp than, say, Jonson's in *The Alchemist*; Randolph's sectaries are good-natured comics who can be won over to approve of plays with the right moral.[17]

Randolph, perhaps through Holland's influence,[18] apparently became regular dramatist at the Salisbury Court playhouse in London around 1629–31, and had two plays produced there, though he was back in Cambridge soon afterwards.[19] Overton is very likely to have known him, since Thomas Pestell of Queens', his fellow-actor in *Versipellis*, must have been at least acquainted with Randolph.[20]

We do not know what Overton was doing in the later 1630s, before we hear of him late in 1640 as printer and pamphleteer, nor whether he ever had any links with the professional theatre, though Southwark, where he was living about that time, was one of the main centres of the popular theatre. All we can say is that he was connected with Cambridge dramatic circles, especially with anti-Laudian ones, and that some contemporary college playwrights certainly did become London theatre poets. Moreover, his pamphleteering activity begins around the time when the theatres were in difficulties in 1640 and increases after they closed. It would not be surprising, however, if Overton later kept quiet about any theatre link, since his opponents among the right-wing Parliamentarians would certainly have used it against him. John Harris was never allowed by the Royalist newswriters to forget that he had once been a 'player's boy'.

III

Vox Borealis or the Northern Discovery, a left-Parliamentarian pamphlet-cum-newsbook of late 1640 or early 1641, is probably the earliest of Overton's writings that we have. Like some of his better-known tracts of 1645–6, this bears the bogus imprint of Marprelate:[21]

> Printed by Margery Mar-prelat, in Thwackcoat Lane, at the Sign of the Crab-tree Cudgel; without any privilege of the Cater-Caps, the year coming on 1641.

And even more than the original Marprelate tracts it is full of references to the theatre. In form it is a colloquial dialogue, supposed to take place in the English camp at Berwick, between Jamie, a dialect-speaking Scotsman recently returned from London bringing the political news, and Willie, who has been with the English army during the disastrous Scottish expedition. They both hate the Bishops; believe the English were defeated because the Scots had a good cause and they had not; and complain bitterly against the officers for their treatment of private soldiers, and especially for discharging them to find their own way home with 'but four or five shillings apiece to travel three hundred miles'.[22] At the end they look forward to seeing the Long Parliament, which is about to meet, bring down the power and pride of the Bishops when they get home.

After a brief run-down on the foreign and general news, Jamie describes several incidents where the Bishops have interfered with the London actors and put down their plays. The writer evidently knew a good deal about what was actually going on in the theatre world.

> In the meantime let me tell you a lamentable Tragedy, acted by the prelacy, against the poor players at the Fortune playhouse. . . . For they having gotten a new old play, called *The Cardinal's Conspiracy*,

whom they brought upon the stage in as great state as they could, with altars, images, crosses, crucifixes, and the like, to set forth his pomp and pride. But woeful was the sight to see how in the midst of all their mirth, the pursuivants came and seized upon the poor Cardinal, and all his consorts, and carried them away. And when they were questioned for it, in the High Commission Court, they pleaded ignorance, and told the Archbishop *that they took those examples of their altars, images*, and the like, *from heathen authors*. This did somewhat assuage his anger, that they did not bring him on the stage; but yet they were fined for it, and after a little imprisonment got their liberty. And having nothing left them but a few old swords and bucklers, they fell to act the *Valiant Scot*, which they played five days with great applause, which vexed the Bishops worse than the other, insomuch, as they were forbidden playing it any more, and some of them prohibited ever playing again.

Some details here may well have been added for satiric effect, such as the title *The Cardinal's Conspiracy* (referring to the common Puritan charge that Archbishop Laud expected to be made Roman Catholic Cardinal of England) and the reference to *The Valiant Scot*, a real play-title but intended here to recall to readers the defeat of the English by the Scottish Presbyterians in the Bishops' War, which in fact occurred much later than the players' fine.[23] But the attack on the play really happened, as we know from a letter of 8 May 1639 from Edmund Rossingham to Viscount Conway (C.S.P.D., 639, pp. 140–41).

Thursday last (2 May) the players of the Fortune were fined £1000 for setting up an altar, a bason, and two candle-sticks, and bowing down before it upon the stage, and although they allege it was an old play revived, and an altar to the heathen gods, yet it was apparent that this play was revived on purpose in contempt of the ceremonies of the church.

Thus the actors had personally confronted Laud in the Court of High Commission, and had to argue their way out of it or risk losing their ears. We usually think of Laud now as the persecutor of Puritan preachers and theorists. But he was equally the terror of actors and dramatists who dared to criticise or satirise the regime or the Church, and this may be one reason why he is such a favourite personal target for Overton's satire in the early 1640s.

Vox Borealis goes on to recount another more recent incident

of censorship and prosecution of players, though this time the
reference is less clear. Jamie says:

> There has been brave branding amongst the boys there [at London]
> upon this business, and they have divided themselves into three
> companies, the Princes', the Queen's and the Duke of York's; the
> first were called the English, the second the French, and the Duke of
> York's were called the Scots company, who like brave blades were
> like to beat both the other two. And I can tell thee, that there has
> been such hot service amongst them, that some of their youngest
> soldiers have been fain to be carried home out of the field:
> whereupon it was blabbed abroad, that boys had done more than
> men durst do here at Berwick.

Probably what's being discussed here is the recent
prosecution of William Beeston and his boys' company, who in
the spring of 1640 had produced a play commenting on the
King's expedition against the Scots and not licensed by the
Master of the Revels.

> On Monday the 4 May 1640 William Beeston was taken by a
> messenger and committed to the Marshalsea by my Lord
> Chamberlain's warrant for playing a play without licence. The same
> day the company at the Cockpit was commanded by my Lord
> Chamberlain's warrant to forbear playing, for playing when they
> were forbidden by me and for other disobedience. . . .

> The play I called for and, forbidding the playing of it, keep the book
> because it had relation to the passages of the King's journey into the
> North and was complained of by his Majesty to me with command
> to punish the offenders. (*Dramatic Records of Sir Henry Herbert*, ed.
> J. Quincy Adams, 1917, p. 66.)

The issue was red-hot, and it was bold indeed of Beeston to
risk handling it on the stage – perhaps he thought the feeling
against the Scottish expedition was so strong that he could get
away with it. If so he was wrong. He was imprisoned for some
time in the Marshalsea, ousted from his position as manager of
the King and Queen's Young Company, and replaced there by
the courtier Davenant. The Court persecution of anti-bishop
theatre was thus on a level with that of anti-bishop preaching: in
both cases people lost their jobs and their means of influencing
opinion.

This is not the last theatre reference in *Vox Borealis*, however.
For good measure, in attacking the 'carpet knights' who came

to the camp 'for fashion not for fighting', Willie singles out Sir John Suckling, leader of the 'précieux' court dramatists, as the type of these elegant idlers: 'but if it had once come to knocks, then you must have expected a tragedy instead of a comedy, as *The Loss of a Loyal Subject*, *The Prodigal's Repentance*, *The Suckling's Succour*, *The Last Lover*, or some such pretty piece.'[24]

Whether or not Overton was reporting the army's grievances from first-hand experience (as Wolfe suggests),[25] the amount of factual detail he gives about theatres and censorship suggests inside knowledge.

Two of the anti-Laud pamphlets of 1642 Overton actually signed: *Articles of High Treason Against Cheapside Cross* (1642), a dialogue between Mr Papist and Mr News, describing the pulling down of the 'popish' cross by 'the rabble rout', and concluding with the Cross' last will and testament ('Item, I bequeath the iron about me to make a clapper for his Holiness passing bell. Item, I give and bequeath all the lead that is about me, to the hostile Catholics in Ireland, to make bullets to confound that cursed crew of heretics'). The will is signed (a zany Overtonian touch!):

'The Cross † her mark.'

The other signed pamphlet, *New Lambeth Fair* (1642), describes the selling-off of the bishops' now useless stock of accessories – lawn sleeves, robes, caps and beads – as fairings for children. References to these two in other contemporary tracts, repetition of particular devices, and stylistic echoes help to identify many other examples of Overton's work.[26]

The pamphlet which most strikingly shows the *dramatic* influence on Overton's writing is *Canterbury His Change of Diet* (1641), a six-page playlet satirising Laud (by this time a prisoner in the Tower), which refers in the text to 'Lambeth great Fair', and seems pretty certain to be his.[27]

The playlet is thus summarised on the title page:

1. Act. The Bishop of Canterbury having variety of dainties, is not satisfied till he be fed with tippets of men's ears.
2. Act. He hath his nose held to the grindstone.
3. Act. He is put into a bird-cage with the Confessor.
4. Act. The jester tells the King the story.

The humour is visual, slapstick and brutal, rather like that of *Ubu-Roi* (or of Marlowe's *Tamburlaine*). Thus in the first scene the

Archbishop at table petulantly rejects a banquet of twenty-four
dainty dishes, including cock and pheasant, quail and partridge.
He demands something 'rare', like a carbonadoed cheek.[28] And
when the pious divine wants to ask a blessing on the meat, Laud
roars 'ho, ho' (like the Devil in the old interludes). 'He knocking
there enter divers Bishops with muskets on their necks,
bandoliers and swords by their sides.' Doctor, divine and lawyer
are pinioned by this grotesque guard, while Laud cuts off their
ears 'to be dressed for his supper' and departs 'after a low
curtsey' – a burlesque staging of the vicious martyrdom of
Bastwick (doctor), Burton (divine) and Prynne (lawyer).

The rest of the play is a fantasy of revenge. An honest
carpenter, asked by Laud for the use of his grindstone to whet
his knife, instead ties the Archbishop's nose to it; and when his
'Jesuit confessor' (who looks like Bishop Wren in the
illustration) arrives to poultice his wounds, Carpenter and
Carpenter's wife put both these 'cormorants' into a bird-cage
('They that have cut off ears at the first bout, God knows what
they may cut off next'). A spirited wood-cut shows the prisoners
in the cage, 'and a fool standing by, and laughing at them, Ha,
ha, ha, ha, who is the fool now'.[29] In the final Act the jester
(represented in the illustration with the traditional cap and
bells) roars with laughter as he reports all this to the King.

> *Jester* I waited long to hear them sing, at last they began to
> chatter' . . .
> *King* What was the Song?
> *Jester* One sung thus: I would I was at Court again for me. Then the
> other answered: I would I was at Rome again with thee.
> *King* Well sirrah, you will never leave your flouts.
> *Jester* If I should, my liege, I were no Jester.

The King fails to appreciate the joke; but though, like Lear,
he reprimands the fool, calling him 'Sirrah', he does not
threaten him with the whip.

The epilogue is a 'jig' – the traditional song-and-dance finale
of so many Elizabethan plays – between a Parator (Apparitor, or
summoner of the Ecclesiastical Court) and the fool, in which the
Parator agrees, since his master is fallen and he can make no
more profit, that in future 'We'll wear tippet fool – caps, and
never undo men.'

The *form* of the satire may have been suggested by the famous feast given by Laud for the King and Queen at Oxford in 1636, costing over £2,000, and followed by a play, Strode's *Floating Island*, parodying the mutilated Prynne in the play-hating Puritan Malevole ('Locks which I have scorned/Must hide my ear-stumps'.)[30]

Canterbury His Change of Diet is described by G. E. Bentley as a tract 'in the form of closet drama'. But the kind of play whose language and style it uses as model is utterly unlike the 'closet drama' of Fulke Greville and other aristocratic writers. The idiom is obviously that of the live theatre with its sharply-caricatured character types, its jigs, its snatches of folk-song, and its jesters who mix in serious matters and dare answer back to the king. Indeed it is not impossible that in these crisis years performances of this sort of show went on in private houses or barns. Whether this is so or not, the satire is obviously aimed to reach people who ordinarily go to plays, and by someone who knows the theatre well, if he hasn't actually been writing for it. Most of the funny parts would be unintelligible to an audience not familiar with acted plays, since they depend so much on visual effects and slapstick.

The Proctor and the Parator of May 1641, also ascribed by Wolfe to Overton, sounds very close to the actual play staged by the King's Company at the Red Bull in 1639, and suppressed by the Privy Council as

> a scandalous and libellous [play in which] they have audaciously reproached and in a libel personated not only some of the aldermen of the [City of London] and some other persons of quality, but also scandalised and libelled the whole profession of proctors belonging to the Court of Probate, and reflected upon the present Government.

And in *The Whore New Vamped*, also complained of in the same entry, Alderman William Abell, the wine monopolist, was called 'a base, drunken, sottish knave':[31] he too is a frequent target in Overton's satires.

Overton's dialogue between Mr Sponge the Proctor and Mr Hunter the Parator reveals an unholy conspiracy between them to search out offenders against the canon law and either fine them or get bribes from them to avoid prosecution.

> Country wenches would sell their petticoats rather to pay us than to endure a white sheet.' '(I) have gotten good booty from

transgressors against holy-days, of chandlers, ale-houses, taverns, tobacco shops, butchers, comfit makers, gunsmiths, bakers, brokers, cooks, weavers and divers other malefactors against our terrible Canons and jurisdiction.' . . . 'I got no small trading by the Brownists, Anabaptists and Familists, who love a Barn better than a Church, and would come off roundly and secretly . . .'

They do well out of

lecturers, who would be silenced because they supplied their places too diligently; nay, I have got well too by some of their auditors for leaving their own parish churches and minsters, and gadding after strangers . . .

Zealous honest ministers who preach twice a day, and refuse to wear surplices or christen children with the sign of the cross, are a steady source of profit.

We do usually receive some bribe for a New Year's gift, and the Judge he expects a good piece of plate for his favour showed in ending causes according to the proctor's desire.

The broad popular alliance of godly ministers, sectaries, shopkeepers and ordinary sinners is thus evoked to rejoice at the downfall of these rogues, who have fallen on evil times with the decline of prerogative courts and the endless profitable legal business they involved. 'This certainty of the Triennial Parliament cuts our combs for ever doing any great exploits for after times.'

IV

A favourite device of Overton's, from these early tracts onwards, is to write in the name either of real public figures (Laud, Lord Justice Finch, Strafford, Attorney-General Noy)[33] or of caricatures resembling morality-play characters or Jonsonian 'humours' (Sir John Presbyter, Sir Simon Synod, Gaffer Christian). Essentially this is a dramatic technique.

Thus *A Letter from John Lord Finch, late Lord Keeper, to his Friend Dr Cozens, with a Commemoration of favours Dr Cozens showed him in his Vice-Chancellorship*, (1642) is written deadpan to mimic the pompous tones of the judge himself. Finch, a Cambridge man and the Star Chamber persecutor of Prynne, solemnly compliments the high-flying Laudian Cozens for having set up altars, crucifixes and holy pictures in Cambridge chapels;

laments his ejection from office; and congratulates himself on his own brilliance in running away:

> Does the triple crown which you erected in St Mary's illustrate still the vulgar speculation? Sir, if the tumultuary imprecations of the vulgar do oppose you, yet macerate not yourself.

In *Old News Newly Revived*, another 1641 pamphlet-dialogue attributed to Overton, Finch is described on the run, in terms that suggest a comic actor playing the part: 'a brother of the blade, with a tilting feather, a flaunting periwig, buff doublet, scarlet hose, and sword as broad as a lath, he looked as like a Dammee newly come out of the North as could be imagined.'[34] Sir John Suckling too has fled, and 'the Blackfriars Actors have a foul loss of him . . . His coat of mail would not keep out their (the Scots') bullets, though it would Sir John Digby's rapier in the playhouse.'[35]

In *Canterbury's Dream* Laud tells how his slumbers in prison are broken by the apparition of Cardinal Wolsey, who compares their relative skill as extortioners; cites himself as an awful warning ('The ruin of us both was indeed in our times the joy and voice of the people'); and finally departs in a manner recalling Hamlet's father ('Much more I have to say, but this is the third summons of the cock, and to fill the number up, I must return unto the children of the night').

In *The Bishop's Potion*, a spoof dialogue between Laud and his physician, the doctor diagnoses 'certain raw crudities' lying on his patient's stomach. An emetic is prescribed and the Archbishop vomits up the symbols of all his transgressions, including the tobacco patent; the Book of Sports; a parchment with the Star Chamber Order against Prynne, Burton and Bastwick; a bundle of papers presenting livings to dumb-dog clergy and suspending preaching ministers; and finally, after a supreme convulsion, up comes the Mitre ('I had almost broken my lungs!'). As a farcical image this harks right back to the 'Mar-Martin' plays of the 1590s, where the ape Martin was purged on stage, and indeed to Spenser; but the comic doctor with his grotesque cures goes back even earlier to the Mummers' plays, and is a stock figure in college drama like Randolph's *Aristippus*. It's not exactly what one thinks of as Puritan in tone, but the symbolism is impeccable.

The most vivid example of this black humour at its cruellest is

A Description of the Passage of Thomas Lord Strafford over the River of Styx, which again is full of theatre stuff.[36] Strafford is ferried across Styx by Charon, who complains that he's a very heavy ghost, having 'devoured three kingdoms'. Strafford is deposited on the opposite bank in the waiting arms of Attorney-General Noy, who has already devised a fine new money-raising project for the Hades regime: Charon, whose fare is only ½d. per ghost, is to be made to pay a penny a passenger 'as a gratification or ventage to great Pluto'. As Strafford describes to Noy the fall of himself and Laud, the style changes from burlesque to serious, and he speaks in straight and reasonably effective blank verse, using the traditional metaphor of shipwreck much as Clarence does in *Richard III*.

> And thus adventured while my bark touched heaven,
> Seas upon waves, and waves surmounting seas,
> They danced me down into a vast abyss
> Where I lay docked in quicksands to embrace
> A certain ruin.

He goes on to compare Laud's dejection in prison to that of Antony after Actium, in terms which suggest the writer may have known Shakespeare's play.[37]

> He like the Roman Antony, when he
> Tried his last fortunes in sad Actium's fight
> And left the grappling Eagles and his honour
> To fly in's beauteous Cleopatra's boat,
> And quite ashamed that anyone but he
> Should own that fame to conquer Antony,
> His heart quite broken, and his head bowed low,
> Whiles eightscore minutes wear in number out
> Their measured sands in the just glass of time,
> Durst not look up towards Heaven, nor tempt her eyes,
> Her eyes to him ten thousand thousand heavens
> More dear than thousand conquests;
> Just so his Grace, his faded head being laid
> On both his hands, his elbows on his knees,
> Will silent lean two or three hours together;
> And in that posture, sad he now must leave her,
> Stoops to his idol, greatness.

These early pamphlets show no interest in Laud's theology; there's nothing about Arminianism or predestination. The

attack is on the riches of a Church which exploits the poor;
spending of ordinary people's money on 'trinkets' and
frivolities of ceremony; the luxurious life-style of bishops, who
live like lords and eat like gluttons, a complaint familiar since
Chaucer and the Lollards; above all the persecution not only of
Prynne, Burton and Bastwick but of all manner of ordinary men
and women. It's the democratic aspect of the case that already
interests Overton. Though he was not as yet in contact with
Lilburne and Walwyn, the Levelling note is already apparent.

Overton's known and much more famous pamphlets after
1645 are largely monologue or narrative rather than dramatic;
but one of the best of all, *The Arraignment of Mr Persecution*, is in
semi-dramatic form, and is believed to have served as the model
for Bunyan when he wrote the trial of Faithful in *Pilgrim's
Progress*. A. L. Morton has written finely of this tract in *The
Leveller Style*.[38] It is far more ambitious than the brief squibs of
1641–42, with a large cast of persecutors and tolerationists,
judges and jurymen, powerfully suggesting the *mass*
involvement at the peak of the Leveller movement. Moreover
while the earlier pamphlets are bent on punishment for the
persecutors, cruel in their exultation over the fallen and crude in
their anti-Popery, by 1645 the stress is on ending *all* persecution
for religion, including that of Catholics and Jews, although the
arch-persecutors (now personifications in the manner of the
morality plays, Sir John Presbyter and Sir Simon Synod, rather
than actual people) are still consigned to everlasting flames, as
responsible for most of the wars and civil wars in the world. This
tract shows the rapid growth in Overton's thought, under the
impact of Presbyterian and right-wing Parliamentarian
persecution of sectaries like Lilburne, and of his own
involvement with the Leveller movement and with Anabaptism.

The success of Overton's dialogues and monologues also
influenced other Leveller writers. Walwyn was already working
closely with Overton in 1646 when he wrote *A Prediction of Master
Edwards his Conversion and Recantation*, a spoof dramatic
monologue by the embittered Presbyterian author of *Gangraena*,
and *A Parable or Consultation of Physicians upon Master Edwards*, a
complete allegory in which the doctors Love, Justice, Patience
and Truth operate to remove the abscess which has poisoned
Edwards' brain. So popular was Overton's semi-dramatic style
that opponents too seem to have imitated it in the hope of

appealing to his public. Thus in 1649 we find two play-pamphlets on *Newmarket Fair*, coarsely satirising Cromwell and Fairfax and their wives, mourning martyred Leveller soldiers like Private Arnold and showing the crowds brandishing the Agreement of the People as they mob Fairfax and bring back the King.[39] The writer is clearly aiming at a pseudo-radical appeal to the now disaffected and disillusioned among the Leveller rank and file.

All in all, Overton's writing is something new in English prose. Although many of his most brilliant pamphlets (for instance a series on tithes) are presented as monologues by 'Martin Mar-Priest', I cannot agree with Joseph Frank[40] that they are 'traditional and conformist' in style, merely repeating the achievements of Martin and anti-Martinists like Nashe fifty years before. In spite of the similarities, Overton is far more vivid, swift-moving and readable. He has more skill in sustained narrative and dramatisation, he is more consistently interesting and makes his meaning much clearer. It's here that the example of popular spoken drama must have been important.

V

A Leveller writer known to have been directly connected with the stage is John Harris, one time professional actor. In 1634 he performed as a boy player in Norwich, probably on tour with the King's Revels,[41] the London company for whom Randolph had worked, which in that same year borrowed a church robe from a pawnbroker 'to present Flamen, a priest of the heathens' – clearly a bit of deliberate anti-Laudian satire.[42] After the theatres closed Harris became a printer at Oxford.[43]

Harris can be reckoned among the leading Levellers. Under the anagram pseudonym of Sirrahniho, in 1647, he wrote two propaganda pamphlets demanding the release of Lilburne, Wildman and Sir John Maynard[44] (*The Grand Design* and *The Royal Quarrel*), and in 1648 he was one of a deputation of fifteen of Lilburne's friends (including Overton) who protested to Cromwell against his ill-treatment.[45] Harris was the craftsman on whom the Army Agitators relied to print their tracts and petitions during the revolt of 1647, and thereafter became for a time the Army's official printer, marching with his press in the rear of headquarters. As well as editing other newsbooks, he set out late in 1648 to produce an uncensored Leveller newspaper, *Mercurius Militaris or the Army's Scout*, lively and humorous in style and full of dramatic allusions; it ran for five numbers before the censor's harassment forced him to stop printing it.

Harris is one of the most radical and sceptical of the Leveller journalists, catching, as Brailsford says, 'the authentic tone of voice in which the agitators would address the New Model. Here are the clichés, the epigrams, the jokes which formed the common stock of their speeches.'[46] In *Mercurius Militaris* he mocks not only Parliament's proposed treaty with the King, but the institution of monarchy itself. Arguing that Parliament should get rid of the King altogether, he adapts Cassius's republican attack on Caesar, basing his rhetoric on Shakespeare's as naturally as on the soldiers' meetings, and bringing out with remarkable clarity the dislike of the parliamentarian right for the revolutionary situation in which their victories had placed them.

> What doth Parliament but mock his sacred Majesty in proposing anything to him to be confirmed? . . . I wonder what strength it would add, or what goodness to the propositions if he should sign them; can a single man compel 300,000 men to observe them when they are laws? Or can he compel them to break them? What virtue unknown is in this name Carolus Rex? Why is this name adored more than another? Write that and Denzil Holles together, is not this as fair a name? Weigh them, is it not as heavy? Conjure with them, Denzil Holles will start a spirit as soon as the name Carolus Rex: and yet this mere puff of breath, this powerless name King Charles set so high in the vulgar hearts, that what would be vice in others his name like richest alchemy change to virtue and worthiness and the subscribing this name to that which he can neither help nor hinder, must set him above his masters and conquerors, and permit him to bestride this narrow world like a colossus, when you victors must walk like petty slaves, and peep about under his huge legs to find yourselves dishonourable graves: *premoniti premuniti* (*Mercurius Militaris* No. 1, 10 October 1648, p. 5. BM E 467).

Harris' writings are full of these quick, easy references to the plays he must have known so well, and usually to Shakespeare – though Jonson comes in too. Thus in the same *Mercurius* he draws on Jonson's *Alchemist*, telling how Parliament has promised that the King may come to London in safety, freedom and honour:

> This makes me think that the King is an Alchemist, and the Lords are his Mercury; they are his crude and his sublimate, his precipitations and his unctions; he can make them dance the philosophical circle four or five times in an hour, like an Ape through a hoop, or a dog in a wheel.

And the servility Parliament may be expected to show to the returning King is described a few lines later in phrases that echo those of Kent about the sycophant Oswald (*King Lear*, Act II, scene 2, ll. 76–80):

> Most of the members, through fear or hopes, will become his apes, and shall laugh or weep, be hot or cold, change ever the garb, mode or habits as he varies (*Mercurius Militaris*, No. 3 October 24–31 1648, p. 17).[47]

The connection with *Lear*, is, I believe, not just a matter of phrasing, but of the whole line of thought. In the same issue of *Militaris* Harris is also writing:

> What work of the people does he for his wages? What good do they receive from him? He can neither make nor execute the laws, nor distribute any justice amongst them . . . But is it reason that a poor man shall be hanged for stealing 14d. and that a great man shall confess he sent his compeers to break houses, plunder and murder, and that thousands of families have been undone by them, and yet not so much as some reparations to be given them out of his lands.

I am not suggesting that Harris here is directly echoing *Lear*:

> Plate sin with gold,
> And the strong lance of justice hurtless breaks:
> Arm it in rags, a pigmy's straw does pierce it.

But when he is writing at high speed about the pretensions and folly of kings and the injustice of courts, at deeper levels Shakespeare works on his thinking, supplies language and precedents.

In *Militaris* No. 2 (10 October–17 October 1648) Harris notes that 'every tyrant and his sycophants are pretended worshippers of that demi-god Authority' (p. 12). Angelo in *Measure for Measure* seems an appropriate character for a journalist exposing the hypocrisy of the Scottish Jack Presbyters (as Harris is here) to have in mind. As usual one Shakespearean reference triggers another: this time to *Henry VI*:

> He is the Lord's anointed . . . was anybody witness to his anointing? Or must we trust him upon his word only? If so, why might not Jack Cade be as well believed to have been Mortimer and rightful heir to the crown? Surely Jack Cade's tongue was never more double than his (p. 13).

Interestingly, Jack Cade comes in here not as a peasant revolutionary hero but (in Shakespeare's manner) as an impostor, a pretend-King. On the next page Judge-Advocate Whalley is described as Falstaff does Bardolph in *Henry IV*:[48]

> with his face like an ignis fatuus . . . the gentleman had been quenching the fire in his face, and the liquor proved too strong (p. 14).

It is hardly a question here of Harris sharing theatrical in-jokes with his readers. Few New Model soldiers in 1648 would have much experience of plays, as readers of Overton's pamphlets would in 1641–43. Simply, like the playwrights before him, Harris stole freely what served his purpose, thereby strengthening both style and ideas. What the dramatists, Shakespeare especially, provide is not of course any kind of programme or scheme of political thought, but images and metaphors of great power and relevance.

VI

Cavalier culture could not inherit the rich and complex traditions of Jacobean theatre. For even though they required Court patronage and lived under the threat of Court censorship, the players' livelihood (at least in the public theatres) depended on their appeal to a popular audience. It was indeed a well-known charge against the 'common player' that his need for approval by the multitude made him a subversive force. 'Howsoever he pretends to have a royal master or mistress, his wages and dependance prove him to be the servant of the people.'[49] In Elizabethan and Jacobean drama the common people have a voice (even if what they say is not always enforced by the play as a whole), and often provide a sceptical commentary on the main heroic and royal action. One thinks of

Henry V's soldiers before Agincourt, the gravediggers in *Hamlet*, the plebeian gibing of Lear's Fool. In the courtly Cavalier plays of the 1630s this voice is silent, and the structural use of contrast has gone.

Undoubtedly it was primarily the 'low' side of Shakespeare that led to his declining reputation in cultured court circles under Charles I. [50] By the time the Beaumont and Fletcher Folio was published in 1647 (during a brief interval of the wars), Sir John Berkenhead, the leading Royalist newsbook writer, in his commendatory verses spoke patronisingly of Shakespeare's outdated 'trunk-hose wit' as the result of writing too much for the mob, and now surpassed by the more correct and elegant work of Fletcher; and William Cartwright dismissed Shakespeare altogether as obscene and unfunny.[51] And while both Royalist and Puritan pamphleteers were making use of playhouse allusions, it seems that the Parliamentarian writers did so more often – so that Berkenhead himself could jeer at a Puritan controversialist for closing the theatres 'very wisely, lest men should track him, and find where he pilfers all his best similes'.[52]

The many-sided, dialectical embodiment of contradictory social forces and ideas that we find in the greatest seventeenth century drama was no longer possible, given the deepening split in society, in audiences and within people's minds. But something of the dramatists' vitality and ease in reaching a popular audience passed to the Leveller writers.

NOTES

1 Prynne was feted by the crowds, along with Burton and Bastwick, but as a heroic martyr of Laudian repression, rather than for his anti-theatre principles.
2 Lancelot Andrews did not approve of plays, though he did not make an issue of it at Court, probably because for him loyalty to the monarchy seemed the more important issue; and Laud himself seems to have had no great liking for them.
3 E.g. Massinger, *Believe as You List*; Glapthorne, *Albertus Wallenstein*.
4 R. Davenport, *King John and Matilda*.
5 See e.g. G. E. Bentley, *The Profession of Dramatist in Shakespeare's Time*, 1971, pp. 145–96, for an account of plays censored; Glynne Wickham, *Early English Stages*, Vol. II, Part 1, 1963, p. 94, S. R. Gardiner, 'The Political

Element in Massinger' in *Contemporary Review*, August 1876; the Malone Society edition of *Believe as You List*, ed. C. J. Sisson, 1927.

6 Marie Gimmelfarb thinks he may have been imprisoned for debt around 1642 (cf. her forthcoming book on Overton). If he was a playwright this would be very plausible.

7 E.g. J. Frank, *The Levellers*, 1955, pp. 39–40, and the article by C. H. Firth in *DNB*.

8 This has been demonstrated in detail for Leicestershire schools by Joan Simon, *Town Estates and Schools in the Sixteenth and Early Seventeenth Centuries*, in B. Simon (ed.), *Education in Leicestershire 1540–1940*, 1968. Leicestershire was probably Overton's home county.

9 My view on this is confirmed by that reached by a quite different route by Marie Gimmelfarb. She considers that he was about Lilburne's age (i.e. born 1610–15), and dates his Mennonite conversion and declaration of faith, written in Amsterdam, at around 1643. I have benefited greatly from the facts she has made available to me and from discussing parts of this article with her.

10 G. C. Moore Smith, *College Plays Performed in the University of Cambridge*, 1923, p. 85, 109–10. The MS. was seen by J. Nichols, who recorded it in his *History and Antiquities of the County of Leicester*, III, 927, but is now lost.

11 Lambe, along with Laud's other helpmate Dr Duck, is also a favourite target of jokes and puns in Overton's early pamphlets.

12 See Hannah Buchan (ed.), *The Poems of Thomas Pestell*, 1940, which reprints the full report of the 1633 case.

13 For the conflict in Cambridge see H. R. Trevor-Roper, *Archbishop Laud*, 1962, pp. 204–10.

14 E.g. *Copy of a letter from John Lord Finch to his friend Mr Cosins* (1641); *Old News Newly Revived* (1641); *A Rent in the Lawn Sleeves* (1641); *Farewell Mitre* (1642).

15 His father was steward to Lord Zouch, an anti-Spanish peer since Elizabeth's time, part of whose estates lay in Northamptonshire.

16 What G. E. Bentley calls the 'surprising' popularity of this play must have been partly due to the satirical in-jokes. In the BM *MS* (presumably the original acting version) a quack doctor advertises his skills: 'If it had not been treason I had cured Gondomar of his fistula and England of a subsidy.' In the 1630 printed edition the Prologue conjures up the spirit of Show, who is only allowed to present the play if he promises to keep off personal satire, which has got him into trouble before. He swears:

> I will not touch such men as I know vicious,
> Much less the good: I will not dare to say
> That such a one paid for his fellowship
> And had no learning but in's purse; no officer
> Need fear the sling of my detraction . . .
> You need not fear this show, you that are bad,
> It is no Parliament (*Aristippus*, 1630, p. 3).

17 Thus in *The Muses' Looking Glass* two godly playhouse hawkers who denounce plays change their minds after seeing Randolph's edifying one:

Bird: Hereafter I will visit comedies
And see them oft: they are good exercises!
I'll teach devotion now a milder temper;
Not that it shall lose any of her heat
Or purity, but henceforth shall be such
As shall beam bright, although not blaze so much.

The sharper anti-Parliamentarian and anti-Puritan references in *Hey for Honesty* have mainly been added much later by 'F. J.', who revised Randolph's original long after his death, during or after the Civil War.

18 Holland was an aristocrat of Puritan leanings, younger son of the Rich family, brother of the Earl of Warwick, and cousin of Essex. The whole family, headed by the old Countess of Leicester, were patrons of the drama (Arthur Wilson being the family's playwright), and staged plays in their own country houses. Holland was written to by Maw, Master of Trinity, to use his influence to help Thomas Randolph.

Holland's Puritanism was of a decidedly 'courtly' and complicated kind. A well-known anti-Laudian, he was intriguing with the Queen in the mid-1630s as a way to outflank the pro-Spanish and more aggressively pro-Catholic party at court. (It was through the Queen, to whose favour he remained loyal, that Thomas Pestell senior, another Holland client, eventually became a chaplain to Charles I.) He was in no sense a radical. Nevertheless he was a close associate of Pym and Hampden, and well-known as a patron and protector of Puritan ministers. At the outset of the Civil War he took the Parliament side, but deserted it once too often and eventually followed Charles I to the block (see Barbara Donagan, 'A Courtier's Progress: Greed and Consistency in the Life of the Earl of Holland', in *Historical Journal*, June 1976, and R. M. Smuts 'The Puritan Followers of Henrietta Maria in the 1630s', in *English Historical Review*, January 1978).

19 G. E. Bentley, *Randolph's Praeludium and the Salisbury Court Theatre*, in J. MacManaway (ed.), *J. Quincy Adams Memorial Studies*, 1948. See also G. E. Bentley, *The Jacobean and Caroline Stage*, 19, Vol. V, pp. 964–93.

20 The Pestells at Packington in Leicestershire lived only a few miles from the Randolphs at Houghton. They had a common friend in James Duport, a common patron in Lord Holland. One Thomas Pestell (senior or junior) answered Randolph's mock-elegy on his own finger cut off in a brawl with a 'Reply to Mr. Randolph's verses on the loss of his finger'. Plays by Randolph and Pestell were probably both acted at Cambridge in the same season: then as now, drama enthusiasts in different colleges were likely to know one another. Overton may indeed have come from the same district: Marie Gimelfarb traced Overtons living in Lea Grange Manor, near Twycross, and Pestell senior also held a living at Cole-Orton, otherwise known as Cold Overton, near Ashby de la Zouch (H. Buchan, loc. cit., p. XXXI).

21 Don M. Wolfe, *Unsigned Pamphlets of Richard Overton, 1641–49*, (Huntingdon Library Quarterly, 1957), lists additional reasons for assigning it to Overton.

22 The bad treatment of discharged soldiers was already a common theme in

popular drama. See for example Dekker, *The Wonder of a Kingdom*, printed 1636.

23 As G. E. Bentley points out in his account of the affair in *The Profession of Dramatist in Shakespeare's Time*, 1971, p. 181.

24 A later pamphlet of Overton's, *Old News Newly Revived*, returns to gibes against Suckling.

25 Don M. Wolfe, *Unsigned Pamphlets of Richard Overton*, Huntingdon Library Quarterly, XXI, 2 February 1958, p. 128.

26 The pioneering work on these tracts was done by Don M. Wolfe twenty years ago in *Unsigned Pamphlets of Richard Overton*, op. cit. Although I would dispute some of his attributions, I am heavily indebted to this article and to Christopher Hill for drawing my attention to it.

27 It is convincingly identified, on this and other grounds, by Don M. Wolfe, ibid. Wolfe had not noted the possibility that Overton was an actor or playwright and his attribution is not made with that in mind. The signed tract *New Lambeth Fair* (1642) incorporates large portions of the unsigned *Lambeth Fair* (1641), to which *Canterbury His Change of Diet* alludes.

28 Prynne had been branded S. L. on the cheeks – Seditious Libeller.

29 The immediate reference is to Archy Armstrong, official Court jester to James I and Charles I, who had just been expelled from Court by the Privy Council on Laud's instigation for gibing at him ('Who's the fool now?' were among the 'scandalous words of a high nature' complained of). When Laud was in the Tower, Archy, from retirement on his Cumberland estates, issued a volume *Archy's Dreams*, which includes a vision of Laud in hell, and other anti-prelatical fancies. Compared with Overton's semi-dramatic satires it is laboured and unimaginative, however. (See Enid Welsford, *The Fool, his Social and Literary History*, 1968, pp. 172–81.)

30 H. R. Trevor-Roper, *Archbishop Laud*, 1962, p. 29.

31 C.S.P.D. 1639, pp. 529–30. The offender who spoke these lines was Andrew Cane, leader of Prince Charles [II] company and a famous comic.

32 Don M. Wolfe cites stylistic similarities with his known work as 'rather certain signs' of Overton's authorship.

33 Middleton's *Game at Chess*, where Gondomar and the Fat Bishop de Dominis were impersonated on stage, showed how effective this could be.

34 The lath dagger was the regular property of the Vice or comic devil in the old morality plays.

35 Digby and Suckling had in fact fought over a lady, the honours going to Digby.

36 Don M. Wolfe's evidence for ascribing this to Overton is purely internal, based on content and word use. It could equally well – perhaps better – be ascribed to John Harris (see below), in whose writing Shakespearean echoes are common.

37 Direct use of Plutarch would not have provided this image: neither would various Antony plays by the Countess of Pembroke and others.

38 See *The Matter of Britain*, 1966, and the introduction to *Freedom in Arms*, 1975.

39 These tracts are assigned by Wolfe to Overton, but I find this unconvincing both in terms of content and style. Overton in his signed writings at this time shows no trace of Royalist sympathies. There were many Royalist pamphleteers capable of using such a form: the likeliest being perhaps

either John Crouch or John Tatham, who in 1660 staged an actual play, *The Rump*, on very similar lines.

40 *The Levellers*, 1955, p. 259.

41 G. E. Bentley, *The Jacobean and Caroline Stage*, Vol. II, p. 462.

42 *Dramatic Records of Sir Henry Herbert*, ed. J. Quincy Adams, op. cit., p. 64. The broker spent the night in prison. 'The employment of such a robe for "a priest of the heathens" cannot have been innocent in intent' (G. E. Bentley, *The Profession of Dramatist in Shakespeare's Time*, 1971, p. 179).

43 H. N. Brailsford in *The Levellers and the English Revolution*, 1961, 1976 reprint, pp. 410–12, gives a good summary of what is known about Harris, drawing attention to the Shakespearean echoes in his writing. Further detail is given in Joseph Frank, *The Beginnings of the English Newspaper*, 1961, pp. 165, 166, 192 and *passim*.

44 Maynard was a Presbyterian and near-Royalist MP, one of the eleven sequestered members, who became friendly with Lilburne while in prison. He was son-in-law of Sir Thomas Myddleton, formerly Puritan Lord Mayor of London, and had himself written a masque in his youth. His family continued to befriend Lilburne to the end of his life, according to Pauline Gregg, *Freeborn John*, 1961, p. 358.

45 Lilburne, *Legal Fundamental Liberties*, 1649. Quoted W. Haller and G. Davies, *The Leveller Tracts*, 1944, p. 424.

46 Brailsford, op. cit., p. 411.

47 This does not, like the *Julius Caesar* extract, follow Shakespeare word for word; but the unusual use of 'garb' (see *Lear*, Act II, Scene 2, l. 98) and 'vary' in this context makes it pretty certain that Harris had *King Lear* at the back of his mind.

48 Act III, Scene 2, l. 42.

49 J. Cocke, *A Common Player*, cited E. K. Chambers, *Elizabethan Stage*, 1923, Vol IV, p. 256.

50 See the analysis of the Beaumont and Fletcher verses and of Cavalier critical attitudes by P. W. Thomas, *Sir John Berkenhead*, 1969, pp. 135 ff.

51 Among the many commendatory verses prefaced to this volume, the only Parliamentarian piece is by John Harris, who describes himself as too unknown and unlearned to praise Fletcher effectively, and goes on to do so for another 126 lines. He does not mention Shakespeare, but works in eulogies of Essex (recently dead), Parliament and Queen Elizabeth.

52 John Berkenhead, *The Assembly Man*, written 1647; cited in E. Sirluck, 'Shakespeare and Jonson among the pamphleteers of the First Civil War' in *Modern Philology*, Vol. 53, 1955–6, pp. 88–99. Sirluck counts theatrical allusions on the two sides, and concludes that 'the Puritans used Shakespeare and Jonson approximately twice as often in political propaganda as the Royalists did'. He points out that earlier scholars have underestimated Shakespeare's reputation at this date because they failed to examine pamphlet literature.

THE KIRK AND THE CAMERONIANS

WILLIE THOMPSON

In his discussions of Leveller democracy and more particularly his research into the Ranters, A. L. Morton has figured prominently among those historians who have, in the past two decades, rescued the popular movements of the English Revolution from the oblivion – or derision – in which traditional historiography had buried them. With the virtual collapse of the social hierarchy at the end of the Civil War, unprecedented freedom of movement, the armed strength of the radical soldiery, and the abolition of literary censorship, the popular movements came to the fore throughout England and appeared briefly even as contenders for state power. No feature of these movements and their spokesmen is more noteworthy than the speed at which, as the traditional order dissolved, their ideologies developed from their invariably biblical starting points in the direction of secular democracy. Among groups such as the Diggers, Ranters and early Quakers, naive communism, a vision of social equality and property redistribution expressed within a – sometimes very minimal – religious framework, developed to complement more specifically political notions.

In the 1650s, with the imposition of Cromwell's remodelled but still essentially traditional order, with the erasure of apocalyptic social aspirations in this world, the more strictly utopian elements in their outlook increasingly predominated – a hope fixed upon God's direct intervention to secure the holy kingdom, a divine redress for the failed political vision. The monarchical restoration in 1660 and its subsequent consolidation finally extinguished any surviving thoughts of political revolution, or even any possibility that popular feeling would merit consideration from the powers-that-be. As Christopher Hill has expressed it:

> After the restoration officers of the New Model returned to their crafts. Preaching tinkers returned to their villages, or like Bunyan

went to gaol. Levellers, Diggers, Ranters and Fifth Monarchists disappeared, leaving hardly a trace. . . . Fox disciplined the Quakers: they succumbed to the protestant ethic. Property triumphed. Bishops returned to a state church, the universities and tithes survived. Women were put back into their place.[1]

The tendency towards depoliticisation and demoralisation, already evident in the sects under the Commonwealth and Protectorate, reached completion after an abortive Fifth Monarchist revolt in 1661. Paradoxically, in Scotland, where the process of radicalisation had been much less developed, active resistance to government authority grew steadily more manifest and uncompromising. The narrative of affairs of the 1680s recalls irresistibly the anti-guerrilla campaigns of modern times – search-and-destroy operations, intimidation and brutality directed at the population thought to be sheltering the armed nucleus, alternating with concessions aimed at winning the 'hearts and minds' of the masses; torture to extract information. On the opposing side, the intransigent sectarianism displayed by the irreconcilable Covenanters evokes parallels with the Provisional IRA.

Morton, in *The World of the Ranters*, notes of the English reformation that '. . . it is essential to remember the extent to which it began, and remained, a great popular movement'. The observation applies with still greater force to the Scottish reformation of the 1560s and, while the nobility and monarchy soon subordinated it to their own purposes, their grip upon the organisation of the kirk remained less effective than was the case in England. The kirk's genesis in a set of coherent and rigid Calvinist principles combined with the training and traditions of its ministers and an effective system of social discipline to preserve theological unity throughout subsequent decades and provided no room for radically heterodox ideas to take root. A framework of episcopal control and a hierarchy of bishops imposed by the royal authority was accepted with reluctance. By the 1620s the kirk was the only structured nationwide institution existing in Scotland, with popular commitment across the social spectrum in burgh and countryside. Possessing a system of higher and subordinate assemblies, dispensing education, propaganda and poor relief and existing in an ambiguous and delicately-balanced relationship with the state power, it was well-fitted indeed to become the vehicle for political revolution in Scotland. Initially it was the instrument of an aristocratic reaction against Charles I's endeavours to use it to extend his personal authority in Scotland and to threaten noble property, particularly the former Church lands they had expropriated at the Reformation. Under the banner of the National Covenant of 1638 the Scottish nobility and leading gentry secured control over church and state, eliminating the episcopal system while fixing their own authority upon the clergy through the body of elders in each kirk which appointed the minister. They had themselves elevated to life membership in that rank, and by their social authority directed the individual congregations, while the composition of the Committee of Estates, the central organ of government power, placed them in control of state affairs.

Fear of the revolutionary direction which events were assuming in England after the king's defeat induced the Scottish rulers to switch sides in 1648, and conduct an armed foray into England on his behalf. This initiative – the Engagement – was opposed by the more thoroughgoing presbyterian elements, albeit not on any grounds which could be considered radical. Their objections lay in the insufficiently strict nature of Charles's promise to impose presbyterianism upon England. Military disaster followed, and the discredited nobility, other than a small anti-Engager faction, lost its hold on the state, which now fell into the hands of the ministers, except that, in the words of Dr Cowan, 'beneath these classes [the nobility and wealthier gentry] lay a new stratum of lay society – small lairds and tenant farmers – whose wishes could be expressed as elders . . .'.[2] Certainly it was these who furnished the social basis of the resistance movement after 1660, and its clergy who were most distrustful of the ill-fated enterprise – supported by the nobility – of militarily restoring a Covenanted Charles II from a Scottish base.

Following the Restoration in 1660, the nobility, thoroughly chastened by the threat to themselves which the social and political upheavals of the past twenty years had presented, became, with few exceptions, zealous converts to episcopacy and royal supremacy. They included some, like the Earl of Rothes, who had been among the leading initiators of the Covenant in 1638. Neither institution now constituted any challenge to their property rights: on the contrary, through close association with the reconstituted hierarchy, an acceptable means existed to reassert their control over disaffected clergy and their congregations.

Within the Scottish economy in the course of the seventeenth century the centre of gravity was shifting away from the chartered burghs towards rurally based linen manufacture and cattle export, coal-mining and salt-boiling undertaken upon noble estates. The economic weight of the territorial magnates was correspondingly enhanced, their evolution furthered in the same direction as their English counterparts – towards the role of an agrarian bourgeoisie. An equivalent development and consolidation in the legal system was taking place concurrently, represented most appropriately by Lord Advocate Sir George MacKenzie, codifier of Scots law and ferocious persecutor in the government service.

If territorial possession in the advancing sectors of production conferred growing economic power upon the possessors, their role had changed drastically in another respect as well. Until the time of the civil wars, the power of the territorial magnates had resided chiefly in their position as autonomous feudal lords, and had been related as much to the number of armed followers as to the wealth they could command. Under the Restoration an irreversible change had occurred. Political power now depended entirely on the royal confidence, and was exercised through membership of the Scottish Privy Council, steered by the King's Commissioner, usually a Scottish noble. This formed the nucleus of government, incomparably more effective than its rather anaemic pre-war predecessor. The magnates' power was over-riding, but derived from their function as royal servants, no longer in their own right as feudatories.

It is within such a context that the organisation of the kirk in Scotland must be viewed. All contemporary evidence testifies to the profound material greed of the new rulers, and their determination to treat their offices as a springboard for accumulation. But while the problems of labour supply in coalmine or saltwork could be solved by enserfing the workforce, an effective mechanism to extract a surplus from the agricultural producers was less easily obtained, especially in view of the retarded state of development of market relations in the agricultural sector. A stagnant population and the end of the land-hunger of the sixteenth and early seventeenth centuries restricted or eliminated the scope for rack-renting, and indeed stability of tenure and rents was the prevailing trend in subsequent years. In addition, small owners without tenurial obligations were, if not plentiful, not insignificant in number.

In circumstances of this kind, the kirk itself, with its deep penetration among the peasantry, the claims which it could make upon their resources, its structure of courts and the financial opportunities presented to its representatives, would be seen by the ruling class as a proper engine for sucking a surplus out of the basic producers, provided that it was brought under the right management. Moreover, the attenuation of feudal personal loyalty brought forward the necessity for an alternative system of hierarchical subordination and ideological constraint reaching out to every individual. The question of control of the kirk therefore amounted to the question of social hegemony in Scotland – would it be responsive to the small men of the kingdom or to their social betters? An episcopal hierarchy was accordingly instituted, and those ministers who refused submission evicted from their charges.

The nature of the Scottish bishops, now elevated to control of the kirk, was in close conformity with that of their secular counterparts: they were typical representatives of the post-revolutionary ruling class, and of the Caroline clergy in that their attentions were fixed upon ecclesiastical preferment and the incomes to be derived from their clerical office. At their head, James Sharp, Archbishop of St Andrews, a renegade presbyterian, had opportunely changed his convictions in order to gain the Scottish primacy. He was not averse to using his authority to jail lairds with whom he became involved in property disputes. One of them eventually commanded his assassins. Alexander Burnet, Archbishop of Glasgow and Sharp's successor in St Andrews was, of all the politicians, lay or clerical, the most active exponent of military persecution against the resisters. Paterson of Galloway, Edinburgh and Glasgow was credited with inventing the thumbscrew, and was so shamelessly corrupt that he eventually had to be dismissed from the Privy Council. All these three were responsible for insisting upon the execution of resisters, against whom charges were admittedly tenuous even by the standards of the time, or whom the secular leaders wanted to reprieve. Within the scope of their opportunity, the men appointed by them in place of the deposed ministers appear to have been of the same calibre. Even discounting the immoderate polemic with which the

Covenanter spokesmen accused them – drunkenness, corruption, and sexual malpractice – no supporter of the regime had any very favourable testimonial for these 'king's curates'. Preferment and wealth motivated their behaviour, and one, Dalgleish, imitated his superiors in securing the execution of the local laird who had discouraged his tenantry from attending the curate's services.

The majority of the population of lowland Scotland was unquestionably presbyterian in sentiment, but within this standpoint three broad positions can be identified. An overall majority, for the sake of peace and to escape harassment, were prepared to accept the new dispensation. In the areas of strongest presbyterian support, however, this ceased to be true. A majority in these districts – in total a substantial minority of the kirk's membership – pursued a course of passive resistance, by refusing to attend their parish churches, where the curates preached to miniscule congregations or to empty benches. Lastly, there was the element actively organising an alternative religious community and prepared eventually to support their commitment with armed force. These events have to be considered in the light of the almost superstitious regard for constituted authority prevailing at the time, the fact that there was no record of success or prospect of early victory to uphold morale, and the absence in Scotland of the revolutionary and democratic possibilities which had briefly emerged in England. In view of these considerations the determination of the active resisters is all the more remarkable. In the earlier phases to be sure, the insurrectionists were willing, even on the point of execution, to acknowledge the king's *civil* authority. Later on, such qualifications disappeared.

The problem is therefore posed of the social characteristics of the resisters, and the manner in which their ideological theory and practice was related to their social being. Nobody reading through their gallows speeches can have any doubt about the total sincerity of their Calvinist attachments, their unshakeable conviction that they belonged to God's elect and were on the point of entering heaven. Nonetheless, it is reasonable to infer that it was not simply an abstract commitment to theological postulates which motivated their inflexible determination to continue the struggle without any abatement of their claims, in the face of thoroughgoing and intense persecution, but rather that their religious faith and objectives expressed their view of acceptable and necessary relations between themselves and authority, and between social classes.

To attempt a direct interpretation of the social meaning of the Covenanters' ecclesiastical views is impossible: we simply do not know how they viewed the secular manifestations of the social order, the attacks in their writings and speeches upon the authorities being expressed wholly in terms of the latter's religious failings and criminality. What follows is therefore to be regarded as a very tentative and schematic hypothesis, derived from scattered hints and clues, which further investigation may amend or entirely disprove.

In the first insurrection – the so-called 'Pentland Rising' of 1666 – a few men of rank joined the enterprise, though even on this occasion a contemporary noted that very few 'landed gentlemen or ministers' took part. In the even more bitter conflict of 1678–88, the leadership was still more plebeian. Among the most prominent, Richard Cameron, was the son of a burgh merchant, though he cannot have been a very substantial one, another son having become a working weaver. Donald Cargill's father was a minor laird and notary while James Renwick, last of their principal spokesmen, was the son of a weaver. The records of the Privy Council and of local courts indicate that the rank and file of the disaffected was composed principally of tenant farmers, and tenant farmers in seventeenth-century Scotland were men of small means. Numerous too were individuals plying the common trades: weavers, smiths, tailors, masons, skinners, millers and servants. Interestingly, many women figure in these accounts, mostly, but not invariably, dependants of the men charged. One particularly significant fact is that the stronghold of the resistance was in Clydesdale and south-west Scotland. It was a Glasgow weaver who in 1662 was found guilty of treason for wishing 'that the king and his whole party should be hanged or it be long'.[3] It was precisely in this region that was found the highest concentration of 'bonnet lairds' – working landowners too minor to lease their ground or hire labour and scarcely distinguishable from the more fortunate tenantry.

In *Primitive Rebels*, E. J. Hobsbawm has shown that, in the absence of a revolutionary party to mobilise the rural proletariat of landless and labourers, the social stratum most likely to rebel under economic and social pressure is that of the petty owners who have something, though not very much, to lose. What they stand to lose is the margin between an accepted tolerable standard of comfort and status and reduction to penury. This assessment is confirmed by Julian Cornwall's study of the Cornish and East Anglian revolts of 1549, not to mention what is known of the agrarian side of the French revolution. It is not difficult to appreciate the social threat to such persons represented by an alien, plundering and rapacious church – that element of the state apparatus which touched them most intimately. Conversely, in their marginal circumstances, their best security resided in a kirk, with all its social and economic connotations, which at least represented their interests and which at most they might hope to dominate. Above all, they abhorred Erastianism, the subordination of church structures to the civil powers.

The conventicle, the unauthorised, illegal and most frequently outdoor prayer meeting was the focus and cellular unit of the opposition movement. Above all other features of the Covenanters' activities, it represented a standing challenge to the authorities and to the social fabric which they aimed to preserve. It represented an active denial of the hierarchical establishment, and furthermore, any gathering of the populace outside the approved channels was in the seventeenth century inseparably associated in the official mind with subversion and sedition. Consequently, the primary aim of government and hierarchy was to root out conventicling. On every other issue in dispute, the government was sooner or later prepared to consider compromise, but on conventicles they maintained an implacable military assault up to the Revolution of 1688. In the end, mere attendance was made a capital offence.

Prior to this, the standard procedure for rank-and-file attenders was fining and the quartering of troops upon their homes. Such fines frequently found their destinations in the pockets of the military commanders or the established clergy – some bishops were even accused of encouraging them in order to collect the fines. Behaviour of this sort, together with the usual molestations associated with military occupations, provoked the initial rising in 1666, easily supressed and attended with numerous executions.

The efforts of the government were next addressed to splitting the opposition in order to isolate the conventicling element and to concentrate its fire upon them. 'Indulgences' were issued to permit displaced presbyterian ministers to function upon restricted terms. The policy achieved a measure of success and in the 1670s negotiations were started towards a similar sort of settlement on a permanent basis. By the end of the decade, however, positions on both sides had become more entrenched and conventicles were spreading. By 1679 guerrilla warfare was underway in south-west Scotland and in the same year Archbishop Sharp was assassinated. In June, an armed conventicle, where women participated as combatants in the action, defeated the government forces at Drumclog and, reinforced from the surrounding countryside, briefly captured Glasgow. Dissension upon the strictness of the attitude to be adopted towards Indulged ministers and military inexperience rendered the Covenanters incapable of following up their advantage, and they were shortly thereafter annihilated at Bothwell Brig. The government celebrated its success with the customary executions.

The guerrilla struggle and conventicling activity continued nevertheless. A fully articulated resistance movement emerged, identified in particular with the Cameronians, followers of the preacher Richard Cameron who was subsequently killed in another encounter at Airsmoss.

The achievement of the Cameronians in maintaining their organisation and continuing to fight in spite of a string of uninterrupted defeats is impressive, but they were rendered a good deal less effective than they might otherwise have been by their refusal to cooperate with any presbyterians who interpreted the Covenant less strictly than they did, or who showed any disposition to collaborate with the Indulged. In spite of that, their political theory was by no means as unsophisticated as their religious narrowness might lead one to expect. A theoretical justification for resistance – *Ius Populi Vindicatum* – had been produced ten years earlier by one James Stewart, who was respectable enough to become Lord Advocate after the Revolution of 1688. He propounded an essentially Lockean theory of contract between sovereign and subjects. The subjects will not choose to be governed by a regime which places them in a worse condition than they were prior to instituting government. The contract is therefore revocable in principle if the sovereign fails to observe his side of the bargain, and the legitimate right of self-defence is invoked. Religious justification is added. No magistrate can be lawful if he destroys the divine purposes of magistracy, as Charles II and his ministers by their religious policy were said to be doing, and if it is justified to maintain a legitimate king against attempted usurpation by a 'lesser magistrate', how much more so to support God against a usurping king.

A Hind Let Loose (1687) by Alexander Shields is the fullest statement of the Cameronian case. It reiterates the points made in *Ius Populi* and, while polemicising against despisers of government as an institution, goes on to declare that

> In some cases it is lawful and laudable for private persons, touched with the zeal of God and love to their country, and respect to Justice trampled upon by Tyrants, to put forth their hand to execute righteous judgment upon the enemies of God and mankind, intolerable traitors, murderers, idolators, [by] whom the ruin of the country, Destruction of religion and liberty and the wrath of God is threatened. . . .[4]

In accord with these statements the Cameronians expected their adherents to refuse to pay the parliamentary taxation or cess, used in their eyes to support an illicit government and finance the repression directed against them.

The translation of their political principles into practice was begun by the Cameronians in 1680 with the declaration made at the cross of the Dumfriesshire village of Sanquhar, disowning Charles Stuart 'who hath been reigning, or rather (we may say) tyrannising on the Throne of Scotland . . .', and likewise his brother the Duke of York, 'a profest Papist, repugnant to our principles and vows'. The document proceded to issue a declaration of war against the pair and their ministers. A draft paper previously prepared by Cameron's fellow-preacher Cargill had included a demand to discard the royal family and set up a new republic. The Sanquhar Declaration was followed by Cargill publicly excommunicating the king, his brother and four members of the Council at Torwood.

In 1681 the Cameronians established what virtually amounted to a political party by instituting a General Correspondence of their Societies designed to be coordinated by a fortnightly circular letter and a quarterly meeting. Three years later, under their then leader Renwick, the Cameronians issued a further declaration, directed especially against 'Informers and Intelligencers' and promising to punish them 'according to our power and the degree of their offence', which document, according to J. Hewison in *The Covenanters* (1908)[5] 'drove many informers and unpopular curates to flight' and provided the pretext for the authorities to intensify repression. The following year, Sanquhar was again the venue for a further pronouncement disavowing the Duke of York's succession as James VII and II and defining themselves as a 'poor wasted, wronged, wounded, reproached, despised and bleeding Remnant'.

The government's answer to the Societies' proclamations and armed attacks was to let loose a campaign of remorseless terror in the disaffected area. Its officers were commissioned to proceed with 'fyre and sword' against the irreconcilables, and they did so enthusiastically. It is an interesting speculation as to how far any connexion may have existed between the intensified resistance and repression of the 1680s and the simultaneous appearance of bad harvests and downturn in the Scots economy. That question, however, for the present must remain unanswerable. The armed forces swept and harried the south-west, pillaging, molesting and performing arbitrary executions. John Graham of Claverhouse, the most notable of the anti-guerrilla commanders, boasted that he 'rifled so their houses, ruined their goods . . . that their wyfes and schildring were broght to sterving'.[6] Two women were included among those hanged, and another two were sentenced to be drowned. It is not certain whether the sentence was actually carried out, but the balance of probability is that it was. The regular practice of the superior officers was to embezzle the common soldiers' pay, providing an added inducement to the latter for brutality and plunder. The 'Killing Time' was a period, in the words of Hewison, of 'uniformed aristocrats stealing from poor packmen on the roads'.[7]

Furnished with a suitable pretext in the Cameronian rebellion, the Council set to drying out the presbyterian sea in which the guerrilla fish were swimming, taking advantage of the opportunity to extirpate presbyterianism itself. A parallel attack was therefore directed upon the presbyterian non-combatants, attenders at conventicles, and simple non-attenders of their parish churches. They were repeatedly and relentlessly fined, packed together into insanitary dungeons and left to rot indefinitely, or transported to servitude on the American plantations. The authorities hanged an occasional one and withdrew the former Indulgences granted to some of their ministers.

By these means the congregations in the official churches were again filled up, and by 1687 the Cameronians had their backs to the wall, but the government remained unable to secure total 'pacification'. The organisation of the Societies remained in being and conventicles continued to be held. In that year, James II, anxious to secure tolerance for his Catholic co-religionists, initiated a drastic shift in policy. Two Declarations of Indulgence extended to all dissenters, Catholic and Protestant, permission to conduct religious activities, organised according to their taste, provided it was done under the eye of authority. For conventicles and repudiators of the royal authority, however, repression was to be intensified.

The presbyterian majority, and especially the better-off, hastened to accept the concession. The Cameronians denounced it as a 'pretended clemency offering a sort of liberty . . . for bringing in all future snares by taking off some former'. The author went on to make the reasonable point that what had been granted by royal fiat might as easily be removed when opportunity offered: 'All the tenure that Protestants have for their religion is only the arbitrary word of an Absolute monarch . . . outvying the height of Ottoman tyranny.'[8]

However, the initiative proved, in Scotland, a very successful coup: grateful presbyterian divines hastened to proclaim their allegiance and to pray for James, the landowners were entirely won over, and both willingly collaborated in the pursuit of the Societies. Records from 1688 show the landowners in the shire of Wigtown acting collectively to root out conventicles, while their counterparts in Ayrshire agreed to evict any tenant not denouncing conventicles.[9] In such circumstances, the English Revolution of 1688, deposing James II, ensured that a fairly smooth transition from a tolerated to an established presbyterian church could occur, one safely under the command of clergymen fervently loyal to whichever regime would tolerate them – whether it be that of James II or William III – and of socially respectable landowners who retained the power to influence ministers' appointments. The populace was able to show its feelings by violently evicting the king's curates, but the Cameronians were to have no part in directing the new settlement. They were still sufficiently well-organised and disciplined to form from the Societies (though the most intransigent were still opposed to any association with 'Malignants') a regiment which was crucial in stopping an attempted Jacobite restoration from the highlands, but with that episode their effective role came to an end. In subsequent years many of their members reverted to the established church; others divided into ever more minute and theologically rarefied fractions.

The ruling class in Scotland found itself after all well able to adapt to a presbyterian kirk which ran no risk of becoming a centre for social dissension, but developed on the contrary into an effective tool for reinforcing class relationships. Famine in the 1690s and, in the following decade, the Union with England and subsequent transformations at the economic base, liquidated the human potential for popular revolt in the countryside. The Societies could not pass from a revolt in the name of religion to the adoption of a social programme. The binding theological shell in which their philosophy was contained – and from which they unquestionably derived their conviction – was far too rigid for any such development. The re-establishment of presbyterianism therefore left them without any viable perspective or hope of mass appeal, however much they might feel the Covenant had been dishonoured. In the words of Victor Kiernan, they 'never learned to turn [their] pact with God into a pact with the common people against their oppressors'.[10]

Nonetheless, the Cameronians deserve a better understanding than history has normally accorded to them – pious Calvinist saints in one version, or bigoted and murderous brigands in the other. Their revolt can be regarded as a particular variation of the tradition of millenial uprising which bridges the history of popular movements between the end of the middle ages and the emergence of modern revolutionary processes. It stretches from the Czech Hussites of the fifteenth century, through the Munster anabaptists, to the sects of the English revolution. Conversely, the organisational methods by which the Societies conducted their campaign point towards the practice of nineteenth and twentieth-century guerrilla movements. Abortive, sectarian, and religiously blinkered, the uncompromising stand of poor men and women in the face of arbitrary and ferocious state power deserves to be respected.

NOTES

1 C. Hill, *The World Turned Upside Down*, Harmondsworth, 1975, pp. 378–9.
2 Ian B. Cowan, *The Scottish Covenanters 1660–1688*, London, 1976, p. 29.
3 *Justiciary Records of the Court of Session*, edited by W. G. Scott Moncrieff Edinburgh, 1905 (November 1662).
4 Shields, *A Hind Let Loose*, p. 39.
5 Hewison, *The Covenanters*, Vol. II, p. 441.
6 Cowan, op. cit., p. 111.
7 Hewison, op. cit., p. 123.
8 Shields, op. cit., pp. 162–3.
9 *The Register of the Privy Council of Scotland*, 3rd series, July 1688.
10 V. G. Kiernan, 'The Scottish Revolution' in *Scottish Marxist*, no. 8, January 1975.

ROBERT OWEN ON THE FAMILY AND THE MARRIAGE SYSTEM OF THE OLD IMMORAL WORLD

JOHN SAVILLE

Robert Owen lived for eighty-seven years. He was born in 1771 and the first twenty years of his working life his career was that of a successful, self-made business man with a notable capacity for industrial management. His early years in business during the 1790s illustrated the extraordinary profits that were to be gained from the first phase of factory enterprise, and with the capital accumulated during this period he was able to buy the New Lanark mills from David Dale in 1799.[1] Owen married the daughter of David Dale and in 1800 he settled near the mills. His life from this year until 1824 – when he left Britain for America – was perhaps the most interesting, and certainly the most intellectually exciting, of his whole career.

Down to about 1812 he was still relatively unknown; an unusually generous-minded and philanthropic businessman, but not one who had yet attracted national attention. In 1813, however, the first essay was published of what became the *New View of Society*, and the *New View* – the product of a benevolent rationalist educator – was to make Owen known to a European audience. His central argument was the familiar one of individual character moulded by the environment in which the individual lived; given a new, and unfamiliar twist by the practical success of the organisation of the New Lanark mills and community. Between 1813 and 1820, when the famous *Report to the County of Lanark* was published, Owen produced pamphlets and made speeches extending, developing and amplifying his ideas. There took place in these years a remarkable enlargement of his intellectual horizons; grappling intellectually with the post-war problems, he developed a critique of his contemporary society, and offered positive solutions for its economic and social ills that took him steadily towards a socialist position. What has often been missed in commentaries upon Owen in this period is both the

development of his ideas and thinking between the *New View*
and the *Report to the County of Lanark*, and the originality of much
of his analysis. He argued from within the new industrial system,
recognising the enormous productive power now available to
society; he showed a striking insight into certain crucial
weaknesses of the new industrial capitalism – the relationship,
for example, between unemployment and deficiency in
demand; and above all he emphasised the fundamental
contradiction between 'individual interest' on the one hand,
and the public good and social welfare on the other. This basic
conflict between the self-interest of the individual in a profit-
orientated economy, and the purposes and aims of a society
concerned with human happiness, were to be repeated again
and again in his writings; and it represented the earliest
sustained critique of capitalist society in the history of socialist
ideas in Britain.[2]

There were always certain major gaps in Owen's thinking,
and some obvious inconsistencies in his analysis. He was in most
things paternalistic in his approach to social, as well as personal,
questions, and his gentle but authoritarian benevolence
seriously clouded his judgement on some central issues of the
day. He never lost his belief, for example, that the ruling groups
in society would come to appreciate the rationality and the
reasonableness of his own community schemes; although he left
for the United States in 1824 partly, at least, because public
support in Britain from politicians, aristocrats and the Church
had been waning sharply since his famous attack on religion in
1817.[3]

Owen was only in America for five years – between 1824 and
1829 – but the experience was important for the further
development of his ideas. He had put forward the self-
contained community as the alternative to competitive self-
interest in the *Report to the County of Lanark*; but now he was to
experience a community in being. He sunk almost all his fortune
in New Harmony, the former Rappite settlement on the banks
of the Wabash, in Indiana; and while the experiment came to an
end in 1827, Owen returning to Britain two years later, it had a
profound effect upon him. For one thing it established Owen as
a social reformer on both sides of the Atlantic; but more
important, it deepened his radicalism, and enhanced his sense
of community, and its meaning.[4]

When he returned to England he almost immediately entered upon a new phase of his career. Between 1829 and 1834 he was centrally involved in the working-class movement, on two interconnected and related fronts: one, the growth of co-operative organisations, and the second, the permeation of the trade union movement with Owenite ideas. The vigorous and turbulent movements of the early 1830s reached their climax with the meteoric rise of the Grand National Consolidated Trades Union, and its equally rapid decline in the spring and summer of 1834; a dramatic collapse which marked the beginnings of a decline of Owenite influence among the grass-roots organisations of working men, and which for Owen himself involved once more a marked shift in the direction of his own life. From now on Owenism became increasingly a sectarian movement, infused with millenial ideas, especially apathetic towards political activity where not outright hostile, and caught up in anti-religious and anti-clerical polemic. The failure of the Queenwood community in Hampshire and the demise of the *New Moral World* in 1845 brought Owenism to an end as a movement of even minor significance in British politics. Owen himself lived on for over a decade longer, dying in 1858, but while his ideas continued to exercise some influence – albeit in many different forms – their significance in the middle decades of the century which followed the defeats of 1848 was no more than marginal.

Robert Owen has often been described as a man with one idea, a judgement which Leslie Stephen, in his well-known DNB article, did much to foster.[5] Owen, it is true, wrote voluminously and was often repetitive; he reiterated again and again his central idea that character was the product of circumstances; but to suggest that there was little more to Owen than this central axiom of his thought is seriously to underestimate the complexity of his ideas and the range of his social interests. This one-sided emphasis, common to a majority of writers on Owen, has largely come about through a concentration upon a few texts – the *New View*, the *Report to the County of Lanark* and the *Autobiography*. What has been ignored is Owen's many contributions to periodical publications, many of which were later republished in pamphlet form.

The first main phase of Owen's development as a critic of

bourgeois society was summed up in the 1820 *Report to the County of Lanark*. Some parts of what he wrote in the *Report* had been sketched out in his 1815 pamphlet, *Observations on the Effect of the Manufacturing System*, but by 1820 he had gone beyond these earlier ideas. His insistence upon the crucial importance of community stemmed from profound insights into the fundamental contradictions within competitive capitalism between individual self-interest and the public good. Owen vigorously denied the central concept of the liberal theory of *laissez-faire*: that the pursuit of private interest would ensure the maximisation of social welfare. He correctly identified the principle of self-interest as 'the cornerstone to the social system' and he argued, in flat opposition to contemporary opinion, that all the evils of human society could be traced to the operation of this principle in practice. Three years later, in *An Explanation of the Causes of Distress* (1823), he specifically identified private interest in society with the pursuit of profit. He acknowledged that ' a commerce founded on a *profit upon cost price – a minute division of labour – and a competition of individual interests*' had been 'necessary and useful' for an earlier period of human history, before society was able to produce a surplus over basic wants; but with the enormous and rapid growth in productive power, based upon the new industrial technology, entirely new possibilities were now beginning for mankind. In the pre-scientific era, the 'natural wants' of men exceeded their productive power, and it was then that there was a population excess. But with technological innovation and improvement, 'the natural wants of men came to be more easily supplied, artificial wants were then excited, and a new era commenced. A commerce was established, founded *on a profit upon price*, and individual gain became the ruling passion throughout society' (p. 2).

Such an arrangement of society inevitably encouraged all the worst aspects of human nature; personal gain was built into the fabric of society; 'everything became valued by its *cost*, instead of its *intrinsic worth*'. The search for profit, now the central principle of economic activity, could only be assured when demand either equalled supply, or was greater than supply; and while Owen somewhat exaggerated the argument, by suggesting that a profit-making society could only be successful through 'foreign or domestic war, pestilence or famine' (p. 3), he was nevertheless stating a fundamental truth about industrial capitalism. Owen went on to emphasise that it was only the removal of the profit motive that would allow the enhanced productive powers now available to provide '*at all times* an excess of supply over consumption without injury to the producers'. To achieve this desired and desirable end, a new organisation of society was required, by which men would supply their wants by their own labour, and this involved the establishment of self-supporting communities, the details of which he then proceeded to outline in the second part of the 1823 pamphlet.

Owen returned again and again in his writings to the basic and central conflict between private interest and public good. He was not, as will be discussed later, a systematic thinker, and he was not always consistent in argument. In general, however, he applied his analysis of private and public interest to most aspects of social life, and never in more interesting ways than in his writings and lectures on marriage and the family system. His work on these matters was widely read by contemporaries in the 1830s, and when Marx and Engels in the *Communist Manifesto* came to analyse trends and tendencies in the socialist movement, they included Owenite ideas under the heading 'Critical-Utopian Socialism and Communism'. Their criticisms of Saint-Simon, Fourier and Owen attacked sharply the practical proposals offered by these thinkers to overcome the existing disharmonies and class conflicts; but at the same time it was acknowledged that their general critique of capitalist society was searching and enormously educative:

> But these socialist and communist publications contain also a critical element. They attack every principle of existing society. Hence they are full of the most valuable materials for the enlightenment of the working class.

Owen had become interested in the community experiments of the Rappites and the Shakers during the years when he was moving from philanthropy to a more radical understanding of his contemporary world. He had known of the Rappites at least since 1815;[6] and he published Warder's *Brief Sketch* of the Shakers in 1818.[7] Owen visited the Shaker community at Niskeyuna, New York, within a few days of reaching America in 1824, and he was much impressed with what he saw. The following year saw the purchase of the Rappite community at

Harmony, Indiana, and New Harmony was inaugurated. Owen's early opposition to the competitive nature of society led him naturally to accept the idea and the practice of community life. The aim of New Harmony, he wrote, was 'to change from the individual to the social system; from single families with separate interests to communities of many families with one interest'.[8]

Community inevitably involved the reordering of family life. It is, of course, a commonplace of historians of millenial movements and sects that there developed a preoccupation, in some an obsession, with family and sexual relationships and with the position, status and role of women in the community. There were scattered references in Owen's writings before the middle 1830s to these matters, as for example in *The Outline of a Rational Society* published as a Supplement to the *Crisis* of 26 May 1832. After noting that all children would be under 'the especial care of the community', with free access to their parents at all times, the Constitution and Code of Laws continued: 'Both sexes shall have equal education, rights, privileges, and personal liberty; their associations would arise from the general sympathies of their nature, uninfluenced by artificial distinctions.' But nowhere was there anything approaching a comprehensive statement and as so often with Owen, his interest in his own ideas fluctuated from one period to another. The early 1830s, however, were years when radical ideas about the relations between the sexes were becoming increasingly discussed. William Thompson's 1825 *Appeal of One Half the Human Race* was dedicated to his close friend and collaborator, Anna Wheeler who was herself in close contact with Robert Owen in the later 1820s and early 1830s.[9] When James Elishama Smith arrived in London in the summer of 1832 and began preaching, Anna Wheeler was soon among his congregation. Smith published his *Lecture on a Christian Community* in the spring of 1833 and a version published in the *Crisis* of 4 May 1833 illustrated the current thinking of advanced radicals on the relations between men and women:

There would also be a material improvement in the intercourse between the sexes; by the emancipation of woman from the thralldom of man. At present woman is a dependent; then, she would become equal to man in political and personal privileges.

Now, the marriage tie binds together for life two parties, who are frequently destructive of each other's happiness; then, each would be free to make such a change of circumstances as was necessary for their own comfort; love would become a perpetual courtship, and not a domestic prison. Nature oft unites two hearts together; in which case, love is constant, and separation painful. This is the marriage of nature. *She* is the only priest, or rather priestess. Hitherto the world has been ruled by priests; let a priestess be substituted in their stead. Hitherto God has been worshipped as a man; let us now worship the female God; the goddess Nature – the bride – the Lamb's wife; thus fulfilling the words of scripture, 'Behold I create a new thing in the earth, a woman shall compass a man.'

The combination of advanced Owenism and the remnants of Smith's earlier chiliastic beliefs derived from his Southcottian experience would not have sounded at all strange or bizarre to his audience at the Rotunda. The Saint-Simonian missionaries who arrived in London in 1832 were impressed by the reception of Owenite meetings, and especially of Owenite women, to their message. The cause of socialist feminism was growing fast in these early years of the decade and that Robert Owen should have addressed himself to the social questions of marriage and the family system was wholly understandable. Much of his extraordinary statement of the problem would be already familiar to his readers, especially those who had read Thompson; but when all is said concerning the provenance of Owen's ideas – and much in this context still remains to be analysed – there was an important part of the analysis that developed from within his own fertile and original mind.[10]

The 'critical element' that Marx and Engels emphasised as characteristic of the kind of socialism Owen represented was fully developed in the *Lectures on the Marriages of the Priesthood of the Old Immoral World, delivered in the year 1835, before the passing of the New Marriage Act*. The first and subsequent editions were all published from Leeds; the second edition (1838) had the more positive title: *The Marriage System of the New Moral World: with the faint outline of the Present Very Irrational System, as developed in a Course of Ten Lectures*. The third edition with the same title as the second was published in 1839, and the fourth in 1840: *Lectures on the Marriages of the Priesthood . . . with an Appendix containing the Marriage System of the New Moral World*. It is the enlarged second

edition which is used here, together with the important
Appendix to the fourth edition.

Owen began his first lecture by recalling that in previous
discussions he had noted that:

> the chief of the Satanic institutions over the world, though
> somewhat varied in name and form, are the priesthood; the lawyers
> and magistrates; the military; the unnatural and artificial union of
> the sexes; individual and national competition and contest; and the
> single family, or universally disuniting arrangements of society; and
> the metal, or any medium liable to change in value, for the
> circulation of wealth (p. 4).

Owen remarked early in his discussion that any commentary
on the marriage system must reckon with the 'oldest, strongest
and most inveterate prejudices'; and he went on to launch a
generalised attack on the marriage system, accusing it of being
'the sole cause of all the prostitution, of all its incalculable
grievous evils, and of all the violent and most degrading crimes
known to society'. He put the responsibility for this state of
affairs squarely upon organised religion; and it was this
combination of a root-and-branch criticism of marriage and
anti-religion that made Owenism in the second half of the 1830s
a synonym for subversiveness and evil that had to be
exterminated.

At the centre of Owen's critique of the family in a competitive,
individualistic world was his denunciation of the single familial
structure. There was to be no one else in the nineteenth century
who provided such a devastating analysis of the effects and
consequences upon husbands, wives and children of what he
constantly referred to as 'the unnatural and artificial marriages
of the world'. He began with the husband and wife who, before
marriage, were almost wholly unaware of the new situation they
would find themselves in after the marriage ceremony. Before
marriage, man was the wooer, 'his will was in abeyance to the
will of his beloved object'; but usually after marriage the reverse
takes place. Now 'the wife is *expected* to be obedient to her
husband'. Both man and wife are therefore placed in this new
unnatural situation, and Owen dilated at length on the ways in
which relationships could worsen. 'But the poor wife,' he added
'is most generally the most to be pitied of the two'. After
marriage the wife had, legally, a master; 'and she is necessarily

forced to become a weak, cunning, deceptious, inferior being'. Owen, however, went far beyond legal disabilities to explain the inferior position of women; and far further than the advanced liberalism of John Stuart Mill some thiry years later.[11] Owen's understanding of the position of the sexes in bourgeois society was interwoven with his appreciation of the central part which private property occupied in the social structure. The single family unit was inevitably competitive with all other families; it encouraged selfishness and self-centredness; and within this vicious single family arrangement, children were taught:

> to consider their own individual family their own world, and that it is the duty and interest of all within this little orb to do whatever they can to promote the advantages of all the legitimate members of it. With these persons, it is *my* house, *my* wife, *my* estate, *my* children, or *my* husband; *our* estate; and *our* children; or *my* parents, *my* brothers, *my* sisters; and *our* house and property. This family party is trained to consider it quite right, and a superior mode of acting, for each member of it to seek, by all fair means, as almost any means, except *direct* robbery are termed, to increase the wealth, honour and privilege of the family and every individual member of it (p. 36).

Competition between families inevitably encouraged all the worst sentiments within individuals; and the exhortation to 'love his neighbour as himself' became quite impossible. Moreover, the institution of the single family was inextricably linked with the gross economic inequalities of contemporary society. Wealth married wealth and children were born into either rich or poor families; but whatever the material conditions in which children were reared, it would not be possible to inculcate and develop rational, just and kindly attitudes until private property was abolished, religious superstition eliminated, and the social structure of the single-family unit fundamentally re-cast.

Women were not, however, subject only to legal inferiority and the social and personal consequences of the competitive family system. There was a different moral standard for men and women. Husbands 'are allowed unnoticed the full natural sexual animal freedom' (p. 26) while an unnatural emphasis is placed upon chastity for women. It is all, of course, 'the unnatural notions and imaginations of a most degraded order of men, called the Priesthood . . .' (p. 11). True chastity is quite different. It is 'a feeling and sympathy mysteriously implanted in human nature, and exists only between the sexes when in their intercourse they feel a sincere and genuine affection for each other'.

> Real genuine chastity is a sentiment and a feeling far too elevated and refined for their ignorant and gross conceptions [sc. the Priesthood] or they could never have artificially tied bodies in their bonds of wedlock, and then said, 'Be you united, mind and body, for life; or be miserable in this world and everlastingly damned in the next.' What a sacrilege of the best and finest sympathies of our nature! What ignorance of the organisation of man and woman! What horrid sacrifice of the happiness of the human life (p. 12).

Owen linked his attack on what has later become known as the double standard of values for men and women, with a similarly vigorous denunciation of celibacy: 'a virtue of the Priesthood of the world, but it is a vice against nature'; and he gave sound physiological and psychological reasons why enforced celibacy was unnatural and false to the human condition. Owen always used as his criteria for assessing what was right and what was wrong in the relations between the sexes the simple and the genuine and the real in terms of affection and love. If men were not chaste, how was it possible for women to be so? If there was not unadulterated love and sympathy within a marriage, how could hypocrisy be avoided? Prostitution flowed directly from the institution of the single-family marriage, for where there was not 'unbiassed affection' only evils could follow.

It was these arguments that led Owen to advocate divorce. In an appendix added to the fourth edition, 1840, of this pamphlet on marriage, he set down the details of his practical proposals for 'the union and disunion of the sexes'; although it should be noted that he had set out all the details which follow in the *Crisis* for 18 May 1833. Unions between men and women, 'having an affection for each other', should be publicly announced; and if after three months it was intended to continue living together, there should be a further public declaration. Separation, if desired by both parties, should not be allowed until twelve months had passed, and then, after a public statement on intent, they would be required to continue to live together for a further six months, after which, if they still wished to separate, they would announce the fact and register the dissolution of their union. If only one of the parties wished to end the relationship, he or she, after similar trial periods, would be permitted to separate. As for the children, since these were the responsibility of Society, 'the separation of the parents will not produce any change in the condition of the rising generation'.

Owen was writing before the full development of the typical middle-class Victorian attitudes towards sexual questions, but the evangelical movement was already well under way. The hysteria which welled up at the end of the decade against his ideas on marriage and religion was evidence of a notable hardening of attitudes and prejudices.[12] Owen's views on the family, marriage and divorce, allied as they were to his anti-clericalism, undoubtedly represented the most radical of all his many attacks upon contemporary society, but as with so much of his writing the ideas were not developed later in a systematic way, either by Owen himself or by sympathetic observers. It has been suggested that these lectures on marriage and the family system were widely read in the 1830s,[13] and certainly four editions in six years indicate a lively interest. The quite rapid decline of the Owenite movement in the 1840s, however, left little legacy in terms of influencing ideas and attitudes. The revival of political radicalism, for instance, in the decade of the sixties was not linked with radical social, and certainly not radical sexual, ideas; and it is worth at least briefly inquiring why this was so, and how it came about that the extraordinarily acute and critical ideas that Owen was developing about sex, family life and the marriage system evoked no response, or almost no response, from Victorian Britain after the 1840s. It is, indeed, only in the 1960s and 1970s in Britain that Owen's arguments about the 'trap' of the single-family marriage (although he does not use the word) began to receive serious attention beyond small minority groups.[14]

The question concerning the absence of response to Owenite ideas on marriage should, of course, be broadened in terms of the general context and content of social ideas in the second half of the nineteenth century. There are first of all two points to be made about Owen's critical writings. One is that he showed remarkable insights into certain of the basic problems of bourgeois society, in ways which were not repeated or recovered until the twentieth century, at least by British radicals and socialists. The second is that he himself was apparently incapable of enlarging and extending his insights into a comprehensive critique that was internally consistent. There was, within Robert Owen, an extraordinary mixture of realist and utopian, of paternalist and democrat, of conservative and revolutionary. He could produce, on the one hand, a devastating analysis of the relation between private property, the marriage system and selfish individualism, and within the same time period offer a utopian, analytically anaemic and politically innocuous statement of what he would do were he to become Prime Minister of England.[15] The contradictions and inconsistencies in Owen's writings have been often remarked upon; but what is even more important to emphasise is the radical quality and originality of much of his thinking on social questions. From one point of view Owen may be characterised as hopelessly confused and uncertain, encapsulated within a utopian framework of thinking which was unrealistic and irrelevant to the problems of his contemporary world. But to say this without at the same time recognising the profound insights he offered into social questions would be greatly to distort the intellectual contribution that he made to the development of socialist ideas. It is, indeed, the contradictory nature of Owen's thinking and his practice that accounts for the many diverse opinions and judgements that have been made upon him by later writers. He was undoubtedly, for example, paternalistic in his general approach to people and to problems. This characteristic is easily detected in much of his writing, and attested for in his handling of contentious and difficult practical problems.[16] Yet the *Outline of the Rational System of Society*, of which there were many editions in the 1830s, contained many sensible ideas on the self-government of communities; with the responsibility for domestic affairs being in the hands of all members between the ages of thirty and forty, and that of foreign affairs of members between the ages of forty and sixty. This is not paternalism, but good democratic commonsense, not least on the age limits for those controlling the general run of day to day affairs.

There is, indeed, no lack of critical commentary on Owen's thinking and writing, but the failure of his ideas to impress later generations, except in quite limited ways, cannot be wholly, or perhaps even mainly, accounted for in terms of his own inability to develop a systematic analysis, or to overcome his obvious inconsistencies and intellectual limitations. Owenism, as J. F. C. Harrison has rightly insisted, 'was a movement of intellectuals [which yet] failed to attract any really first-rate minds'.[17] There was no sustained development of Owen's ideas, no serious critique within an Owenite framework of reference by sympathetic writers, no attempt to separate out the millennial elements from the realistic analysis of contemporary social issues; no attempt, indeed, to debate what was millennial and what was realistic.[18] Owen's own failure to comprehend the problem of human agency in the transformation of society, 'a vacant place in his mind, where most men have political responses'[19] sharply divided him from the active radicals of his day, and above all, from the movement of Chartism. In the persons of Bronterre O'Brien and Henry Hetherington, as well as those of many less well-known militants, this division was only partial; and this is one among other reasons why the description of Owenism from the mid-1830s cannot be expressed in simplistic millenial terms. But the rejection of politics by Owen and most of his followers, their utopian views of how social change can be effected, cut him and them off from most of the dynamic political radicals of this period. The gap between the politics of the Chartist movement and the imaginative social insights that Owen was offering in the 1830s in particular was never wholly impassable, but contact and bridging were intermittent and localised; and the post-1848 history of working-class radicalism only too clearly reflected the lack of serious thinking and debate on basic social questions. The history of British socialism has been immeasurably poorer for their neglect.

NOTES

1 The most substantial biography of Owen is still Frank Podmore, *Robert Owen: A Biography*, 2 vols (1960; reprinted in one volume, New York, 1968). For details of his business career see: A. J. Robertson, 'Robert Owen, Cotton Spinner: New Lanark, 1800–1825', *Robert Owen, Prophet of the Poor* (ed. Sidney Pollard and John Salt, 1971); and John Butt, 'Robert Owen as a Businessman', *Robert Owen. Prince of Cotton Spinners* (ed. John Butt, 1971). Leslie Morton's many years' interest in Owen resulted in *The Life and Ideas of Robert Owen* (1962), which was an extremely useful selection of Owen's writings prefaced by a 50-page biographical introduction.

2 See the brief introduction by John Saville to the reprint of *A New View of Society* (New York, 1972), pp. iii–xv.

3 *Address at the City of London Tavern on Thursday, August 21 . . . in A Supplementary Appendix to the First Volume of The Life of Robert Owen*, Vol. 1A (London 1858; reprinted, New York, 1967).

4 The most useful study of all aspects of Owenite ideas and community experiments is J. F. C. Harrison, *Robert Owen and the Owenites in Britain and America* (1969). Among the many merits of the volume is a comprehensive bibliography.

5 'Owen may be described as one of those intolerable bores who are the salt of the earth. . . He was essentially a man of one idea; that idea, too, was only partially right, and enforced less by argument than by incessant and monotonous repetition', *DNB*, XIV, p. 1345.

6 J. F. C. Harrison, *Robert Owen and the Owenites* . . ., p. 54.

7 Ibid., p. 53.

8 *New Harmony Gazette*, 1 October 1825; quoted Harrison, op. cit., p. 59.

9 R. K. P. Pankhurst, *William Thompson* (1954) for a discussion of the relations between Thompson, Anna Wheeler and the Owenite movement. See also Harrison, op. cit., *passim*. and for the general background of early feminism in England, the excellent unpublished dissertation of Gail Malmgreen, 'The Intellectual and Social Origins of the Women's Suffrage Movement in England; 1792·1851 (MA thesis, University of Rhode Island, 1972).

10 For bibliographical references to J. E. Smith, see John Saville, 'J. E. Smith and the Owenite Movement, 1833–1834', in *Robert Owen. Prophet of the Poor* (ed. S. Pollard and J. Salt, 1971); and for a good discussion of socialist feminism in the 1830s, Barbara Taylor, 'The Woman-Power: Religious Heresy and Feminism in Early English Socialism', in *Tearing the Veil* (ed. S. Lipshitz, 1977).

11 For which see M. St John Packe, *The Life of John Stuart Mill* (1954) esp. pp. 492 ff; K. Millett, 'The Debate over Women: Ruskin *vs* Mill', in *Suffer and Be Still* (ed. M. Vicinus, Indiana University Press, 1973).

12 Podmore's biography of Owen Chapters XX and XXI discusses the reception of the *Lectures on the Marriages of the Priesthood* and the intense furore they aroused. His latter chapter is headed 'The Holy War'. See also Harrison, *Robert Owen and the Owenites*, pp. 216 ff.

13 By J. F. C. Harrison, op. cit., p. 255.

14 The phrase 'the trap' is used in an interview by Simone de Beavoir, reported in the London *Observer*, 15 January 1978.

15 *Robert Owen's Reply to the Question, 'What Would You Do, If You Were Prime Minister of England'*, 2nd edn, Stockport, ? 1832.

16 See, for an example, the discussion of the conflict between Owen on the one hand and James Morrison and J. E. Smith in 1833–4: John Saville, 'J. E. Smith and the Owenite Movement', pp. 125 ff.

17 J. F. C. Harrison, op. cit., p. 258.

18 I accept Eileen Yeo's criticism of J. F. C. Harrison in this particular regard. See her article, 'Robert Owen and Radical Culture' in *Robert Owen, Prophet of the Poor*, and especially note 2, p. 108 where she writes: '. . . Harrison is very keen to use sociological work on sects and sect formation. But in

depicting Owenism as a secular millenarian sect, he detaches the Owenite movement too sharply from other social and protest movements of the time and brings in misleading (and, to my mind, distasteful) sociological descriptions about "adjustment" to times of severe social dislocation through "withdrawal". This sort of language trivialises widespread and constructive attempts at culture building which left an important legacy for later working-class movements. Moreover, Harrison gives little sense of the actual content of the culture or the social terrain where it took root and makes too little distinction between Owen, the local leadership and the rank and file.'

19 E. P. Thompson, *The Making of the English Working Class* (1963), p. 783.

WORKING CLASS AND NATION IN NINETEENTH-CENTURY BRITAIN

VICTOR KIERNAN

'The workers have no fatherland.' For the Marx of the *Communist Manifesto*, born in a Germany which had only a dozen years before ceased to be the Holy Roman Empire, this was a necessary condition of their historic task; it meant emancipation from the past and all its trammels. In Britain the factory working class started existence doubly segregated, morally and physically shut off in its smoky towns from the rest of the nation. Yet it was being born into a land where the spirit of nationalism had flowered, along with nascent capitalism, earlier than anywhere else. England's most remarkable traveller listened with deep indignation to the King of Brobdingnag's ridicule of his noble country – 'The mistress of arts and arms; the scourge of France; the arbitress of Europe; the seat of virtue, piety, honour, and truth; the pride and envy of the world'.

Gulliver spoke for the middle classes, but many things combined to give those below them a concern with the national greatness. In a heterogeneous labouring population with little in common except poverty, seamen and shipwrights and their dependent trades were always affected by any foreign quarrels. French wars loaded Britain with tropical islands and slave plantations which supplied the man in the street with cheap sugar, tobacco and rum, creature comforts very helpful towards keeping him quiet and contented. Less agreeably, there were always immigrants trickling or pouring in, most of them poor folk coming to compete with native workmen, and arousing the same 'Nativist' resentment as newcomers in the nineteenth-century USA. It was an anomaly of the world-wide British empire to include one colony close at hand, and the great influx from Ireland, the most bitterly resented of all, coincided with the Industrial Revolution. But English as most Englishmen might feel, few of them possessed citizen rights. Defeat of the popular forces in the Commonwealth debarred the majority from participation in the public life of their country. This was a deprivation against which urban masses might react morbidly; Tory mobs and Church-and-State demonstrations were a pathetic attempt to claim a place in the nation by those pushed down or in danger of being pushed down into the limbo of exclusion.

While the new working class was in its formative years Britain was involved in further long spells of conflict abroad. The onset of the Industrial Revolution came a few years after the victorious Seven Years' War, and a few years before the less glorious war of the American Revolution, quickly followed by the contest between 1793 and 1815 with Revolutionary and Napoleonic France. So much fighting, with France always the chief enemy, and with the national energies more and more heavily drawn on, could not fail to have its effect on most minds. When the sailors mutinied in 1797 their manifesto boasted how often they had 'made the British flag ride triumphantly over that of our enemies': all they asked for was the same increase of pay and pensions lately granted to the army and militia. Prudent Tories found ways to confirm the common man in his allegiance. Scott describes in a letter of 1812 how in honour of the battle of Salamanca he treated his labourers to 'an ocean of whisky-punch' and an all-night dance on the banks of the Tweed.[1] He had lately been busy breaking up combinations of workers in nearby Galashiels; now he had a chance to play a more benign part.

Scott's workmen were semi-rustics, easily brought under gentry influence, whereas the factory proletariat which he dreaded was an unknown, inaccessible force, a Frankenstein monster as Kingsley was to call it.[2] It was multiplying in its grimy lair at the same time as the long-drawn wars were intensifying national consciousness among the upper and middle classes and their appendages. Seldom have two such opposites been growing side by side. Social strife smouldered, breaking out at times in Luddite violence and reprisals. But in the post-war years there took shape the movement for parliamentary reform which in 1838 took the form of Chartism. The 'Charter' was devised in London, by representatives of the old type of skilled craftsmen, familiar with England's constitutional traditions. These were as remarkable and unique as its precocious nationalism, and interwoven with it; between them they fostered a conviction that in England man is born free, whereas everywhere else he is in chains. Dickens was to be a spectator at an elaborate London working-class entertainment which included a pantomime depicting the Spirit of Liberty.[3]

Freedom as an English birthright might be illusory, yet it could stimulate efforts to bring reality into line with the ideal. Only in England would a mass movement of workers think in terms of an enlargement of constitutional rights, and only there would it be allowed to run its course. Lovett and his London Workingmen's Association were trying, under the pressure of changing times, to secure their status in society, and to this end had to enter into an always uneasy alliance with the northern mill-workers.[4] Chartist leadership was taken over by men like Feargus O'Connor, a lawyer but an Irishman, from outside the English pale, and ready to talk of force. In between these two camps were the cottage industries scattered about in villages and townships. Hand-weavers unlike many other craftsmen were being crushed by the new machines. Hitherto politically null, these men had some share of culture, unlike the uprooted millworkers whom they were inclined to look down on but with whom they now often felt compelled to make common cause. Collectively all Chartists were claiming a place in the national life, guaranteed by votes; but the factory workers, most restless and radical because newest, most ambitious because of the sense of strength brought by concentrated numbers, wanted – if dimly – more than this, and would use their power to transform society as well as government.

With Chartism by 1850 virtually at an end, the failure of the new working class to enter and remould the national life left it shut up in the 'labourism', the self-absorption and political apathy, from which it has never really recovered. Mill life was by now familiar and accepted, but those living it were still cut off from other sections of the labouring classes, as well as from the rest. Marx expected a fairly rapid dissolving of the middling strata of society into the proletariat, which would thus come to constitute the bulk of the population: it would be the People, confronting as in 1789 a small class of exploiters. In fact industrialism, and the proletariat with it, were growing fairly slowly. And while hand-weavers disappeared many other craftsmen in old, small-scale trades survived; new skilled occupations emerged, bringing a new, successful type of trade union and leadership; these were capable of bettering their position, and so 'ceased to be estranged from society'.[5] There was the fact also that the country's political and intellectual metropolis lay far away from its main industrial areas. In France the two were closer; in Germany each region had always been more self-contained, though there too the distance between the Ruhr and Berlin may have had some harmful effects. This division immunised the industrial north of England from some metropolitan infections, but deprived it of much political stimulus, and both it and the London working class suffered through lack of the mutual reinforcement that Chartism had given.

'There is really no bond of union amongst the working men of England,' *The Beehive* wrote in 1872. 'There is no determined well-defined thought as to any necessary work. . . . They originate nothing; have no hearty faith in any understood policy'.[6] But the instinctive desire of any class or group to feel that it belongs to a wider community is a deeprooted one, and if not satisfied in a healthy, positive way is likely to find partial substitutes of a worse kind. Carlyle's or Ruskin's conviction that the masses were longing to be ruled and guided by their natural superiors had some corroboration in the rise of the Tory working-man, or 'deference voter', and above all in the conversion of a once fiery Lancashire to Toryism. This seems to have happened largely under religious suasion,[7] aided by the gulf between English and Irish. It was a bizarre re-creation in a new environment of the acquiescent torpor of the cottage-workers of old. 'A member of the aristocracy,' Bright wrote disgustedly in his diary in 1857, 'or anyone willing to act with the aristocracy and *for them*, is accepted by the people as if he were the friend of the people.'[8]

As part of Tory demagogy's design to content the workers with an illusion of citizenship, in an old society varnished over, flourishes of drum and bugle figured prominently. Warlike distractions came promptly on their cue: the Crimean War in 1854–6 was closely followed by the second Opium War with China, and in 1857 by the Indian Mutiny. As an organization combining all classes the army made a suitable emblem of national unity, of the nation as a big family. All imagery or ideology of nation and State has derived a great deal from the family; in the factory districts it must have had more persuasiveness as family life there recovered from its disruption in the early days of industrialism. No one felt the link more warmly, or could better embody the 'motherland', than Queen Victoria. During the Crimean War, for the first time in English history, soldiers of all ranks were collected to shake hands with their sovereign and receive their medals from her. As she wrote lyrically to her uncle Leopold, it was an exalting experience to feel 'the rough hand of the brave and honest private soldier. . . . Noble fellows! I own I feel as if they were my own children; my heart beats for *them* as for my *nearest and dearest*.'[9]

Most of the Chartist papers had faded away, though for 'the thinking section of the working class' *Reynolds' Weekly* still upheld the old cause and was also well primed on foreign affairs.[10] David Urquhart, with a mixture of the Russophobia he shared with Marx and the current myth of a constitutional golden age in Anglo-Saxon times, was able to reach the radical artisans of the west midlands and north-west during the Crimean War, and his Workingmen's Committees proliferated.[11] Straightforward jingoism found it easiest to reach London labour, always within earshot and with a considerable *lumpen* ingredient. Music-halls growing up in London suburbs and the provinces were patronised by better-off workers, and might purvey on a more modest scale the exhilaration the Covent Garden audience got from 'The Fall of Sevastopol', music imitating 'the deafening noise of exploding mines . . . the shrill sound of the trumpets, the ships blown in the air, the cries of the fugitives and the shouts of the victors'.[12]

But it has been noticed that music-hall gatherings were apt to applaud any stirring or striking song or spectacle, whether its political moral meant anything to them or not. What happened in the wide world was outside their sphere. For the solid bulk of the working class 'labourism' served to muffle all ideas from outside, bad as well as good. Perhaps indeed an Indian crowd's enjoyment of any *tamasha* or show, which has misled both Viceroys and communists, has been typical of common folk everywhere. It stands out all the same that when the electorate gave Palmerston's China war a vote of confidence in 1857, and Bright lost his seat at Manchester – he was bottom of the poll in every ward, despite the fact that Manchester and Salford at that date were supposed to muster a fifth of all working-class votes in the country. This was in late March. Immediately afterwards the

Indian Mutiny broke out and threw Britain into another fit,
worsened this time by rabid racialism. Common soldiers and
sailors putting down the rebels displayed the same revengeful
temper as their superiors. An inbred contempt for the Irish
among English workers must have predisposed them to take an
arrogant view of other colonial races.

This and the China war were scarcely over before there was
fresh sound and fury about an invasion that England's late ally
Napoleon III was alleged to be plotting. Out of it came the
Volunteer movement. There was little ground for the scare,[13]
and it must be suspected that it was welcomed and made the
most of by those who still thought the workers dangerous. Of
the something like a hundred thousand serious recruits, most
were middle-class or rural,[14] and would furnish a reliable
National Guard in case of social disturbance. Significantly there
was nowhere more keenness to enroll, or readiness to work
under the army authorities, than in Manchester and other
Lancashire towns.[15] Carried away by detestation of Louis-
Napoleon and love of soldiering, Engels threw himself into the
drilling and training with immense ardour and, one must think,
an odd lack of realism. In one of his many articles on the subject
he complains of the 'shameful' behaviour of some in a crowd
watching a review, who threw stones and tried to break it up.[16]
They may have been hooligans, but it seems as likely that they
were old-fashioned radicals. In general the effect of this stir and
bustle would be to draw the classes closer: these amateur
warriors were protecting rich and poor from the dreadful
French, and their parades were animating spectacles. When the
Scottish Volunteers were reviewed by the Queen in Holyrood
park at Edinburgh on 7 August 1860, while the royal standard of
Scotland floated above the summit of Arthur's Seat, a crowd of a
hundred thousand 'made the welkin ring with their reiterated
cheers'.[17]

Britain is still sprinkled with public-houses entitled Volunteer
Arms. The movement continued, on broader lines, with the
government taking over more of the costs and direction, until it
became something like an army reserve. By the later 1870s there
were 200,000 on the rolls, of whom three-quarters may have
belonged to the working class, almost entirely to its better-off
categories.[18] This meant that these upper strata were being
brought under strong conservatising influence, an important

antidote to the voting power conferred on the workers by the second Reform Act in 1867. As to the regular army, it offered young men an alternative in bad times to unemployment. They came mostly from the lowest levels of casual labour, and were often illiterate.[19] Ex-servicemen drew small pensions; they usually found themselves unemployable, and were numerous among 'the homeless and the inhabitants of common lodging houses'.[20] But civic receptions for home-coming troops, the attraction of uniforms to young women, so frequent a theme for banter in *Punch*, and regimental associations, particularly active in martial Scotland, helped to invest army life with a certain glow.

All this beckoned in the direction of empire, which many were eager for many reasons to popularise. In retrospect there may appear to have been no deep social crisis in Britain in the later nineteenth century, but there was quite enough social tension to make imperialism a useful as well as profitable diversion. Two politicians very conscious of this tension, first Disraeli and then Chamberlain, took the lead in promoting imperial sentiment. There were fears that the working class now being enfranchised would prove indifferent, if not hostile, to empire and its costs and risks. They were expressed in 1887 by an American proponent of the idea, fashionable on both sides of the Atlantic, of an 'Anglo-Saxon' league. In a fresh conflict with Russia, he wrote, Britain might be compelled to abandon Asia, because its domestic problems were so urgent and its workers took little interest in remote possessions and frontiers. 'The cry of "Perish India" is sometimes heard. . . .'[21] During the eastern crisis of 1878 the two biggest peace meetings, in Hyde Park, drew the bulk of their attendance from radical working-men's clubs.[22] But most workers' notions about all such things beyond the narrow horizons of daily life continued hazy and unstable, symptomatic of a class half in and half outside the nation. It has been remarked that the average workman was not religious, but did not like to be dubbed an atheist; his patriotism may often have been of the same order.

Poets of the people like Capern and McGonagall tuned their lyre to the same conquering themes as poet laureates like Tennyson, sometimes not much more feebly. Willingness to back the government against colonial rivals had primitive precedents in crowds of workers brawling with one another at election-time to get their respective employers into parliament. Another parable of the common man drawn into his betters' quarrels may be found in a story from Lakeland of a fight between gangs of labourers employed by two landowners at odds over a right of way.[23] More rationally, some workers as well as capitalists could benefit from the captive market provided by a colony, most bountifully by India for Lancashire cottons. In the late nineteenth century two-fifths of the county's cloth exports were going to India, and this was all the more satisfactory in view of the prevailing depression.[24] Even though not the prime cause of Lancashire's political stagnation, this advantage must be supposed to have deepened it. Perhaps as time went on it may have helped to bring English and Irish mill-hands closer together, as well as labour and capital.

There was little in the equipment of the ordinary labour spokesman to enable him to resist the insidious appeal. He came into politics by way of his trade union, grew dependent on it as a career, was always immersed in petty detail.[25] He was easily induced to regard an empire as a good thing for his rank and file, so long as they got their share of the proceeds. There were indeed labour spokesmen of a very different calibre, such as Tom Mann, and those through whom the British working class played its part in the formation of the First International and the development of the Second. On the level of articulate debate, however, the Fabians supplied a prophylactic against Marxism by adapting socialism to the capitalist outlook, 'especially to the new Imperialist phase of that outlook'.[26] Meanwhile a wealth of propaganda resources were being mobilised on its side. Chamberlain dismissed any talk of 'manufactories of political opinion, where zeal and unanimity are produced to order', an observer remarked in 1902, but they were in fact busily at work.[27] A new-style cheap press was one; another, of course, primary education. At a Suffolk village school when Empire Day was celebrated in 1907 'Her Ladyship kindly lent 20 flags and the children were taught to salute the Union Jack. Lessons were given on the Union Jack and the "Growth and Extent of the British Empire". Several patriotic songs were sung . . .'.[28]

There is no doubt a problem of psychology as to what hold ideas put into heads artificially can have over them. Images of tropical colonies were necessarily superficial, not rooting and growing in the consciousness. A recent analyst speaks of 'the almost total lack of impact made by colonial matters upon the lives and interests of the British populace'; surveys in 1948 and 1951 showed that more than half could not name a single British possession.[29] Nevertheless, even very blurred impressions can be persistent, and affect behaviour potently, at least at moments of excitement. Religion has swayed multitudes ignorant of the latitude and longitude of heaven. Beery euphoria might deposit a gradual sediment of loyalty.

Moreover empire feeling was buttressed, in a way not shared with any other country, by the colonies of white settlement, to which legions of workers had migrated. They wrote to their relatives at home, and described their new lives;[30] many must have sent home remittances, as Irish emigrants did. In a Jubilee poem[31] Tennyson evoked, side by side with Canadians and others,

> the hardy, laborious,
> Patient children of Albion – [31]

part of an imperial family, brought out for the occasion like well-washed children at a party, and looking more respectable than the working class usually did in his poetry. There was also of course that former colony, the USA. To the workers their facility of emigration was far the best of the 'crumbs' bestowed on them by imperialism, and the real aristocracy of labour was to be found in Toronto and Chicago and Melbourne.

A test came in 1899 with the Boer War, whose advocates were anxious to draw labour into a united front, and felt they were succeeding. 'Great Britain,' the *Scotsman* with somewhat fatuous logic pronounced, 'is not expanding because it is greedy of territory; it is expanding because it must find outlets for its teeming population and employment for the workers at home.'[32] One of its staff reported complacently that pro-Boer speakers were appealing to labour in vain, and 'discovering that the British working man whose name has been taken in vain contributes his quota to the discussion by means of brickbats.'[33] Brickbats are all right when thrown in the right direction. 'Some of us,' Norman Angell wrote a few years later, 'have seen a pro-Boer aristocrat running for his life before a howling mob of working-class "patriots".'[34]

But in all such cases, part of the incentive is the plebeian's relish of being licensed for once to mob his superiors. In Britain generally workers showed far less frenzy about the war than the middle classes. On the other hand, organized labour made no attempt to oppose it. Working-class newspapers were mostly critical of the war, and had much to say about soldiers' hardships and their officers' incompetence; on the other hand workers could not be got to believe that the soldiers, their fellow-toilers, were behaving barbarously.[35] In Scotland at any rate no pro-war songs were heard in music-halls;[36] workmen's clubs everywhere had a tolerant ear for anti-war talk, yet they were quite prepared to join in celebrations like Mafeking night.[37] Inconsistency, non-Euclidean logic, is very far from being confined to any single class; but Price has good ground for stressing its part in working-class attitudes to the Boer War, and for pointing out that historians are less familiar than anthropologists with how 'what appear to educated minds to be two seemingly contradictory opinions can be held at the same time about one event'.[38]

One channel through which the working class was being accosted was the chapel: Rosebery courted Dissent on behalf of Liberal Imperialism, and the *Methodist Times* succumbed readily, but the average Nonconformist minister was faithful to his pacific past.[39] It would be worth while to ask how much of the working class's deafness to any abstract principle, good or bad, might be ascribed to the fact of most of it having little or no religious grounding; in a negative sense a fact not to be regretted, since most religion was Anglican, very Tory and jingo, or Catholic. In the long run, in any case, it seems that flag-waving was only effective when accompanied by more tangible inducements. Unionists had been talking, as Halévy says, of social legislation to avert socialism, even if Chamberlain's 1895 proposals were much less comprehensive than their Bismarckian model. In 1897, to cover up the Jameson raid fiasco, he pushed through a workman's compensation measure; but having managed to light his South African fire he felt no need to fulfil his pledge of old-age pensions. Altogether the social legislation of this Unionist government was unimpressive.[40] Disappointment with it must have assisted the landslide victory of the Liberals in 1906.

Pensions now made their appearance. Conditions remained bad enough. Prices rose gradually between 1904 and 1914, wages barely kept pace with them. On the eve of the Great War 'it was stated on high authority that there were eleven million people living on the verge of starvation'.[41] Once again some friends of order detected a whiff of revolution in the air. It is only when two halves of a ruling class each feel that the other is mishandling the masses that they hate each other as acridly as Tories and Liberals did in the years just before the Great War. But unrest was still elemental, little transformed into socialist thinking. Levels of literacy were as low as standards of living. In 1907 an inquiry into reading habits among two hundred households in Middlesbrough – during the war a big armaments centre – found only twentyfive individuals reading any sort of serious books; cheap papers and novelettes were the usual pabulum.[42] On trade-union and bread-and-butter issues the working class was an increasingly solid, firmly anchored force; politically it might be as volatile as the small middle classes, because it had so little of a political tradition to orient it. Brailsford remarked that it could be swayed by speeches about fraternity with workers abroad, but equally by anti-foreign claptrap.[43]

Germany had suddenly become the country to be hated. Unlike France it was not an old antagonist, and there were no time-honoured memories to play on; but to make up for this there were now means of indoctrination which could be brought to bear in all sorts of ways. A rising politician, who looked upon war with Germany as a historical inevitability, treated his company of Territorials to a visit to the theatre to see a play which expounded a suitable moral.[44] Not all such propaganda sank in. Blatchford, preaching a combination of socialism and patriotic preparedness, was not making much impact with either; he met with a 'continued mass indifference to the growing threat from Germany and its navy'.[45] What may have sunk in far more than prophecies of a German invasion was the bogy of a Germany bent on ruining Britain by cut-throat competition. Britons had no experience of being invaded, but loss of jobs in some corner of the economy because other people were making the same things cheaper was familiar enough.

We hear one of Tressell's workmen, a reader of the Tory *Obscurer*, grumbling about the country being beggared by foreigners. 'Just go to a shop to buy something; look round the place an' you'll see that more than 'arf the damn stuff comes from abroad.'[46] Foreign competition had not stimulated British capitalists to keep up with the times, but it had long inspired them to eloquent calls to labour to realise that they were both in the same boat. That Britain deserved to be the workshop of the world, and British workmanship was the best in the world, was comfortable doctrine for both. Without much success William Morris tried to warn labour that 'desperate "competition"' might soon turn into 'desperate war': that talk of the necessity to prepare for a fight was 'no longer confined to the honour-and-glory kind of old Tories, who if they meant anything at all by it meant that a Tory war would be a good occasion for damping down democracy'.[47]

On the eve of the war labour unrest was acute. 'In this respect we started the War under a heavy handicap,' Lloyd George was to confess.[48] Yet this quickly seemed to be vanishing amid a rush to enlist; at Middlesbrough, for instance, where employers were helpful and families were given half-pay, with the other workers contributing a levy.[49] It was much the same nearly everywhere. H. G. Wells thought he heard the host of volunteers saying to themselves: '"Thank God! we can serve our country at last instead of some beastly profiteer".'[50] Some such vague but uplifting sensation there must indeed have been, a substitute for the socialism which had failed to blossom. In a more earthy vein a farm labourer recalled in after years: 'We were all damned glad to have got off the farms', away from grinding toil and callous treatment.[51] But these men were also staunchly patriotic, being more directly exposed than the industrial workers to thought-control by the society which exploited them. Gallacher surmised that his fellow-Clydesiders were joining up under yellow-press hypnotism, but even more from a craving for excitement, 'the illusion of wonderful adventure', escape from 'the deadly monotony of working-class life'.[52] This too must account for a great deal.

It is only fair to the peoples of Europe, working classes and middle classes alike, to say that they all believed themselves, however deludedly, to be engaged in a defensive war. It is only fair to the British people in particular, so long deluged with imperialist propaganda, to remember that it thought it was going to war in defense of a small neighbouring country barbarously invaded, not in pursuit of any fresh colonies or markets. In this atmosphere it might appear as if a whole estranged class was suddenly finding its way out of limbo into the national fold. Before long several labour leaders were entering the government. Ben Tillett's visits to the front to promote morale were 'a task he greatly enjoyed and carried out superbly'.[53] By contrast with the French wars a century before, integration seemed to have been achieved. Reality was far more complex. Not all labour leaders were prepared to take the war at its face value, and as it dragged on this face value grew less and less convincing. In South Wales at first well-known militants from the mines could be heard making recruiting speeches.[54] But when Mrs Pankhurst was there before the end of 1915 she found the Welshmen very unresponsive: 'they are sulky and difficult to handle, and will not sing the national anthem . . .'[55]

Out of ten million men of military age only six million were physically fit for 'general service'.[56] Most of the unfit must have belonged to the working class, which thus got some recompense for the crippling existence it was condemned to. Before conscription began to be introduced in January 1916, two-thirds of the six million had joined up. Men in reserved occupations were exempted; again these were mostly workers, miners and gun-founders and the like, especially numerous in Scotland. When comb-outs had to be resorted to they proved awkward; there was an obstinate feeling that if labour was to be conscripted, the same must happen to capital. Dilution of labour too was bitterly disliked. A left-wing union activist like Thomas Bell, himself anti-war, has scarcely anything to say in his record of the war years except of trade-union stands over grievances like this.[57] The workers' whole equivocal place in the nation was finding the sharpest possible expression; the class was divided, to a considerable degree emotionally as well, between the men at the front and those at home, painfully defending their own trenches, the small collective rights painfully won by generations of struggle. Meanwhile outside their dugouts empires crashed, revolutions erupted, history took giant strides.

Milner wrote at the end of the war of 'the lurid picture of approaching Revolution, in which critics of the Labour Party usually indulge'.[58] In reality the party, despite its nominal adoption in 1918 of a socialist programme, came out of the war patriotically conformist instead of radicalised.[59] There was enough radical impulse to inspire – with the aid of war-weariness, no doubt – the Hands Off Russia campaign, and the founding of the Communist Party. The General Strike might be viewed as a belated epilogue to the war, an outburst of all the smothered feeling it and its profiteering had stirred up; a swing from integration to the opposite pole of secession. As against this, something of the working-class dichotomy of the war years was perpetuated by ex-servicemen's organizations, under conservative guidance. Those who have made sacrifices for a cause seldom find it easy to admit to themselves that the cause was worthless, the sacrifices made for nothing.

It is moreover a fact of developed industrial societies that war can bring social progress on some lines, or accelerate it more than any peacetime effort is likely to do. During the Great War health in Britain improved and mortality was reduced;[60] it was agreed that more care had to be taken of mothers and children, because so many were left on their own, or if only to ensure that there would be enough soldiers for future wars. The Second World War brought a much bigger, but again fortuitous, advance. Since then, with the dwindling of empire and navy, and the entry into the EEC, the old siren-songs have faded almost into silence. More and more, governments and capitalists are compelled to provide, or appear to be providing, material benefits for voters, instead of rhetoric. On these benefits labour has strenuously insisted; but little of a more rational social consciousness and purpose has grown up to replace the old half-accepted false consciousness.

England's proletariat was recruited from a countryside where the degradation of the farm labourer had destroyed the old folk arts. Its lack of any culture of its own has been a permanent factor in helping to keep it *incommunicado*. In place of it, since Nature abhors moral as well as other vacuums, there has been a growth of the cult of sport which would have astonished Marx and Engels even more than the rise of nationalism in the world; though it was already in their time an important go-between of the classes. In Manchester on 22 May 1977, a thousand people collapsed in the press when three-quarters of a million thronged the streets to cheer a football team which had defeated Liverpool, and a few days later there was as ecstatic a reception for the Liverpool team returning from Rome with the European cup. This naive hero-worship is of course not to be mistaken for the sum total of working-class allegiance or aspiration. In itself it may be said to represent a sturdy independence, deserving of respect in a world of increasingly machine-made values. These crowds might have been filling the streets to applaud far worse men than a football team. Symbolically they were turning away from the higher collectivities of Nation, State, Church, always artificial and in part fraudulent, to the simpler spirit of tribalism. It would not be hard to find a parallel between this and the relationship of women to the man-built world they have lived in, seldom positively challenging it and its ideologies or laws, but equally seldom, perhaps, whole-heartedly accepting them. Women in Nazi Germany offered no collective resistance, but neither did they identify themselves with the Third Reich in the way a strenuous indoctrination sought to make them do.[61] German women proved less malleable than German working-men. In Britain, in the course of the long interaction between a new class and an old nation, each has, but only very limitedly, transformed the other. From this imperfect incorporation, this autonomy which the working class has preserved, negative as it may often seem, fresh beginnings can always be hopefully looked for.

NOTES

1 Scott to Lady Abercorn, 2 September 1812.
2 Charles Kingsley, *Alton Locke, Tailor and Poet* (1850), Chap. 33.
3 *The Uncommercial Traveller* (1861), Chap. 4.
4 Z. Bauman, *Between class and elite. The evolution of the British labour movement* (translated by S. Patterson, Manchester, 1972), pp. 39–40.
5 ibid., pp. 125–6.
6 4 May 1872; extract in J. B. Jeffreys, ed., *Labour's Formative Years 1849–1879* (London, 1948), p. 197.
7 P. F. Clarke, *Lancashire and the New Liberalism* (Cambridge, 1971), p. 25.
8 *The Diaries of John Bright*, ed. R. A. J. Walling (London, 1930), pp. 224–5.
9 25 May 1855; *The Letters of Queen Victoria*, ed. A. C. Benson and Viscount Esher, Vol. III (London, 1908), p. 127.
10 Kingsley Martin, *The Triumph of Lord Palmerston. A Study of Public Opinion in England before the Crimean War* (revised edn, London, 1963), pp. 92–3.
11 Olive Anderson, *A Liberal State at War. English Politics and Economics during the Crimean War* (London, 1967), p. 149; cf. pp. 153–4.
12 P. M. Young, *The Concert Tradition* (London, 1965), p. 210.
13 Admiral Sir H. W. Richmond, *The Invasion of Britain. An Account of plans . . . from 1586 to 1918* (London, 1941), p. 65.
14 W. H. Chaloner and W. O. Henderson, eds., *Engels as Military Critic* (Manchester, 1959), pp. 2, 4, 33.
15 ibid., p. 36.

16 ibid., p. 37.

17 J. Grant, *Cassell's Old and New Edinburgh* (London, n.d.), Vol. 2, pp. 319–22.

18 H. Cunningham, in a discussion on 'Jingoism and the Working Classes 1877–8' (Society for the Study of Labour History, *Bulletin*, no. 19, 1969), p. 8.

19 E. M. Spiers, *The Reform of the Front-line Forces of the Regular Army in the United Kingdom, 1895–1914* (Ph.D. thesis, University of Edinburgh, 1974), pp. 3–6.

20 G. Stedman Jones, *Outcast London* (Oxford, 1971), p. 79; cf. Spiers, op. cit., pp. 27, 37.

21 W. D. Foulke, *Slav or Saxon* (1887; 2nd edn, New York, 1899), p. 41.

22 Cunningham, loc. cit., p. 7.

23 S. Johnson, 'Disagreements by the Duddon, 1825–1832' (*Transs. Cumberland and Westmorland Antiquarian and Archaeological Soc.*, 1966), pp. 379–81.

24 Clarke, op. cit., p. 79.

25 J. A. Spender, *The Public Life* (London, 1925), pp. 156–7.

26 John Strachey, *What Are We to Do?* (London, 1938), pp. 74–5.

27 M. Ostrogorski, *Democracy and the Organization of Political Parties* (English edn, London, 1902), Vol. 1, p. 211.

28 R. Blythe, *Akenfield. Portrait of an English Village* (1969); Harmondsworth edn, 1972), p. 169; cf. pp. 171, 173.

29 D. Goldsworthy, *Colonial Issues in British Politics 1945–1961* (Oxford, 1971), pp. 68, 399.

30 G. M. Trevelyan, *English Social History* (London, 1944), p. 583.

31 'On the Jubilee of Queen Victoria', 1887.

32 2 November 1899.

33 25 September 1899.

34 N. Angell, *The Great Illusion* (1908; London edn, 1933), p. 264.

35 R. Price, *An Imperial War and the British Working Class . . . the Boer War 1899–1902* (London, 1972), pp. 46, 86.

36 G. Best, in 'Jingoism and the Working Classes 1877–8', p. 8.

37 Price, op. cit., p. 92.

38 ibid., p. 4.

39 É. Halévy, *A History of the English People in the Nineteenth Century*, Vol. V (English edn, London, 1951), p. 104.

40 ibid., pp. 231, 235–7.

41 Viscount Milner, *Questions of the Hour* (London, 1923), p. 64.

42 Lady Florence Bell, *At the Works* (1907; extract in P. Keating, ed., *Into Unknown England 1866–1913* (London, 1976), pp. 285 ff.

43 Cited by H. B. Davis, *Nationalism and Socialism. Marxist and Labor Theories of Nationalism to 1917* (New York, 1967), pp. 112–13.

44 *Journals and Letters of Reginald, Viscount Esher*, ed. M. V. Brett (London, 1934, 1938), Vol. 2, p. 438.

45 L. Barrow, in 'Jingoism and the Working Classes 1877–8', p. 10.

46 Robert Tressell, *The Ragged Trousered Philanthropists* (London edn, 1955), p. 20.

47 *Signs of Change* (London, 1888), p. 6.

48 D. Lloyd George, *War Memoirs* (1934; London edn, 1938), p. 1141.

49 W. Robertson, *Middlesbrough's Effort in the Great War* (Middlesbrough, n.d.), pp. 6–7.
50 *War and the Future* (London, 1917), p. 200.
51 Blythe, op. cit., p. 42.
52 W. Gallacher, *Revolt on the Clyde* (London, 1936), p. 26.
53 F. Williams, *Ernest Bevin* (London, 1952), p. 64.
54 M. Foot, *Aneurin Bevan*, Vol. 1 (London, 1962), p. 32.
55 *Lloyd George. A Diary by Frances Stevenson*, ed. A. J. P. Taylor (London, 1971), p. 64.
56 Lloyd George, op. cit., p. 1561; and see J. M. Winter, 'Britain's "Lost Generation" of the First World War' (*Population Studies*, Vol. 31, 1977).
57 T. Bell, *Pioneering Days* (London, 1941), Chaps. 8–11.
58 Milner, op. cit., p. 109.
59 See R. McKibbin, *The Evolution of the Labour Party, 1910–1924* (London, 1974), Chaps. V and VI.
60 J. M. Winter, 'The Impact of the First World War on Civilian Health in Britain' (*Economic History Review*, 1977), pp. 502, etc.
61 See Jill Stephenson, 'The Nazi Organisation of Women 1933–1939', in P. Strachura, ed., *The Shaping of the Nazi State* (London, 1978).

WILLIAM COBBETT'S
TWOPENNY TRASH

EDGELL RICKWORD

William Cobbett founded his weekly *Political Register* in 1802, when he was nearly forty. He edited it and was its main contributor until a few days before his death in 1835. For two years (1810–12), he conducted the paper from prison, where he was serving, in fair comfort, a sentence for seditious libel; and for nearly three years from the United States, where he had been obliged to take refuge (1817–19) from Sidmouth's new and sterner Press laws. But the only break in publication was during the twelve weeks of his crossing the Atlantic and the return to London of his copy for the first issue of the revived *Register*. No other journal bears its editor's stamp so unmistakably throughout a whole epoch, one of formidable upheavals and unpredicted change.

For most of these thirty-three years he was the bugbear of successive Governments, but long before their end he had become the most influential of the Reformist leaders. It was not the consistency of his policies (which were variable) but his consistent regard for the people's welfare which gained him wide-spread confidence throughout the labouring classes.

Cobbett's return from the United States in 1819 was celebrated by a dinner at the Crown and Anchor tavern, attended by over 400 paying guests. The Chairman was Henry Hunt, then awaiting trial for his leading part in the Peterloo meeting, who proposed the toast to the guest of honour in the following terms: 'The health of William Cobbett, the ardent and zealous defender of our rights and liberties, by whose luminous and incomparable writings the public opinion of the people of this country has undergone a change unparalleled in the history of the world.' An encomium of which the company showed their approval by drinking the toast (in water) 'with almost nine times nine' (*Black Dwarf*, 8 December 1819).

But the *Political Register* and all reformist newspapers were entering difficult times. Under one of the notorious Six Acts (20

George III, c. 9), the obligation to pay the Newspaper Stamp tax
of 4d. was extended from papers carrying news, to those merely
commenting on 'affairs in Church and State' – an obligation
which immediately rendered the twopenny edition of the
Register illegal.

Thus the much loved and much hated *Twopenny Trash*, which
had been a source of political enlightenment for tens of
thousands, was extinguished. The eloquent oration which
Cobbett composed for its funeral can be read again on page 7 of
its successor, ten years later.

The finest flowers of polemic wither quickly unless we can feel
we have a share in the issues. It is a sense of involvement even in
remote controversies that Cobbett communicates. He is
immediately responsive to every material circumstance, to every
variation of scene or mood. His tactics won him the reputation
of a prize-fighter; but he had besides, a delicate touch at
command. It could perhaps be said that it was his magnetic style
that kept the *Register* alive through difficult years. 'The
Reformers read him for what he had to say, the Tories for the
way he said it.' And many who were indifferent to Reform would
have approved his lambasting of the parasites, the loan-
mongers and sinecurists, who weighed on the necks of the
middle-classes only less heavily than on those of the poor.

It was about two years after Cobbett's return from the United
States that he began the series of horse-back tours which did
much to spread his influence and the cause of Parliamentary
Reform, and during which he immensely enlarged his
knowledge of the conditions of the working-people. And it was
from this experience, with the necessity of expounding his views
at almost every stopping place that he acquired a new mastery –
proficiency in the art of public speaking. His descriptions of
these journeys were sent off to the *Register* from any convenient
hostelry, written whilst the impressions of the day were still fresh
upon him, to be inserted in that week's *Register*. Cobbett
collected them into a book in 1830, and *Rural Rides* has seldom
been out of print since. But there are others of his books which
might also achieve popularity if restored to circulation – *A Year's
Residence in America, or Advice to Young Men*, for instance.

Cobbett was only a few years' younger than Rowlandson and
Gillray, two masters of another art, both sharing with Cobbett a
genetical kinship with the England which best survives in the

caricatures and his prose. But whilst the climax of Cobbett's career was still to come, they had run their course. In 1830 he was still in full vigour, his capacity for work seeming to increase with his years, his style as resonant as ever. The approaching climax of the struggle for some measure of Parliamentary Reform supplied him with fresh stimulus to action. Each new attempted imposition on the working people brought out the old lion in him, bristling for the attack. And there was no lack of provocation whilst the *Twopenny Trash* was in existence, whether a Whig or a Tory administration held the reins.

Once or twice, though briefly, Cobbett refers to the possibility of his retirement, 'to close the *Register*' and to publish, 'as the work of another year', those long, eventful *Memoirs*, not yet transmitted to paper. Had he retired, it is still doubtful if he would have written any Memoirs. His farm or garden would have claimed him. He could never have become a reflective writer, even without a journal to edit. Consecutive narrative damped his ardour – witness his *History of the Regency and Reign of George IV*, which should have been glistening with spite.

It needed the goad of controversy, the scent of opposition, to bring out his characteristic vehemence. When he wrote, his bodily processes were involved. With him, composition was a physiological exertion. When he says 'my blood boiled', it seems no metaphor. He could write with concentration whatever his surroundings and in fact preferred to work when at home in the midst of his family, to one or other of whom he would often dictate an article. His daughter, Anne, who became the publisher of his books after his death, must have observed him numberless times: 'He *felt* as he wrote, would look pale with earnestness in the subject, folding his hands which would seem to get thinner and thinner, colder and colder, and his voice would falter.' On the platform he would often act out an argument with an absent opponent, taking each side with a suitably altered voice and routing him with comic gestures.

When Cobbett first announced his intention of issuing a cheap political monthly he referred to it as *Politics for the Poor*. His final choice of title is an improvement since it recalls his earlier defiance of the Government in 1816, when he first published the twopenny edition of the *Register*. The entire contents of this famous issue was 'An Address to the

Journeymen and Labourers' and came at a time when sporadic rioting and incendiarism were spreading through the country. His basic message to the workers in this, as in the succeeding issues, was that they should turn all their energies to a movement for immediate Parliamentary Reform. Here, says G. D. H. Cole, was really the starting-point of his great career as a working-class leader. But in 1830 the tough restrictions of the Gagging Acts of 1819 were still in force, and hampered all periodicals 'commenting on Affairs of Church and State'. The Act, by making sixpence the lowest price at which a periodical might be sold, had curtailed the sale of the radical weeklies, and finally extinguished them. The two most influential, Wooler's *Black Dwarf* and Carlile's *Republican* succumbed in 1824 and 1826 respectively. But the struggle of the 'great unstamped' was soon to begin. Doherty's *Poor Man's Advocate* was founded in 1829; Hetherington's *Poor Man's Guardian* in 1830. Even so, the recent rise in trade union activity and the stimulus it lent to the Reform movement was without adequate guidance. This accounts for the tremendous efforts made by the national and local leaders to instruct, enthuse and organise their followers by means of public meetings.

The Press laws inhibited, as they were intended to, the growth of political discussion among the 'under-privileged'. The Whigs saw a stage further ahead than the Tories, and set about providing a substitute for political discussion, a filling of the hungry minds, potentially explosive, with a pabulum of soothing or diverting information. A steady flow of cheap, even gratuitous, tracts was set in motion by means of subscriptions raised by the Society for the Diffusion of Useful Knowledge and other charitable bodies.

These tracts were widely regarded among the Radicals as deceptive nostrums. Their denunciation by Cobbett was inevitable. The moving spirit behind the Society, in the movement for popular education generally, was Henry Broughham who as a Scot and a utilitarian philosopher, Cobbett already found doubly obnoxious. He was himself no novice in the employment of the 'tract' or pamphlet. He had increasingly in the past ten years reprinted the most topical or cogent articles from the *Register* as penny or twopenny pamphlets, and he clearly intended *Twopenny Trash* to be a regular antidote to the stupefying potions handed out at cottage doors by ladies from the Squire's mansion or the Rectory. Whereas the *Register* at fourteen pence a week could not hope to penetrate these cottages, the twopenny monthly which carried many of the same articles, received a wide response.

The strength of Cobbett's feelings against such insidious propaganda is graphically illustrated by the full-scale attack which he mounted in the *Register* against the Society for the Diffusion of Useful Knowledge, as a prelude to his announcement of the imminent launching of its twopenny adversary. This provides a key to the motivation of some of Cobbett's most violent and obsessive phobias.

As matters turned out, *Twopenny Trash* was not to bear much resemblance to that systematic exposition of the causes of poverty which Cobbett had envisaged in the first flush of enthusiasm. Better, it became a documentary record of the tragic dénouement of the economic-political system, whose instability Cobbett had been fore-telling for years.

Events had overtaken him from the start. Even in the first issue he was obliged to turn aside to comment on unforeseen happenings. There was the sudden death of the long-ago tarnished Regent, hardly to be recognised as George IV, but faithfully recalled by Cobbett. No black mourning borders round the *Register* that week! And such a casual brushing aside of a royal nonentity coming from one who was generally favourable to the system of monarchy! The next month, Europe was shaken by the July Revolution in Paris, and it was as enthusiastically welcomed by this once vociferous anti-Jacobin as if he had been an international socialist. He helped to raise funds for the widows of those killed on the barricades; and gave a course of lectures at the Rotunda, Blackfriars, on the deeper causes and significance of this overthrow of the restored Bourbons. In October the Fires began. Ricks and barns blazed in Kent, Sussex and Hampshire. The Government panicked. Strong measures were adopted. Cobbett had to repeat what he had been saying for years about the plight of the labourers and their need for help. The Whig government appointed a Royal Commission to tour the disturbed areas and to intimidate the hungry with hangings and transportation. Cobbett refused to blame the labourers and begged the government not to embitter the starving people further by the shedding of blood. His words were twisted so as to provide an excuse for issuing a Bill of Indictment against him, charging him with seditious libel.

The first year's *Trash* ends with a remarkably unexpected and, for Cobbett, unusual production, a three-act play, *Surplus Population*. It is, as its ironic title might suggest, anti-Malthusian, a high-spirited melodrama about a villainous Squire, Sir Gripe Grindum of Grindum Hall and his wicked designs against lovely Betsy Birch, the buxom sweetheart of Dick Hazel, whose union promised to be most dangerously prolific by Malthusian standards.

The issue for June 1831 should logically have contained an account of Cobbett's trial, but this is not referred to until August, which opens the second year of *Twopenny Trash*. This continues with a good deal of material bearing on the circumstances of the labourers' revolt. This material serves to discredit semi-official allegations of a nation-wide conspiracy under a Captain Swing, and reveals it as a measure of the labourers' desperation to ward off the rigours of the approaching winter. Some small increase of wages was in fact won from local employers in some districts. It is notable that not a life was lost during the so-called riots. Incendiarism admittedly was rife, but was intended as an earnest of their need, not bloody terrorism. Yet the account on the Government side reads direly. Nineteen were hanged, and over two hundred suffered the agony of waiting whilst under sentence of death. Nearly five hundred were transported to New South Wales and Tasmania. From Cobbett's accounts we can infer how haphazard the judgements were, dependent on the flimsiest evidence as to personal responsibility, the merely having been with a crowd being crime enough. Some sentences are seen to be motivated by personal spite or political partisanship; the first in the hanging of the young ploughman Cook of Micheldever, who knocked off the hat of Bingley Barham, landowner and financier; the second, the transportation for life of Joseph and Robert Mason. These two brothers had regularly taken Cobbett's *Register* and had read it aloud to twenty or thirty villagers at a time. Joseph had also organised a petition for Parliamentary Reform and walked the hundred miles or so to Brighton to present it to the King.

The long account of the law-suits between the Barings and Mr and Mrs Deacle vividly lights up the feudal mentality of the land-owners. Between the Squires and their clerical relatives, who filled for the most part the bench of magistrates in the country districts, the uninstructed labourers had little chance to free themselves from the legal chicanery which entangled them.

There is much more in this volume which the historian will value and the disinterested admirer of Cobbett enjoy. For instance, in the first issue for 1832, his *Address, to the Yeomanry Cavalry, on the Fires*. This opens quietly but menacingly: 'I cannot call you *friends*; and I will not call you *gentlemen*.' And Cobbett argues closely what their function is, in this period of unrest. It is not only intimidation, but in practice it is also provocation. To go prancing vaingloriously through sad villages, stared at by hungry women and children, that could only enrage their toiling menfolk. Other historians have untangled the squalid intrigues attending the struggle to get any sort of Reform Bill into Parliament, and then its whittling down by both parties to a mockery of the adult suffrage intended by the Radicals; but who other than Cobbett would have been roused to denunciation of a Bill to legalise the sale of the dead bodies of paupers; or to write eloquent pages on the merits of mangle-wurzle beer and the multiple virtues of Cobbett's Corn; and maledictions against the FOOL-LIAR, the Preston Cock, the Reform Candidate for Preston, his one-time ally, Henry Hunt, of Peterloo fame?

There is a fine set-piece to close the volume. It is the promise of a CHOPSTICK FESTIVAL,* a rich vision of abundant food and drink, and perhaps some dresses or blankets for the wives, to celebrate the Reform Bill becoming law. Let these hard-driven men for one day eat and drink their fill. They have more than earned it.

For that day Cobbett stifled his forebodings. But he had no illusions as to what the Whigs intended, and indeed some pages here hint of the struggles to come when, almost alone in Parliament, he will denounce the new Poor Law and the opponents of the Bill to restrict the children's working day to ten hours.

Cobbett is definitely a writer to be savoured in quantity; in tit-bits the flavour is lost. His conclusions are never enunciated as principles; the meaning resides in the whole passage, and loses much of its significance out of context. In this, Hazlitt contrasts

---

* CHOPSTICKS – Cobbett's favourite word for the labourers.

him with Thomas Paine, of whom he writes: 'You cannot open a
page in any of his best and earlier works without meeting with
some maxim, some antithetical and memorable saying which is
a sort of starting-place for the argument, and the goal to which it
returns. There is not a single *bon-mot* or sentence in Cobbett that
has ever been quoted again.' This is not a dismissal of Cobbett;
indeed, Hazlitt warms to the man as he does to no other
representative of the Spirit of the Age. He grants him to be 'not
only the most powerful political writer of the present day, but
one of the best writers in the language'. Cobbett has 'vast
industry, vast information, and the utmost power of making
what he says intelligible, yet he never seems to get at the
beginning or come to the end of any question'.

Perhaps Hazlitt might be answered by saying that Cobbett's
principles are expressible only as contingencies. It is not the
three abstract nouns painted over the porch of the Mairie, but
more food in the peasants' bellies that signifies for him the
French Revolution. Aphorisms are to be admired for their
elegance, like *La propriété, c'est le vol* ('Property is theft'). But they
often require volumes for their interpretation. It is sometimes
equally possible to get to the point by Cobbett's road.

So, let us admit that we look for different virtues in Paine and
in Cobbett. Cobbett's empiricism was responsible for more than
one volte-face that scandalised his contemporaries. His egotism
is frank and open, not stupid self-complacency, but it is an
awkward propensity in a political leader. It has been said that he
was backward-facing, that his Merrie England had never existed
in fact. But a reformer must present his followers with some
palpable vision as the goal of their strivings, and nothing in the
way of modern innovation seemed to him so good as the life he
had known in his childhood, before paper-money and taxes and
speculation had eroded the rough but ample economy of the
self-sufficient village.

This projection of Utopia into the past survived to a degree in
the propaganda of English socialism, at least until the time of
the First World War. It was only when scientific socialism hitched
its waggon to the triumphal progress of industrial technology
that the past became finally discredited. Now it is apparent that
technical innovation carries menaces as well as promises, some
rehabilitation of earlier dreams might plausibly be expected.
Appreciation of the complexity of environmental relations has

exposed the fallacies in much of the 'advanced thinking' denounced by Cobbett, of Malthus and the Utilitarians, which inspired the punitive legislation of the time, particularly after the Reform Act. His instincts served him better than erudition.

It must be said that Cobbett relied too exclusively on his own phenomenal powers; he trained no disciples and bequeathed no body of doctrine to any followers. But even by his presence, by the warmth of his humanity, not excluding an ineradicable pugnacity, he demonstrated the bankruptcy of the Establishment politicians and the shallowness of Party distinctions. He would have survived as a legendary figure even if his writings had been forgotten.

The original numbers of *Twopenny Trash* were flimsy enough, and passing through many hands, and the vicissitudes of poverty, very few of them survived. In their pages two crucial years of English History are reenacted. No overt successes are scored up. The farm labourers were beaten to the ground. The industrial workers were only beginning to organise against the inhuman conditions to which they were subjected. But a process had been set in motion which is a dominating factor in today's world; it has to guide the technological miracle for the benefit of men in general. In its broadest aspects this many-sided process owes very much to Cobbett and his writings take on fresh significance whenever basic social values are brought into question.

EBENEZER JONES, 1820–1860
– AN ENGLISH SYMBOLIST

JACK LINDSAY

The least explored period of our poetry is that between 1830 and 1850. The Romantic surge had died down and the Victorian middle-class synthesis had not yet emerged. The two decades saw much violent upheaval and deep-going change. They began with rick-burnings and the Bristol riots, then saw the rise and culmination of the Radical and Chartist movements, the Poor Law riots and the risings at Devises, Birmingham, Sheffield, Newport and elsewhere, the great mass-meetings of the Chartists, which reached their climax and breakdown in 1848. They saw the decisive construction of British capitalism; the old forms of popular resistance were crushed and struggle was able to reawaken effectively only with the expansion of trade-unionism that went on from the 1880s.

Dickens comes out of this period, expressing many of its pressures, dislocations, anxieties, and the reassertion of human solidarity. But what of the poets? There was a considerable number who did their best to tackle the situation, aware of a pervasive crisis in human relationships, which they expressed and illuminated in varying degrees; but none of them was able to encompass the issues in their full reach. The best name yet found for them is that of Gilfillan: the Spasmodics. The term expresses well enough the way in which their moments of penetrating vision came in unstable bursts, but it hardly suggests the remarkable insights which they could not sustain.

Philip James Bailey's *Festus* of 1830 first definitely revealed the new turn that was being taken: 'the hero is the world-man.' Indeed the idea of Faustus brooded over the epoch, though mostly in secondhand forms derived from Carlyle or the like; a lesser though important archetypal figure was Byron's Cain. The conclusion may be said to come with Alexander Smith's *A Life Story* and his *Glasgow*, in which the industrial city is realised from within for the first time. Among the poets who made valuable contributions were 'Orion' Horne, John Stanyan Bigg,

W. H. Smith, Sydney Dobell, D. B. Starkey, J. E. Reade, A. J. Symington, Gerald Massey, with Darley as forerunner and Beddoes as off-sider. The first works of Browning and Tennyson, *Paracelsus* and *The Devil and the Lady*, belong to the movement, but with these two poets the deep striving element, in which the poets seek to grasp what is happening tumultuously among the uprooted people, dies out or is diverted to lesser ends. Hopkins and Meredith alone can be said to have carried on to some extent from Spasmodic bases.

The Spasmodics were keenly aware that the systems which had held men together in previous ages were being disintegrated and that new ways were being opened up. They knew that it was necessary to fight all along the line for human values if the new ways were not to be wholly destructive. Their poetry, in both its virtues and its vices, is conscious of a fierce disruptive pressure, which they can only partially understand and control. They lacked an adequate philosophic instrument and could grasp the threatening forces at work only in momentary intuitions. Their imagery, owning much suggestive vitality, fails to cohere in the comprehensive vision they wanted. Still, taken all together, they reveal richly the nature of the crisis they confront and the new possibilities opening up in culture, in human relationships; at their core is the quest for the new kind of union that will overcome the evil effects of the dehumanising forces at work throughout society.

In this quest the poet who goes furthest and deepest is Ebenezer Jones. He was born on 20 January 1820 in Canonbury Square, Islington, and he died after a cramped and miserable life on 14 September 1860. His father was Welsh; his mother Hannah Sumner came from an Essex family. The family lived in comfortable style, though with harsh Calvinist restrictions. All contacts with the corrupt world were seen as a backsliding. Ebenezer's brother, Sumner, tells us:

> Dr Watts and Kirke White were permitted in our Parnassus; but Shakespeare and even Milton were left in rigourous quarantine. Of Byron we had a mysterious notion, gathered from hearing our elders now and then speak of him shudderingly, as of some Satanic spirit who had been permitted visibly to stalk abroad. Of Shelley we had never heard.

Ebenezer went to a school at the foot of Highgate Hill under a nasal dissenting minister, Snipe. Then his father fell ill and the family fortunes collapsed. The boys began to fight the dark Calvinist controls, aided by reading Carlyle's *French Revolution* and Shelley's poems. A sister to whom Ebenezer was deeply attached died at the age of twenty-two. He tried to stay on at school as junior usher, but at seventeen had to take a city-clerk's job in a tea-merchant's house. He worked from 8 a.m. to 8 p.m., without counting the time taken in getting to work and coming home. The tea-trade, he found, involved grossly dishonest practices.

The rest of his life was spent in this sort of drudgery, against which every fibre of his being revolted. We hear (from T. Watts) of an unrequited love for a woman 'who passionately loved another man – a man to whom Ebenezer was very dear – and who soon afterwards died'. He was saving what money he could in the hope of publishing his poems: which he did in 1843 under the title *Studies of Sensation and Event*. The book 'utterly failed of public appreciation' (Linton). Sumner says that the misery of the lost love had led him to 'throw the medley of his poems into the cauldron of his ill-fated book'. He sent copies to several leading authors, from whom he is said to have received slighting or unkindly responses, Proctor and Horne being the exceptions. He was deeply depressed by the book's reception.

In time he was to gain the interest of other poets: Houghton, Barry Cornwall, W. B. Scott, Allingham, Swinburne, Browning, and above all Rossetti, but too late to help him on his way as a poet. The conventional-minded keenly disliked his work. Thomas Hood imputed to him an 'impure motive' and accused him of 'shamefully prostituting the gift of poetical powers'. Ernest Jones, one is sorry to say, granted him power and originality, but attacked him for 'unintelligible obscurity', for neglect of the harmonies of rhythm, and for setting 'his heroes in the most preposterous and extraordinary situations'. Worse, he endangered 'the dignity of the democratic character', indulging in indelicacies and obscenities, 'which, in plain prose, would subject the writer to contempt and disgust'.

It was in the later 1840s that Rossetti chanced to pick up a copy of *Studies*; he was fascinated and finally sought Ebenezer out. The book left an indelible impression on him and in 1870 he wrote:

I met him only once in my life, I believe in 1848, at which time he was about thirty, and would hardly talk on any other subject but Chartism. His poems had been published some five years before my meeting him, and are full of vivid, disorderly power. I was little more than a lad at the time I first chanced on them, but they struck me greatly, though I was not blind to their glaring defects, and even to the ludicrous side of their wilful 'newness'; attempting, as they do, to deal recklessly with those almost inaccessible combinations in nature and feeling which only intense and oft-renewed effort may at last approach. For all this, these *Studies* should be, and one day will be, disinterred from the heaps of verses deservedly buried. Some years after meeting Jones, I was pleased to hear the great poet Robert Browning speak in warm terms of the merit of his work.[1]

Helped by his response to Carlyle and Shelley, Ebenezer had been deeply stirred by the popular movements of protest and revolt. He became an Owenite sort of socialist. Rossetti found him obsessed by Chartism, though Sumner and Linton, presenting his work later to the Victorian public, tried to minimise his political passion. Yet even Sumner speaks of him as 'picturing a leader of revolt (such as he could himself have been) in lines of startling force'. At least one of his poems, *A Coming Cry*, was 'thrillingly recited from the platform by W. J. Fox'. This poem, which contrasts the great constructive powers in men with the degraded ends to which they are put, and with the denial of human dignity by unemployment, has a darkly menacing line at the end of each stanza: 'We'll go on building workhouses, million, million men.'

We know the sort of ideas he set out to Rossetti; for in 1849 he published *The Land Monopoly, the Suffering and Demoralisation caused by it; and the Justice and Expedience of its Abolition*. He writes passionately throughout, demanding an 'equitable distribution to the people of what may be produced'. The wage-system he denounces as essentially evil; it 'demoralises the entire people', and is a form of slavery. But society conspires to conceal this deep truth. The parties

try to pass it off by misuse of language, as 'having to earn one's living', 'getting one's bread by honest industry', 'gaining one's bread by the sweat of one's brow'; meaning by these phrases, working for capitalists, employers, masters. There is, however, all difference in the world between having to earn a living, and having to depend on an employer for permission to do it. . . .

As a remedy, 'The Right to Labour', has been demanded, and fought for, and consecrated by the blood of thousands of martyrs; and though the foolish and the vicious have succeeded for a time in suppressing the demand, it, or some similar one, will yet triumph, if there long enough remains in heaven God, and in man the human soul. Ay, triumph! though the blood in the next struggle be the blood not of martyrs. The victims of social wrong must be politically curbed, or they would soon render illegal their social victimisation.

As things are, everyone in society is forced to accept the distorting pressures of a morally evil situation, which pervades all relations. Society is divided into robbers and robbed, and the result is a demoralisation of all concerned. The final horror comes when efforts are made to turn the suffering working class 'contented with their inferiority'. Baseness can sink no lower. If the wage-system and monopoly-forms are indeed eternal, then 'let poets cease their singing, or raise only protests against fate, or elegies over prohibited grandeur', and let the workers cease to propagate their enslaved kind. But Jones does not believe that the movement into intensified degradation is fated; it can be halted and reversed; monopoly can be expropriated. And he calls for the expropriation.

There is however a confusion in his thinking, which appears in the very name of the essay. He sees Monopoly as solely vested in land, certainly influenced by the tradition of Spence; yet he pours his fiercest wrath on the wage-system and the enslavement of the workers by the capitalist employer. Indeed he bases his whole moral thesis on this point. However, when he comes to the steps needed to end the situation, he thinks only of the land. The monopoly-forms in industry seem to him so insecurely developed that they will fall away if only the land is handed back to the people. (His only direct reference to Communism shows that he thinks of it as a utopian system in which all property is shared out equally.)

He proposes then that the land be taken over by the people and vested in commissioners periodically elected by the whole nation. The rent from the land is to be used wholly for social purposes such as Education, Recreation (Gardens, Libraries, Music Halls, Ball Rooms, Picture Galleries), and Science. Landlords and their children are to be compensated with a life-interest. Thus the burden of land-monopoly will be removed from the 'wages of the working-man, and the profit of the trader, manufacturer, and merchant'. Jones instances corporations such as the University or Crown Lands, declares that the French Revolution made the fatal mistake of sharing the land out capitalistically, and attacks Feargus O'Connor's scheme for getting every Englishman an acre of land.

As a political thinker he is then only an advanced radical attacking the landed interest; but his moral and social analysis is primarily concerned with the essentially dehumanising nature of the capitalist wage-relation, anticipates attitudes of Ruskin and Morris, and is in the key of what his contemporary Marx was thinking about the alienations of class-society. (Sumner refers to a work by Ebenezer on the Condition of England Question, but this did not reach print.)

The engraver-poet W. J. Linton was a close friend of both Ebenezer and Sumner. He tells how he was freed from orthodox religious views by a stockbroker's clerk who seems certainly to be Sumner and with whom he read Voltaire's *Philosophical Dictionary*. In 1841–2 he edited a weekly newsletter, *Odd-Fellow*, put out by Hetherington as one of his unstamped penny-ventures, with a small circulation among the independent friendly societies of London; but it was not scurrilous enough for the lodges or political enough for the Chartists. When he dropped it, Ebenezer edited it for the short while before it died. He was a very handsome man: Linton calls him 'the type of Alcibiades but with an idea of duty which the Greek had not, which made him heroic in a time of severe martyrdom'. They went once on a ramble in the Lake country.

How well to this day I can retrace our steps and recall the pleasant bright companionship, that, like the sparkle in wine, made that pleasure-draught but more enjoyable; our delight in the moon-light walk from the Windermere Station by the Lakeside to Ambleside, that loveliest five miles in all England; our next day's climb (the track missed) over the Stake Pass, after bathing under the fells in a pool at the head of Langdale; how we lingered dallying with our joy, on the mountain tops till night came on, a cloudy night of late September, after a day of autumn glory, overtaking us before we could reach the Borrowdale road; how, unable even to grope our way, we lay down together on the stones to sleep, and awakened by rain, crept under an overhanging rock, and cold and hungry, smoked our pipes and talked till the dawning light enabled us to find a path to Stonethwaite; how we sat in a cottage porch to await the rising of the inmates and welcome a breakfast of bad coffee and mutton-ham so salt that it scarified our mouths. No grave-minded man was either of the pair who went laughing and singing, if somewhat limping, on their way; nor was there much disposition to gravity two evenings later, when, after supper, at the little Fish Inn at Buttermere, we amused ourselves with improvising verses (certainly never printed) not exactly in honour of

William Marshall, William Marshall,
Cotton-Spinner of Leeds.

Verses of more rhythmical extravagance in proper poetic execration of the factory-owning plutocrat who had the impudence to possess the one grand house in pastoral Buttermere. Full capacity for enjoyment, whether of his senses or his intellectual faculties, characterised the man in his day of health: delighted with all he saw, from the rugged bleakness of Wastdale to the pastoral repose of Buttermere, enjoying equally a row on Crummock Water and our evening walk beside the golden woods to Keswick. . . . His week's holiday over Jones returned to London, in order that a fellow-clerk in the same house might take his turn at recreation. This young man went with a friend into Scotland, and four or five days later, the two were found dead on a hillside, having, as Jones and I had earlier, lost their way and laid down to sleep in the cold air.

That is the one living glimpse we get of Ebenezer. In 1844 he married Caroline Atherstone (niece of Edwin Atherstone, author of the *Fall of Nineveh*). The marriage was a total failure; Linton and Sumner speak of Caroline in terms of bitter reproach, but give no details. Ebenezer continued to write verses, but as so much of his later work seems to have been unpublished or destroyed we cannot properly estimate his development, though it is clear his powers did not weaken. He meant to issue a second book, *Studies of Resemblance and Consent*, and at least some of it appeared in the 1879 book of his poems. Sumner depicts him as carrying on through desolate years, detesting the money-world to which he was tied and struggling to carry on as a poet: strolling with his dog Fool (named after the Fool in *Lear*) and talking feverishly, after he had blown out the candles to save pennies, in his parlour in Paulton Square, to which he moved in 1856. There he was excited by his nearness to Carlyle, though he could never bring himself to speak to him. The Rev. T. Mardy Rees of Chelsea adds that he 'might be seen in his latter days walking on the sunny side of the square', that he burned many poems before his death, and that 'what Mary was to her brother no one can declare' (I have not been able to find the year of his sister's death). He died of consumption while wintering in Jersey.

Now let us look at his poetry. We might begin with the late poem which found its way into the *Oxford Book of Victorian Verse*. Here we find the strangeness to which Ernest Jones objected. As in all his work there are clumsy touches; and yet in his very clumsiness we feel his originality, his attempt to evade conventional poeticality and romantic cliches. The poem has no title, but a prefatory statement tells us that it was written for music. Its theme is that the world ends, not with a bang, but a whimper; or rather something more subtle than that: that world-end creeps upon men without their being aware of it, so that they are unable to distinguish the disastrously ubiquitous death from the normal processes of nature, of their world, and therefore make no effort to do anything about it. That such a conception should be found in a poem on the 1840–50s brings us sharply up against Jones's unusual angle of vision.

> When the world is burning,
> Fired within, yet turning
>   Round with face unscathed;
> Ere fierce flames, uprushing,
> O'er all lands leap, crushing,
>   Till earth fall, fire-swathed;
> Up amidst the meadows,
> Gently through the shadows,
>   Gentle flames will glide,
> Small, and blue, and golden.
> Though by bard beholden,
> When in calm dreams folden, –
>   Calm his dreams will bide.
>
> Where the dance is sweeping,
> Through the greensward peeping,
>   Shall the soft lights start;
> Laughing maids, unstaying,
> Deeming it trick-playing,
> High their robes upswaying,
>   O'er the lights shall dart;
> And the woodland haunter
> Shall not cease to saunter

When, far down the glade,
Of the great world's burning
One soft flame upturning
Seems, to his discerning,
Crocus in the shade.

The rhyme-scheme, we may note, long antedates Swinburne.

Studies of Sensation and Event deserves to be analysed poem by poem; indeed no other way can fully bring out the force and interrelation of Jones's ideas and images. But here we can deal only with three main points: (a) the strong sensuous pictorial effect, which clearly had much effect on Rossetti and played its part in bringing about the key-ideas of Pre-Raphaelitism, (b) the strange or bizarre situation, image, event, which dominates in each poem as did the unrealised doom-fires in the poem cited above, (c) the dialectical interrelation of ideas and emotions, which has affinities with Blake's method and leads on to a doctrine of symbolic correspondences linking Jones with the French *symbolistes*, with Baudelaire and Rimbaud.

First then the peculiarly precise pictorial definition, which at the same time has a dynamic quality. The long blankverse 'A Crisis' will serve here. Amid all its broken form, which seeks to express and directly evoke the distraction of love, we find a steady elaboration of visual detail which builds up the complete image. It is not a question of naturalistic accretion, but of a sharpened awareness that sees the world of forms stirring and infused with new energies in all its 'minute particulars': a new relation of the parts and the whole. The movement of the seemingly detached eye is one with the movement of a strong almost-tranced emotion, bringing about a unity of observer and observed, of isolated object and the totality of scene and episode: a sort of comprehensive dream-state merged with a near-sight realism. Such an approach to the image is based on a distrust of past generalisations, a need to reconstruct the world afresh from the smallest possible units or facets inside a unifying vision.

The evening church-chimes had dispersed the mowers
From all the fields of toil; the evening sun
Slanted his golden light, as he did lapse
Towards underneath the earth; his light was ray'd
So gorgeously upon this sacred meadow,
It's yellow buttercups, its ruby sorrels,

Its milk-white clover, and its cool green grass,
Seem'd blended into one rich colour'd woof
Changing in hue, as waved beneath the breeze; –
When leaned therewithin, against its fence,
A form white robed, which the whelming sunshine
Show'd to be fullest symmetry of woman
Swelling thro' girlhood's prime. Fronting the mead
She stood; against the fence her shoulders rest;
Above it gently her head and neck bend back;
Her long brown hair behind her straightly fall'n
Leaves unconcealed her twin-breasted bosom,
Thus raised against her vest; her pertinent feet
Pressingly side by side, are forwarded
Into the mead, and planted firmly there;
And from her planted feet to her fall'n back head,
One proud full arch she arches.
                A large wind
Came o'er the mead, and flaggingly on her fell,
Weighing her vestments downwards and around;
Sleeker than apples show her round young knees;
Show beauteously together twined her limbs:
The frontage of her body broadly orbs;
The sunlight whelmeth all: – loosely her head,
Loosely her neck falls backward; her round chin,
And its rich blood-red lip, now idly sink
Down to the upwardly curved lip above;
While round the corners of her idling mouth,
Slow smiling dimples, when her basking eyes,
A little uplifting their nigh-closed lids,
Thrill with voluptuous light, – above her cheeks
Like opening crevices to measureless splendour.
Bounds she out thus on firmly-planted feet
Her enjoying form, and thus her face is naked
In glowing rapture. . . .

The detail is used throughout to make us feel the plasticity of the girl's form, and the movement of light and of wind is used to harmonise her with the scene, to beget a unity of the human being and nature. The outer movement is again one with the eager eye of the absorbed lover before the girl and with the love stirring inside her, communicated to every part of her body. The sloping form is one with the slanted sunset-light, and the lapsing curves are one with the deeply-felt moment of surrender, of intense union.

And spake
Of the meadow sleeping goldenly before, –
The trees around – the richly slanting sunlight;
And as she spake, her shoulders to the fence;
No longer curved she out as sail wind-filled,
For her exquisitely supple body revolved
Over its ample throne; and negligently
Her feet slid out apart into the mead
And to her bosom, with low dropping lids,
Her face declined; and down from her propp'd shoulders
Her arms fell loosely; and her slackening limbs,
Loosen'd out all her form; and, there towards him,
She sloped. . . .

And so on and on. The moment is drawn out into an endless realisation of its components of body and spirit, and yet is concentrated into a single sustained movement of union. We can see how Rossetti was affected by the plastic effect gained by a continuous precision of detail, and by the use of the love-union as the sensuously organising centre of the image. Though Jones's verse then was by no means the sole stimulus of Pre-Raphaelitism, it cannot be omitted in considering the origins of that movement. An enthusiast like Rossetti would have read the poems to his friends and associates, one of whom, W. B. Scott, had later much to say of them.

Next we may take another poem where a strange situation is used to get inside the 'normal world' and to show its extreme abnormality, its distance from human truth and meaning. Here are what Rossetti called inaccessible combinations. The first poem in *Studies* is 'The Naked Man', which describes a high tower-room in the midst of fashionable London.

> The winds uncheck'd around it swept:
>   And o'er all others high,
> Straight into it the sunshine stept
>   Stark naked from the sky.

This stripping of light sets the key for the lonely man in the tower, who himself strips and paces round.

> Twelve times the lonely chamber round,
>   This naked man doth pace,
> His globing eyes growing more profound,
>   Scorn fixing more his face.

The light breaks over him with a sheen that 'kills every shade and haze', and, 'multitudinous and keen', picks out his naked form. Watching the people who pass below, he laughs in his contempt.

> Why seeks this man the lonely height?
>   His fellows sport below:
> Why is he naked, what doth he write,
>   Nakedly crouching low?
> What means the scorns that swiftly surge
>   O'er his expanded eyes?
> Why do his mind-strung muscles urge?
>   What is their mind's emprize?
> What means the room, of life's stuff bare
>   As mountain-hollow'd grave?
> The naked manhood, nerving there
>   Like a tongue in its dark red grave?

He carries out the bidding of his dying father, an old lord who had led armies 'through this world, like sea-snakes through the sea', and who on his deathbed realised something of the truth of things. 'I die a fool, a duping fool; I leave a veiled world.'

> I sink within the senseless tomb, –
>   The shapes I seem to leave,
> Now strike their masks, and midst the gloom,
>   Some real glimpses give . . .
> I thought I fought for man, – I know,
>   'Twas for the thing man seemed;
> I thought to man my blood did flow, –
>   It flowed to dreams I dreamed.
> With armies I have lashed the world,
>   And at my will it flew,
> I know not what the power I hurled,
>   Nor that I did subdue.
> I die deceived, but one shall tear
>   The masks that lied to me . . .
> Through him I hurl detecting scorn
>   At life's old harlot zone,
> I crush her masks for centuries worn,
>   I strip her, on her throne.

So, while the careless passers of Kensington chat below, the unknown man brooding above men, the naked man at his vigil in stark light, the son who must redeem his father's blood-guilt

and tear off the masks of the power-world, struggles to achieve a
new depth of consciousness, meditates in anguish.

> His body writhes beneath the strife,
> To make men keenlier see . . .

'Beyond earth's creeds', he is alone even in the arms of love.

The next poem, 'Egremont', seeks to break through the
tormented loneliness of the poet who is concentrated solely on
discarding the masks of men's false consciousness. It opens with
a sketch of evolutionary growth and depicts primeval days, then
declares that the time is ripe for changing life by 'competent
energies'. The poet's task is to

> Leap with passionate reason down the depths
> Tempestuously tossed, of human nature,
> Seeking the masked demons, that invoke
> Suffering and wrong.

Now he is no longer inturned. He desires storm, the violent
convulsions of revolutionary change.

> 'So that my soul may widen to her fate,
> And throb exultingly against the storm . . .'
> The moon slants bright on his sky-lifted face,
> Haggard with eager intellectual toil,
> Beautifully haggard as the face of a corpse,
> That, peering through its riven sepulchre,
> Lists to the resurrection-trumpetings.

Through struggle the New Man will be born. The poet cries to
the Moon (which for him as for Keats expresses transformation
and love-union, union with nature), but offers no 'parasitical
and insulting worship of terror-wrenched thanks'. He wants
'the discords of a deepening harmony': a powerful phrase that
goes to the heart of Jones's aesthetic and social positions. 'Like
thee, do I arise in life's dark night.' But not to soar aloft above
the earth. He needs a chaos, he declares, to subdue and organise
by his grasp of the new harmony arising from the discords, the
resolution won by the fully fought-out conflict of opposites:

> I know creation rapture: what creation,
> Save harmonising elements! . . .
> I claim, by virtue of the peace I make,
> Some dim, disorganised, sullen star,
> That I may be to it in place of thee,

Teaching its hearts all musics; through thy world
Dismiss me glorying!

A voice answers: 'Come up hither.'

Next, in 'The Waits', Jones seeks to state the positive aim born
from the struggle to unmask evil. His image of uncorrupted
union comes from childhood, from Baudelaire's *paradis
enfantin*, in a perspective of snowlight and all that is loveliest and
strongest in nature:

> I have seen the snow sink silently to the ground;
>   And beauteously its white rest
> Quieted all things; and the hushing sound
> Murmuring and sinking everywhere around,
>   Blessed me and was blest.

He had been lustrously greeted by the moon coming through
"the dark cloud-flight'; he had heard 'the ungovernable sea',

> I had mark'd afar his raging radiancy,
> And proudly, in his pride, had felt that he
>   And I were twain god-born.
> But than the under-uttering hush of snow,
>   Than the moon's queenly reign,
> Than ocean's pride, more beautiful did glow
> One other beauty, – even now bending low
>   I adore to it again.[2]

In a lonely house the Child steals down a dark gallery into a
room of 'mellowed moonlight blown', where a little girl lies on
a couch with 'the sleeping light, pleasuring beneath her eyes'. In
a leap of music he kisses her and she wakes. He tells her that
again has come the music they feared never to hear again.

This vision of the Child, he says, gives joy and hope in a
'strange world', fierce and mean, alien to happiness, where is
'throned the wrong' that destroys hope. It persists through
terror and madness, through the loss of love, in a world of
palsied mechanistic science and maniac muttering poetry. In
the drear of the storm the boy's voice is still heard murmuring,
'Listen.'

Now we turn to the creed of dialectical correspondences. This
indeed pervades the poems, but is set directly out in *Two
Sufferers*. In a rich ancient garden of the dusk stands a lily, its
'alone star'. At the lily-root gnaws an invisible worm. 'Distant a

moth-flight from the suffering lily' is a temple of pleasure with 'lights dazzlingly undulating it within ever with varying hues'.

> Like one gorgeous opal
> It glowed, and in its vast capaciousness
> Exquisitely nerved life sought all sensation,
> Crises, and tides of pleasure . . .
>   Its broad mirrors
> The company multiplies, the space disbounds,
> And its music strangely wantoneth, and aye changeth
> The hue of its light.

(We meet here the *symboliste* derangement of the senses: the aim of which is to fuse the sensory material in a new unity.) The dancers sweep on, wreathed with music and filled with lights; the 'secret hurrying notes bewilder sense'.

> The merciless music
> Sweeps eddying on, and on each lady whirls,
> And whirling aloft her draperies, her limbs
> Startle the hall with symmetry, like sea surge
> The light lace heaped above each shelterless knee.

At last the music swings the dancers into the culminating love-embrace. But the loveliest girl comes out alone under the acacia by the lily and leans on the tree. 'The universe is the millstone round her neck.' She wants to sink back into the life before men evolved:

> When no ocean rolled
> Her serpent form in continent-strangling folds
> Around the struggling earth, thus torture claspt,
> Compelled to struggle its endless orbit round,
> The jaws of its still tightening enemy
> Plunged deep into its heart: when no false spring
> Summered with flowers –

She wants to return to the other side of the world of lies where all hope and desire are betrayed; she alone is not deceived by the pleasure-whirl. Then she has a vision of the cataclysm inherent in that sphere with its masks and cheats. She sees the moon, 'suddenly stayed, turn a dead face amidst the skurrying clouds as a drowned man on the waves'. The moon that once lighted the poet's face, the face of the dead about to be resurrected, in 'Egremont', is now the face of death itself, its transformative powers gone.

Suddenly would my heart befit its death time
By wonderful growth, and suffer mightiest thoughts
Of the glory of its storm; – the stricken world
Grinding its atmosphere to thundering surf
As wild it plunges: – with enormous joy
Feeling itself last-life, I'd hear all cease;
And when the air grew icy, when the darkness
Abolish'd vision, into the deepening silence
Would I expire.

Then the wind blows the moonlight through the garden; the lily snaps; the hidden worm comes out.

Oh, friends! what secret woe
Has blooded the vision of the pagan lady,
That she saw nought but wounded suffering
In our glad world! Children of earth! believe,
That though but a moth-flight distant yonder temple,
It was no chance that led the lady suffering
To impart her fate to a like suffering flower;
For it may make sacred every nook in space,
May annihilate despair, alleviate sorrow,
To believe in a rule unseen.

The 'rule unseen' is the system of dynamic correspondences, the discords of a deepening harmony. The discovery of the veiled connections forces into the open the worm gnawing at the root of life and makes possible a new consciousness, an uncorrupted series of relationships. (The poem strongly suggests *The Sick Rose* of Blake.) From one level Jones draws on the opposites of pagan enjoyment and Christian repression, but he makes clear that he rejects both opposites in terms of a higher synthesis of organic harmonies or realised correspondences. The pleasure-temple is the space of those who seek to enjoy the world without facing its lies, cruelties, parasitisms. To stress this point Jones follows with the 'Song of the Kings of Gold', which shows the pleasure-world stript of its pretences and openly dominated by the rulers of the cash nexus, the economic system treating people as things and turning all relationships into reifying deathforms. The Kings of Gold possess the earth and its fullness, but transform it into a hell, with all relationships become those of prostitution:

And all on earth that lives,
Woman, and man, and child,

> Us trembling homage gives;
> Aye trampled sport-defiled . . .
>
> On beds of azure down,
> In halls of torturing light,
> Our poison'd harlots moan,
> And burning toss to sight.
> They are ours – for us they burn;
> They are ours, to reject, to hold;
> We taste – we exult – we spurn –
> For we are the Kings of Gold.
> > We cannot count our slaves,
> > Nothing bounds our sway,
> > Our will destroys and saves.
> > We let, we create, we slay.
> > > Ha, ha! who are Gods?
> In a glorious sea of hate,
> Eternal rocks we stand. . . .

Even the few poems I have cited will suffice to show what Rossetti meant by speaking of Jones's vivid, disorderly powers and his reckless effort to deal with almost inaccessible combinations of nature and feeling. I have treated the poems as making a consecutive argument, and this approach is justified by the poet's own theory of dynamic interrelations and by many of the titles, which make explicit his use of opposed states or emotions. Thus, 'A Pagan's drinking chaunt' leads on to 'A Christian's drinking chaunt'; 'A Plea for Love of the Individual' on to 'A Plea for Love of the Universal'; 'Feminine Spite' on to 'Feminine Goodness'. Often the resolution of the conflict is made in a third poem, though at times the triadic movement occurs inside a single poem. At times the links are tenuous, but it is clear that Jones has a definite dialectical principle in his mind, which links the notion of the unity of opposites with that of organic correspondences. How he arrived at these positions it is hard to say; he belongs to the tradition of Smart and Blake, but certainly did not know these poets.[3]

I must omit many of his poems that I should like to discuss, but cannot here ignore his 'Ways of Regard' (different levels of consciousness), which opens:

> Sharks' jaws are glittering through the eternal ocean
> Now, even as ever; through the topmost seas
> That mightily billow, through the secrecy

> Of its abysses, where the waters bide
> Omnipotently shuddering – scattering fear,
> Onwards they go; their illuminating teeth,
> Perpetually parting . . .

An image of ravening divisive forces that looks back to Keats but is developed with fuller insights. Slaughter, says Jones, sways earth and ocean, jungle and town. And 'dire is the woe when first the vision of slaughter' breaks in on the young who have just left the shared love of home. Such a person stumbles, reaches for aid; 'then the howl of the world arouses him.' He stares 'through heavens and hells, eternities and times . . . seeking the power that bids this terrible reign . . . Baffled, his gaze retreats.'

> He strips his being of all control and veil,
> With which men gird themselves; and he thinks his teeth
> Could grasp Earth's wretched breast, and that he could leap
> With her to oblivion. And while thus he dreams,
> Steals sensual pleasure to him. The nakedness,
> To which in noble rage he smote his being,
> But exposes him to her dalliance.

Thus emerge the conflicts of adolescence. The lad hides from bloody reality in pleasure and ignominiously sleeps: if we can call it sleep, this stupor into which keeps descending 'the vision of possible and gentle glory That circles brightly round his youth' – if we can call it sleep from which he rises to murder 'these entreaties', or from which he wakes to watch with sane intellect his moral idiocy. Many persons remain at this level of unresolved conflict. They accept the murder-principle and try to use it for their own profit. If all goes well, they think that everything is right; if they founder, they accuse life of being a torture-house, and stab 'a poisoning blade into the hearts of their brothers'. Many become quite inhuman in their acceptance. They drift along with a false consciousness of freedom:

> Otherwise, haughty steps,
> Of men who tread with appropriating feet
> Earth and its causeways; and of beauteous women,
> Who walk our pavements, and our terraces,
> And our swung bridges, as though hoveringly
> Their scornful feet the fitness questioned

> Of every spot they press, – would drop to a shuffle
> Of slaves and tools.

Yet there are some who face the truth and what it implies in act and thought. Such a man,

> Commanding time,
> And extinguishing space, and past the furthest reach
> Of the five senses reaching, – he beheld
> Within this earth, where night was dark, a cavern,
> Peopled with slaves contemplating revolt.
> Under the light of many a lurid fire
> That burned on upper ledges of the rock,
> The countless slaves stirred noiselessly; the light
> Fell on the mass, as eagerly it upturned
> Its face to the chief, who on a ledge
> Above them stood.

This is the reality of revolt gathering at the heart of an alienating and exploiting society. A woman rushes in to tell the leader that his daughter has been ravished while she herself had to watch helpless. He cries out in utter repudiation of a world where rape and murder are the way of life and where the ravished ones end by being fascinated by the process of demoralisation, where the raped virgin shades off into the harlot. 'Slaves! Brothers! are we already thus cursed! Damned are we to endurance, to acquiescence, to content?' The ultimate horror is to become blinded to the murder-rape process surrounding and conditioning them.

> Oh! being men, they who would hold you slaves,
> Do murder you alive! They blind your minds
> With writhing toil, and say you have no sight;
> They break you from the majesty of man,
> Into gaunt monsters, crooked miseries,
> And call you brute-like, – trample down your hearts,
> And say you have none, – banish from your souls
> The light of knowledge, and proclaim you soulless . . .
> Because they have so damned us,
> That we've endured these shames! Oh for *this* murder,
> This poisoning, this pollution, this dead life,
> What, what revenge?

Thus he addresses the working-class, who break into an 'answering tumult,' and an upraised light burned lurid on his face, like the reflection of a burning kingdom.

The vision changes. The poet goes on to deal with the ways in which reality is evaded, veiled, distorted. A young man and a girl slip from the cave of the class-war. He is of the ruling-class, but compassionate, and the girl follows him through love.

> Oh monstrous contradiction! – these, possessing
> A curst identity, yet having no power
> To self-determinate, – a tortured tool
> For others' usage.

He swears that he'll attack his own class in the senate.

> If I move not the king to piteous thought,
> His lips shall whiten. All their boasted order,
> Their laws unbroken, all the deep submission
> Of their whipped slaves – is terrible disorder;
> Disorder of the universe, and of the heart.

The defenders of the system reply: 'The nation flourishes, its power is vast.' 'Its wealth supreme.' He cries: 'Oh, idiot knaves and liars! Say, is a flag a nation? is an army? Do half a million traders make a nation? A thousand lords? The people is the nation.' Yet, though education is made a weapon of human debasement, the truth will triumph and evil be defeated. However the dissident aristocrat can see only a mad violence in revolution.

> Man cannot pause. –
> Go! bid the sun to rot within the heavens!
> Arrest the marching melodies of stars!
> Chill every river into stagnancy!
> Deracinate the fruitful earth of growth!
> Though infinite space grow dark, the soul of man
> Shall soar triumphantly. Within this cavern
> Are thousands, sworn to rise from out the mire,
> Whereto you damn them; they will rise – will rise,
> Though war may hew their pathway; though their march
> Be in blood to the armpits! Oh, that it were mine
> To lead them bloodless conquerors! They will rise,
> But with the chains they shatter from their limbs,
> Must they do hellishly. A vessel, laden
> With captives fettered with famine and plague,
> Now is this land; the slaves force-freed, will make
> A burning wreck; themselves, amidst the flames,
> Maniacs, wild dancing. Oh, who, who can know,
> How to redeem this people?

In answer to that cry we meet the Statesmen. No fool, he knows that sooner or later the people will cast their fetters off. Detached, he scorns the governing class as fools,

> To whose whim
> Aye I must pander, and the pandering call
> Government; for whose robbery of their fellows,
> That have no gold, I will forge dutiful tools
> And term them law.

His ambition makes him turn from the truth, so that by cheat and oppression he may gain the name of 'wise, bold statesmanship', and thus hold the people down for a while. After him speaks the Middleclass Man who interprets all political and social realities in terms of his own mean grovelling plans for security and family-advancement: a creature who cannot see beyond his own petty schemes. To preserve his easy life he will defend slavery to the last. So we are returned to the cave of the class-war. There a tumult breaks out and a radiance of released powers streams circling out on high, with the chant: 'Soon will be complete Auxiliar changes, and one mighty change.' The struggle will converge on total revolution.

But at this point the poet's understanding breaks down. He cannot imagine just how the one mighty change will come about through the revolt of the workers. 'Big is the earth with the superior creatures waiting to displace man.' The spirits keep on crying their joy in free process, looking to the great moment:

> All things intensify; and we must ever
> Intenselier contemplate, intenselier joy.
> Rest we above the cave. Rejoice, companions!
> Brightly speeds on the baptism of the earth.

Jones writes as if some *Übermensch* is to appear spontaneously; but he must in fact mean that the men of an unalienated and free earth will live such a different life from that of the present with its inner and outer divisions that they will seem a different species. In any event we see that while he has faith in a total revolution he cannot conceive the forms through which it will take place. This final weakness however does not detract from the depth of vision in the rest of the poem.

We must now glance at his final poem in the book with a title taken from Georges Sand: *Car la Pensée a aussi ses ivresses, ses extases, ses voluptés célestes, dont une heure vaut toute une jeunesse, toute une vie*. Here at sunset a child comes out of a cedar-grove. His mother asks what has upset him. He tries to tell her of an overwhelming experience where stand 'terracing the mighty trees'.

In the shadowy depths he remembered the priest's blessing; ecstasy went oceanic through his brain and, 'cresting, raised my hair'. The grove and the lifted hand were fused in a single image; in his mind a thunder-cloud burst 'in bright wild rain, torrenting through my limbs, and for its goal, mounting back mightily to my brain again'. Now in the ebbing rapture, panged, he tries to explain the revelation, which concerns the dynamic correspondences at work in the whole universe and uniting the most sundered things. The child, says Jones, has shown himself

> one of that band
> Who, telling the sameness of far-parted things,
> Plants through the universe, with magician hand,
> A clue, which makes us following, universe-kings.
> One of the seers and prophets who bid men pause
> In their blind rushing, and awake to know
> Fraternal essences, and beauteous laws,
> In many a thing from which in scorn they go.
> Yea, at his glance, sin's palaces may fall,
> Men rise, and all their demon gods disown;
> For knowledge of hidden resemblances, is all
> Needed to link mankind, in happiness, round love's throne.

He knows, however, as he shows in *The Land Monopoly*, that the realisation of the dialectical nature of the life-process must be linked with the struggle of the victims against the Kings of Gold, if 'fraternal essences' are indeed to be realised. (The title of the projected second book, *Studies of Resemblance and Consent*, shows that he meant to explore further the question of correspondences and union.) The Child of 'Car la Pensée' looks back to the Child of 'The Waits', and his *ivresses* are those of the *Bâteau Ivre*, his idea of universe-kings with magical hands is thoroughly Rimbaudean. Indeed the whole poem may be called a prophecy of 'the marvellous boy'.

We are thus brought back again to the fact that Jones was trying to bring about in England the development of Romanticism into *Symbolisme*, which was being effected in France by Baudelaire. (It was no accident that R. H. Shepherd, editor of the 1879 reprint of his poems, published one of the first translations of Baudelaire in English.) We see then that the English tradition had all the elements needed for a development of its poetry in the nineteenth century into an expression fully adequate to tackling the human condition brought about by the consolidation of capitalism, a fearless confrontation of the vastly intensified alienating pressures. But the forces of Victorian middle-class society were too strong; they cut off English culture into a relatively parochial situation (where the French novel from Balzac to Zola and the Russian novel from Gogol to Dostoevsky had no impact whatever). Jones's work remains as a remarkable, though broken, monument of what might have been, of a poetic effort to face what was happening to people in all its fullness and to affirm a concept of total revolutionary change. Hopkins and Meredith, we noted above, conserved elements of true dissidence; the Pre-Raphaelites concentrated on the aesthetic aspects of Jones's vision which Rossetti had taken over.[4] (The early William Morris has affinities with the work of Jones, which Morris probably did not know. Take Jones's lines: 'Around her mouth a new smile grew', or 'Its smooth slow ankles, very slowly'. Here we have the hypnotic effect, the visual intentness, which Morris achieved so powerfully in *The Defence of Guenevere*.) But it is only now, with the question of alienation come to the forefront of serious social thinking, and with Jones seen against the following development of European culture, that we can truly estimate what he tried to do. It is of great interest that the poet who could make this particular aesthetic attempt was the social thinker who wrote *The Land Monopoly*.[5]

Achievement and failure, reinvigoration of poetic form and collapse into confusion, characterise his work throughout. The critics of his own day who saw him as rising to heights of eloquence, then writing weak or bad lines, failed altogether to get inside his work. His strengths and weaknesses are intertwined. He has staked everything on a wholly new grasp of the formative aspects of the life-process; he continually makes us feel he is coming through and as continually sinks down just short of his goal. His work is thus, as Rossetti recognised, singularly difficult to define, and yet, once known, it haunts us with its sense of deep potentialities, with its insights into the alienated condition of men and with glimpses of a liberating union, a truly human harmony.[6]

NOTES

1 Such Victorian critics as commented on Jones's poetry were usually more vocal about the weaknesses than the virtues, which they defined only in very general terms. Thus Lord de Tabley: 'When Jones writes a bad line, he writes a bad line with a vengeance. It is hardly possible to say how excruciatingly bad he is now and then. And yet at his best, in organic rightness, beauty, and, above all, spontaneity, we must go among the very highest poetic names to match him.'

2 It was typical of the New Poets (as the Spasmodics preferred to call themselves) to use adjectives in an active way rather than for mere description. Hence phrases in Jones like 'globing eyes', light 'pleasuring' beneath the eyes, 'whelming sunshine', and so on. Present participles are thus often used for novel effects.

3 Some deep thinking was going on about art and psychology in the 1840s. Thus Bulwer Lytton in his preface to *Night and Morning*, 1845, remarks on the need to explore 'new regions . . . lying far, and rarely trodden, beyond that range of conventional morality in which Novelist after Novelist has entrenched himself – amongst those subtle recesses in the ethics of human life in which truth and falsehood dwell undisturbed and unseparated'. But Jones carried this discovery of deep ambivalences further, relating them to the struggle to become human.

4 Jones's 'wrenching of rhythm', his particularized diction, and his concern with the 'thisness' of the object described seem to point (through the superficial concern with the realistic presentation of detail in the Pre-Raphaelite aesthetic) to the more intense attention to singularity in Hopkins's inscape. Hopkins, by the way, may well be the one poet, following the Pre-Raphaelites, who actually realised the cardinal principle of Pre-Raphaelitism'. (Michael Wolff, editor of *Victorian Studies*, in communication, 4 December 1963).

5 He has an incessant sense of the pressures of renewal, rebirth. 'He is born; again he is born . . . The flesh flakes in his face.' (*Zingalee*, a poem apparently based on his marriage.) Again his strength and weakness lies in his overwhelming sense of being only a moment of history, compelled by the forces of the people. 'Who wrote the *Revolt of Islam*? Not Shelley: 'Tis the mighty utterance of a society whose eyes have just opened to the glory of truth, and she made him her poet.'

6 Note on Sources: *DNB*, 'E. Jones,' by Richard Garnett; W. J. Linton: *Memoirs*; introductory memoir to Shepherd's edition, 1879; 'Reminiscences', *Prose and Verse*, xix, New Haven, 1879. See also F. B. Smith, *Radical Artisan, William James Linton* (Manchester Univ. Press 1973). D. G. Rossetti in *N. and Q.*, 5 February 1870. T. Watts, *Athenaeum*, September–October 1878 and W. B. Scott in *Academy*, November 1879. In 1878 Shepherd issued a small brochure with a brief account of Jones and a few poems; W. M. Rossetti's review started off litigation between Shepherd and the *Athenaeum*. A second volume of prose and

poems (preserved by E. J.'s friend Horace Harval) was promised, but did not appear. Poems were given in Monckton Miles's anthology, Vol. V; a few in Stedman; the two directly political ones in H. Salt's *Songs of Freedom.* Sumner, who emigrated to Australia, also wrote poems. Garnett speaks of E. J. working for the radical publishers Cleave and Hetherington.

ON AN UNPUBLISHED
IRISH BALLAD

A. L. LLOYD

BBC S21899[1]
Title: Lord Leitrim
Inf.: Thomas Moran
Orig.: Mohill, Co. Leitrim
Coll.: Seamus Ennis (1954)

O you boys of the shamrock, pay attention to my ditty.
Be alive to your duty, be wise and be witty.
Keep your powder dry, and we'll make the tyrant fall,
And we'll give them what Lord Leitrim got below in Donegal.
   With me riddle-addle-day-ri, fol-ol-the-riddle-al,
   Riddle-addle-day-ri, fol-the-rol-the-ree.

It being on the 2nd of April, this old debaucher left his den,
He left bailiffs, bums and harlots in the castle of Lough Rynn.
To Makim and Kincaid he gave a hellish bawl,
Saying: 'We'll tumble down the cabins in the County Donegal!'
  With me riddle, etc.

'Twas two crafty-looking renegades old Shiney did obey,
Saying: 'We'll hurl out the Papish and we'll drown them in the
    sea.
As Cromwell did in days of yore, we'll waste 'em, great and
    small,
And we'll desolate their farms here below in Donegal.'
  With me riddle etc.

'Oh, me lord, I'll feel so horrified,' poor Makim he did say,
'For my mind it has foretold me we'll meet Rory on the way.'
His lordship then made answer in the presence of Kincaid:
'Of Rory or the devil, sure, I never was afraid!'
  With me riddle, etc.

So they druv away together on that unlucky day,
Until they come to Cretlagh Wood, near an angle of the sea,
Where bold Rory he was standing there, just threatened by a
    squall,*
All for to protect the widows in the County Donegal.
  With me riddle, etc.

When young Rory seen him coming, his heart did jump for glee.
He give three cheers for Tenant Right, Home Rule and liberty.
'Our maiden fairs and Colleen Bawns that was proper, straight
    and tall,
Caused by you they were sent o'er the seas, far far from
    Donegal.'†
  With me riddle, etc.

Oh, this monster's face began to foam. His venom he did spew,
And roared out in a hellish tone: 'Sir, tell me who are you?'

---

  * Other versions have: 'who never feared a ball'.
  † The version of Miles Duggan, of Beleek, Co. Fermanagh (BBC S19536)
has:
    'And then as he approached them, he did 'em then salute,
    Saying: "Where are you going today, you dirty ugly Orange brute?"'

'Well, my Lord, I'm Rory of the Hill, that makes you welcome all
To a hearty dose of bullet pills below in Donegal.'
  With me riddle, etc.

Oh, young Makim cries: 'Spare us our lives, Mister Rory, if you please!'
'No, no, for when you lie with dogs you're sure to rise with fleas.'
The boys was laughing at the joke, they stood behind the wall,
Saying: 'We'll pepper 'em up with powder and smoke this day in Donegal.'
  With me riddle, etc.

'Oh, go on, my boys,' says Rory. 'Make ready, present and fire!'
At his old brain they took fair aim and they hurled him in the mire.
To revenge the joke, his head they broke, and his carcase there did maul.
They stuck him in a pool, his head to cool, below in Donegal.
  With me riddle, etc.

'Well done, my boys,' says Rory, as he turned to the sea,
Where the men they jumped into a boat that there at anchor lay.
'We can paddle our own canoe, we've got a speedy shawl,
And hooray, me boys,' says Rory, 'for the maids of Donegal?'
  With me riddle, etc.

Oh, the policemen like beagles gathered round this dirty beast,
And the devils all, both great and small, they had a sumptuous feast.
He was dissected like a bullock down at Manorvaughan Hall,
And the devils ate him, rump and stump, that night in Donegal.
    With me riddle, etc.

William Clements, Third Earl of Leitrim, was born in Dublin in 1806. After graduating from the Royal Military College at Sandhurst, he served in the British army in Gibraltar, Portugal and elsewhere, and retired with the rank of Lieutenant Colonel. In Parliament he represented a Co. Leitrim constituency (1839–47). He was a tall, powerful man, lame for much of his life through a fall from a horse. He succeeded to the title and estates on his father's death in 1854, becoming landlord of Bobey, Clooncahir, Breanross, Drumgeldra, Errue, Derreen, Cashill, Tulcon, Towneymore, Lough Rynn, Bornacolla, Clooncarn, Farnaught, Gortletteragh and other townlands in Leitrim and Donegal as far west as Gweedore.

On 2 April 1878 he left his residence in Manorvaughan, near Milford, Co. Donegal, on his way to the Quarter Sessions at Manorhamilton, Co. Leitrim, with ejectment orders against a number of tenants. He rode in a post-car driven by a 19-year-old youth, Charles Buchanan. On the other side of the car sat John Makim, the earl's clerk. His personal servant, William Kincaid, followed with the baggage in a second car driven by Michael Logue. They had travelled but five miles from Manorvaughan, and were passing through a thickly wooded spot by an arm of the sea on the shore of Mulroy Bay when they were ambushed by three men armed with shotguns and pistols. Buchanan was killed instantly; Makim died shortly after by the roadside; Lord Leitrim, twice wounded by gunshot, was battered to death.

A police notice was issued from Dublin Castle, 15 April, 1878:

Whereas it has been represented to the Lord Lieutenant that, about the hour of 9.30 o'clock on the morning of Tuesday the 2nd day of April 1878, William Sydney, Earl of Leitrim, John W. Macken or Meekan, and Charles Buchanan, were brutally murdered at Cratlagh Wood, about 3 miles from Milford, in the County of Donegal, by some persons unknown: His Grace, for the better apprehending and bringing to justice the perpetrators of this outrage is pleased hereby to offer a reward of
FIVE HUNDRED POUNDS
to any person or persons who shall, within six months from the date hereof, give such information as shall lead to the arrest of the persons who committed the same, or any of them.
                    By His Grace's Command, T. H. Burke.

Three brothers, Anthony, Bernard and Thomas McGrenahan, their cousins Anthony and Michael McGrenahan, also Michael Heraghty, Manus Trainor and Charles McTaggert were arrested in connection with the assassination. Trainor and McTaggart were soon released, no evidence against them being offered.

The Earl's burial took place in Dublin on Wednesday, 11 April 1878. Accounts of the funeral vary somewhat in sobriety. A particularly vivid report appeared in *The Freeman's Journal* on the following day.[2]

The hearse was a closed one, topped with white plumes. At twenty minutes past two o'clock a derisive yell announced that the short procession had reached Church-street. The crowd closed around the hearse as it approached the graveyard, groaning, cheering and hissing. The occupants of the mourning coaches on descending from their carriages were jostled about and scattered. The police in vain sought to clear a passage for the coffin. The most violent sections of the mob broke the line with a rush, and groans made the scene a horrible one. Not more than 100 rowdies of the worst class either laughed or jeered. The rest looked on without any overt act of misconduct, but without any violent demonstration of disapproval. A reinforcement of thirty more men of the D Division hurried up at the moment and recaptured the hearse. Under their convoy it was piloted to one of the entrance gates, and it was evidently intended to bring it through the gate to the church door. No sooner was the gate unfastened, however, than the mob burst through the cordon of police and was almost pouring in when the gate was forced out in their faces. Over a quarter of an hour elapsed before the coffin could be finally removed. In the meantime the mob hooted and groaned, and voices came from the worst of them saying 'Out with the old b—,' 'Lug him out,' 'Dance on him.' With the utmost difficulty, by the aid of a double line of policemen, the mob was held in check while the coffin was unhearsed and removed on men's shoulders through the gate. A great yell of execration was raised as the coffin passed in. Then came another rush, in which the chief-mourners were rudely jostled against the railings. The new Lord Leitrim, who was not recognized, was separated from his friends, hustled, and crushed severely, before he could get safe inside the gate. Lord James Butler also came in for rough usage, and one of the Donegal mourners, who got jammed against the wall, shouted that they were breaking his back. At last the funeral procession was safe within, and the gate slammed to. The organ of St. Michan's played the Dead March in Saul as the coffin was borne to a place opposite the lectern, the congregation standing the while. Two of the Royal Irish Constabulary from Donegal had been ushered into the church shortly before, and it was whispered that they were there on special service . . . The last prayers being over, the coffin was borne through the southern door, towards the vaults. A furious rush was made through the church after the coffin, and the confusion was for the moment scarcely less indecent within than outside the church. Immediately that the bareheaded mourners were sighted by the mob outside the railings, a new howl of execration went up, and amid hisses, cheers, and indecent jests, the coffin of the unfortunate nobleman was hurried to its last resting-place.

Deposition of William Kincaid at the Petty Sessions, Milford Courthouse (April 1878):

'I was in the employment of the late Earl of Leitrim at the time of his death. I was groom and coachman. I remember ordering a car from Michael Logue at Carrigart. The car was at Manorvaughan on Tuesday morning, April 2nd. Two cars were drawn up before the door at the same time, a few minutes after eight. Charles Buchanan drove the first car. The Earl of Leitrim and John Makim were on that car, one on each side, and Buchanan on the dickey. Lord Leitrim sat as usual on the side next the sea. There was no luggage on that car except a small black bag on the right hand of his Lordship, a stick and an umbrella: the bag was tied to the car with a leather strap.

Michael Logue and I were on the second car. I was on the side next the sea. My car started immediately after the other. For some time, the distance between the two cars increased. The mare was lame. The first car was several times out of my sight.

I know a place called Cratlagh Wood, near three miles from Milford, five from Manorvaughan. I know a place at Cratlagh Wood where there is an incline on the road. When I came to that, my attention was attracted by a shot. When I heard that, I could not see the first car. I was not quite at the top of the incline at the time. My car went on for a bit after I heard the shot. I saw smoke from the wood at the waterside; the smoke rose from opposite the rise of the hill. The next thing I heard were two shots. There was very little time between them and the first shot.

I was in sight of the first car then. I saw smoke again from the waterside. The car itself was moving up the little hill. There was only Lord Leitrim on it, going up the top of the hill. I had not seen any person on the road up to that time. The first person I saw on the road after the two shots was Makim coming running to meet me. He was nearer the first car than to me when I saw him. My horse had stopped then. The horse stopped after the first two shots were fired. I could not say whether the horse stopped itself or was stopped by the driver. I got off the car and went to meet Makim. When I met Makim, Lord Leitrim's car was at the top of the little hill and Lord Leitrim was still on it. I saw a black object on the road when Makim met me.

When I turned round from Makim where I met him first I saw two men just behind Lord Leitrim's car. Lord Leitrim was in the act of getting off the car. One of the two men had something that appeared red in his hand. I afterwards saw the black thing, which I afterwards found was Buchanan. I heard two other shots fired after Lord Leitrim got off the car; immediately after and when the men were on the road. I saw the smoke on the road. I had not removed from Makim up to that time. The car I had been on had come up. I put Makim on the car before I heard the last two shots. Makim came off the car immediately; he was wounded at the ear and there was a little blood. He grew weaker as he was talking to me. When he got weaker I called to Logue to take him up to the ditch. I saw a man taking up something red and striking Lord Leitrim. I saw only one stroke; I seen no more of them then. I placed Makim to the ditch and when I looked back they were gone. I could not see the car either. From the time I heard the first shot till I saw the blow given with the red thing, two or three minutes only elapsed.

The next thing I observed was a boat on the water. I was on the road beside the ditch where I laid Makim, nearer to Manorvaughan. I went to bring Logue on with his car. I observed two men in the boat: it was going straight across the bay to Fannett (Fanad). I left Makim then. He was still alive. I wanted to get him on the car but Logue wouldn't have him on the car because he might die on the road. I then went and found Buchanan lying. He was dead then. There was blood, but not much, near him. I lifted him from the centre of the road to allow the car to pass.

I went on further and saw Lord Leitrim lying. He was lying partly on his face. He had no hat on. He was dead then. The water in which he was lying appeared bloody. I seen a pistol lying on the road about two feet from Lord Leitrim. I afterwards overtook the car Buchanan had been driving about half a mile from where Lord Leitrim was lying. A boy had the car stopped. I drove on that car to Milford. I know where John Clarke lives, a little piece off the road. I met a female standing on the side of the road before I overtook the car: I don't know who she is. I called Clarke. Going on in the direction of Milford I met some carts and two policemen. I spoke to the police and went on to Milford.

I could not see the features of the two men on the road. They appeared to have soft felt hats on. Lord Leitrim's hat was off at the time they were striking at him. The colour of their clothes appeared to be grey. I could see Lord Leitrim's legs and body when he was getting off the car. When I turned round I could see the top of the wheels; the back of the car was in my sight and I could see as far down as the top of the wheels and the shaft. When Lord Leitrim got off, I could see his head and shoulders. He was facing me and the men were quite close to him. I don't believe the men were as tall as Lord Leitrim; his Lordship was a pretty tall man.

I only saw the heads and shoulders of the men at first; there's not much of a hill where the car was. I saw the man rising the red weapon in his hands. I saw his head and shoulders still. The other man was on the road along with him at the time. I have been acting as the personal attendant of the Earl. I attended to his things and assisted him that morning to put on his outside coat. He usually carried his pistol in a belt under the inner coat. I brought the black bag out and tied it. I believe there was a pistol in it. It was known at Manorvaughan by every servant in it that Lord Leitrim was to leave that morning. I have seen M'Bride whose boat was found. He was painting at the castle some time ago; I can't say what paint he had.[3]

Testimony of Dr John Osborne: That I am Medical Officer of the Milford Dispensary District. I remember on April 3rd last making a post mortem examination of the bodies of Lord Leitrim, John Makim and Charles Buchanan. Lord Leitrim's body and that of Makim were in a house of Lord Leitrim's at Milford; the body of Buchanan was at his father's house. On Lord Leitrim's body, commencing with the shoulder, there is punctured wound about two inches from the vertebral column on the left side and on a level with the fifth dorsal vertebra. There were about eight or nine other wounds between that and the top of the left shoulder. They did not all pierce the skin; some of them did. The wounds appear to have been caused by gunshot or gun slugs. From the position of these wounds they were probably caused by the same discharge. None of the wounds was of such a character as to cause death. They were on the left side of the back, near the shoulder. On the left arm I observed about thirteen punctured wounds and the flesh a good deal torn. Those wounds appear to have been caused by a single discharge. The first group of wounds could not have been inflicted by a gun before him; the second group of wounds were caused by a discharge from the front of Lord Leitrim. The wound in the arm seemed to have been inflicted from a very close range. The clothes were carried in under the skin of his left ear, and on the bridge of his nose I observed small lacerated wounds; they appeared to have been caused by something bluntish and having corners on it. About the left side of the head and face there were bruises apparently caused by a bluntish weapon. The principal wound was on the top of the head. It was three inches in extent. It caused a fracture of the skull. The same blow could not have caused all the wounds I saw on the head. The wound on the top of the head, the fracture of the skull, was the one that caused death. I should say that death would be very speedy.

With regard to Buchanan, all the wounds were gunshot wounds. They were on his right arm, right breast, right back, and one upon the left breast. I think there were about thirty altogether. A number had penetrated the right lung and would have caused almost instantaneous death. I think the wounds on Lord Leitrim and Buchanan were caused by regularly-formed round shot. There was a little bit of metal got in Charles Buchanan's right lung; the metal appeared like brass.

I found a punctured wound above and behind Makim's ear. I found a small grain of shot. I found the cause of death in his case to have been an effusion of blood on the brain. There was nothing else but that one shot to cause the effusion; there was no other external mark to cause it.[4]

Deposition of John Clarke: About nine o'clock on the morning of the 2nd April I saw Kincaid on the road and in consequence of something he told me I went with John M'Bride in the direction of Manorvaughan. I know Cratlagh Wood and Woodquarter. At Woodquarter I saw Lord Leitrim lying in a pool of water on the side of the road; his head was lying towards Milford.

I saw blood on the crown of his head, and on the side of the face he appeared to have got a blow of a blunt weapon. I saw a pistol lying on the side of the road close to where he lay in the pool. I saw the stock of a gun from which the barrel was severed. I took up the pistol and gun-stock. It had a guard on it, fastened with two flat-headed nails which loosened while I had it in my hand. I did not examine the pistol to see if it was loaded. I lifted his lordship out of the pool and laid him on the side of the road.

I went on to the face of the little hill, and about the centre of it I found the cardriver; there was blood on his face. I did not go into the plantation at that time.

A little over one hundred yards I found the third man, Makim, on the side of the ditch. There was life in him but he was not able to speak a word. M'Bride was with me; there was no one else there then. I think I met two men with a cart and another man with a cart; I had no conversation with any of these men I met. After I had seen the three men I looked over a fence and saw a gun; it was lying about halfway between where Lord Leitrim and the driver were lying, and on the shore side, inside the fence. The fence was of whin bushes. The gun was about a yard from the fence. I did not go inside the fence until the police came. I went inside the fence with the police. I remained till the corpses were removed. His Lordship's hat was lying beside him, and there were two hats lying beside where Buchanan was lying. Buchanan had no hat on him, nor had Makim. One of the two hats was hard.

I examined the gun-stock and noticed that it was not made by a mechanical hand. I put my initials on it. The guard was on it, there was a split in it, and I have nothing more to say about it. It was all down in the water but a short bit of the butt-end; there was just as much of it that I thought it was a powder-flask. I noticed no blood on it. The dead body of Lord Leitrim was lying at full length in the water, not halfway covered. There might have been a foot of water. I saw no appearances as if a body had been dragged. If a man had sworn that he had done his best to take that body out of the water, my reply would be that he would have done it easily if he had someone to help him. I had someone to help me. The head was in the water, the same as every other part. I don't know if it would be true if a man swore he had taken the head out of the water.[5]

Evidence of James Doak, of Ballymagahey: That I live at Ballymagahey. I am a carpenter. I know a man called Heraghty. The man nearest me in the dock is Micky Heraghty. He is a tailor and has worked occasionally at his trade for some days at a time in my father's house. I remember his bringing a gun to my father's house. It was not three or four months ago. He asked me to put a new stock on the gun. I agreed to do so. I made the stock myself of sycamore. I painted it with red lead, red cart paint. I fitted the barrel to the stock. My brother done some ironwork, that was before the fitting took place. The barrel and stock fit, but not very well. The stock is split now; it was not split when I gave it up. It might be a month or less or three weeks in my house. Micky Heraghty was in my house occasionally while the gun was there, but I can't say how many times. I gave that stock and barrel to Micky Heraghty and he took it away with him; that might be two months ago, it might be, two months ago or less. I never saw it as a perfect gun since I gave it to Heraghty.

I was arrested for giving witness on the stocking of a gun. My brother was arrested along with me. I was in custody a night and two days. There were no hand-shackles on me. I was asked something before I was arrested by the man who arrested me. I was told to dress myself, that I had to go to Milford. I was not cautioned. I gave in a statement and after that my brother and I were let out. We had a fire in the room where we were kept. I gave the statement to more than one in the barrack, there were two or three or four there. I was not there of my own will.[6]

Evidence of Thomas Peter Carr, County Inspector, R.I.C.: I remember April 2nd last. In consequence of information received I went to Milford. As I went through Milford I saw the bodies of the murdered people; that was about five perhaps ten minutes to one o'clock. They were then in Lord Leitrim's house. The clothes had not been removed. The bodies were apparently the same as if they had been taken off the road. Lord Leitrim's body had on it two coats, his gloves were on, and a pair of wrist-bands over them at the time. I did not examine as to whether he had arms on him. I did not see the bag at that time.

I went immediately to Woodquarter. I rode to the scene accompanied by a mounted orderly, and I sent Kincaid and two police on a car to meet me at the scene. Kincaid pointed out to me the places where Lord Leitrim's body had been lying, where Buchanan's body had been lying, where Makim's had been lying against the bank and hedge, and where the second car was when Kincaid heard the first shot. There was a mark on the side of the road where Lord Leitrim's body had been, and not very much blood on the road. There was a pool of water and it was much discoloured with blood at the place where Buchanan's body was found. I saw a round spot of blood and a stream of blood about eighteen inches long trickling from it.

I continued down the plantation about thirty-two or thirty-five yards, then I came to a round knoll in the plantation. That was not easy to go up, there was a lot of tangled wood there. That knoll was covered with stunted larch, some gorse and long heath, directly opposite the place where Buchanan's body had been found. I observed a round place in the long heath where evidently some person had been lying. The heath had been pretty well cleared away by the person who had been lying there; it was pressed down. About seven feet from that in the Manorvaughan direction there was an exactly similar hole in the heath. At either of these two places a man standing erect could have been distinctly seen from the road. Before one of the holes there was a larch tree on the Manorvaughan side, and before the other a gorse bush on the Milford side. Sub-Inspector Doudican, who was with me, picked up a pistol and handed it to me. The pistol was a foot and a half from the hole on the Milford side and about midway between the two holes. The ramrod had been sprung as if fired from an overcharge. It had the appearance of having been recently fired. I found the powder had been recently burned. We did not find anything else in that particular hole on the Milford side.

I then went to the constable to go on his knees to search the hole. He picked another hole, and the same constable lifted a hat from the ground. That hat was lifted from between the front of the hole and the road. He then took a piece of paper out of the round place and handed it to me immediately. It was folded and I found it had recently contained lead in some granulated form; I have often seen the appearance presented on paper by lead being rolled up in it; the granulation was perfectly distinct when I took the paper first. In the same place there were two pieces of blue cartridge paper rolled in such a shape as if intended for wadding. A little on the right of the hole on the Manorvaughan side the constable found a soda water bottle which had recently contained whiskey.

There is a Sub-Inspector Bailey at Rathmullen. On the morning of April 3rd I got a copybook from him. It is described as 'Vere Foster's Copybook'. It is headed in print the words 'Written by', and in writing, 'Mary McGrenahan, Third Class'. 'Third' is written, 'Class' is in print. The number is 6 of a series. I observed through that book, on the top and middle, lithographed lines for a copy. Under these lines there is the handwriting of some person all through. On each page there is written 'Mary McGrenahan' and the date, purporting to be the date on which the copy was written. The first date is the 7th December 1876, the figure 6 not being very distinct. The two lithographed lines on that page are 'Diligence is the mother of good luck', 'Drive your business, let not that drive you'. Taking the piece of paper that I found on the ground, I found that there are portions of these two lithographed lines on either side, and under each of those lithographed lines are written copies as in this book, and at the bottom of each page there are portions of dates – '6th December' and '10th' on the other side, and before these dates part of a name – 'Grenahan' on one side and 'enaghan' on the other, as in this book.

I have compared the handwriting of the copies and dates on the book. I am able to say that they are in the same handwriting. I am clearly of opinion that the same hand wrote these two. I have a No. 6 Copybook of Vere Foster's as issued to the National Schools. The back of that book is identical in every respect with the book that I have already been describing. On the third leaf the two lithographed lines are 'Diligence is the mother of good luck', 'Drive your business, let not that drive you'. On the page preceding, the lithographed lines are 'Blessed is he that considereth the poor', 'Continual dropping wears away stones'. On the reverse of the same page the lines are 'A bad workman quarrels with his tools' and 'Be slow to promise and quick to perform'. Upon the paper that I found I observed the words 'Be slow to promise and', and upon the back, 'wears away stones', on the top lithographed lines the letters 'works' and on the other side the letters 'reth the'. These four pieces of lithograph are identical in position, words and writing with those in the perfect book.

I got another piece of paper, almost circular, from Constable Kelly. On this piece of paper there are on the top of it on each side portions of lithographed words; on the one side the letter 's' followed by 'with', on the other side the letter 's' followed by 'be' and 'ing' and underneath writing on such side; on the one side plainly on each line 'rrels with his' and on the other side on each line 'is he that'. I have compared this circular piece of paper with the paper found at the place. The handwriting is the same as that of the copy in the Copybook; the circular piece appears to me to supply a portion of that piece which was found at the place.

I saw the small bag on April 2 and sealed it at the request of Captain Dopping in his presence. I broke the seal on a subsequent day. I found a six-chambered revolver in a case, with a belt in the bag; it was loaded in each chamber. A small double-barreled pistol was handed to me by a policeman on the day of the murder; it has two barrels and both were loaded. I don't know to whom that hat belongs. There was no paper found inside the hat. I made as close a search as I could but found nothing more than I have already enumerated. I know the gorse bush on the side of the road; I found nothing there. If anyone swore that on the Wednesday he found a quantity of hair, portion of a newspaper singed, I would not be surprised. Some hair was brought to me and I found it to be cow's hair. There was not a piece of paper the size of a crown beside that bush when I left it on the day of the murders. I searched the road near where Lord Leitrim was found. I saw no hair there; there might have been; the ground was wet and a good deal tramped.[7]

Evidence of Edward Bailey, Sub-Inspector, R.I.C., Rathmullen: On April 2nd last about ten minutes past eleven o'clock I received information of the murder of Lord Leitrim. I went to Wood-quarter. I know Anthony, Bernard and Thomas McGrenahan, the three brothers; they are the sons of a Thomas McGrenahan, and live at Gortnatra North in Fannet (Fanad). I know the Hawk's Nest. From the Hawk's Nest to Gortnatra North is about fourteen English miles by land; there is no difficulty in going there. I know Anthony and Michael McGrenahan, two brothers; they also live at Gortnatra North between five and ten minutes' walk from where the three already named live. I know Michael Heraghty.

I remember on April 3rd going to the house of the first-named of the three McGrenahans. I had several men of my force along with me. I reached the house about six o'clock in the morning. I found the father Thomas in bed. His wife and two daughters, Mary and Margery, I think were in the house. The prisoner Thomas was in the house. On our way to the place we met Anthony and Bernard and two sisters near Kildrum; we met them about five or six o'clock; they live in the father's house.

There were three rooms in this house and a kind of loft above. The kitchen is the room as you go in from the door; there is a bed in the room. There is a room off the kitchen for storing things, and off that there is a sleeping apartment. There were two beds in the apartment as far as I recollected. I found Thomas McGrenahan the prisoner in a bed off the lumber room. The father was in the bed in the kitchen. I searched the house. In the room in which Thomas was, coats and trousers was found. I searched the trouser pockets and in them I got some tow. I also got a bar of hammered lead; it was in a drawer in the lumber-room. I believe it is hammered lead. I got some caps and blue paper on the table in the lumber-room. There was a saucer on the table with shot in it. It was half full, and I brought some of it with me. There was a gun also found and it appeared to have been recently discharged. I saw a rude stock in the lumber-room as well as I remember.

I made no arrest on that day. On the morning of the 11th day of April I was at the house of Michael and Anthony McGrenahan, brothers, between half past one and two in the morning. I found the prisoner Michael there, a woman and a girl. I arrested Michael on that occasion. When I met Anthony and Bernard in the morning I had no conversation with them. I think a Sub-Constable spoke to them and had a nod from him. I have never known anything against them. I have heard of something against them. I have heard that they are noted smugglers in the district. I don't know of any conviction against them. I also heard that they were poachers. I took nothing away from the house of Michael and Anthony. No conversation that I recollect occurred about the skin of an animal.[8]

Evidence of Sub-Constable John Sherry, Kindrum: On the 3rd day of April last I went with Sub-Inspector Bailey to the house of Thomas McGrenahan. I knew McGrenahan's house before that day. The father Thomas, his wife, and his three sons now in the dock, three or four daughters and a grandson lived in the house at the beginning of April. One of the daughters is named Mary, between 12 and 14 years old, and attends Cashel Glebe School.

I was in Kindrum on the 3rd. I met Anthony McGrenahan, Bernard McGrenahan and their two sisters Margery and Maggie on the road that morning. I had a conversation with them. I bid them the time of morning, asked them if they were going far and they told me they were going to Milford or Ramelton, I am not sure now. I don't remember that they told me what they were going for; I believe they told me they were going to buy clothes. Their father and mother told me they were going to Milford or Ramelton to buy clothes for going to America.

I was at the house of Anthony and Michael McGrenahan with three Sub-Constables. I saw the skin of a rabbit in the house. I said it was a good place for rabbits. I could not tell that the rabbit had been recently killed. The skin was hanging up. I was shown a gun by one of the two McGrenahans.

I was in the house of old Thomas McGrenahan on April 6th last. I found three copybooks in the top drawer of a press. After finding these books I went to Cashel Glebe National School. I saw Mrs Dolan the schoolmistress there. In consequence of something I said to her she searched for a copy-book in the school, the copy-book of Mary McGrenahan. She did not find it.[9]

Evidence of Ellen Dolan: That I was a schoolmistress at Cashel Glebe in Fannet in the County Donegal during the whole of the month of April last. I know Mary McGrenahan. I know Thomas McGrenahan, her brother. I know three of her brothers by eyesight. Mary McGrenahan was a pupil of mine in 1876 and has continued to be my scholar since for part of each year. She was last in my school as a pupil on the 3rd of April last. She was there as an ordinary scholar on that day. I saw her copy-book on that day; it was a Wednesday. I collected it with the other copy-books about half past eleven, that is the rule. The rule is, when copy-books are finished the pupils give them to me to keep for the annual examination. After they are finished, every day they are collected and put in a press and given out next morning. I last saw Mary McGrenahan's copy-book in my school when I collected it on the 3rd. On the following Saturday my attention was called to it by one of the police. He asked me to produce the book. I searched for it but could not find it. Between Wednesday the 3rd and the following Saturday I had not missed the book. Mary McGrenahan was in the school on Friday morning, but it was before school hours; she did not remain for school that day, and on the next morning I missed the copy-book. The hand-writing 'Mary McGrenahan' at the top of the copy-book is my own.[10]

Evidence of Mary McBride, of Turlaghan: The road from Cratlagh Wood to Rawross is the road that passes my house. I know Michael Heraghty right well; I see him rightly and kens him rightly. I remember the day Lord Leitrim was murdered; it was on a Tuesday. I saw Michael Heraghty on that day in my own house. He came into my own house, and would come always when going the road. It was about two years before since he was in my house before that time.

We get dinner in the middle of the day. A bell rings at Manorvaughan at one o'clock; that is the time we have our dinner. They get their breakfast before they go out in the morning. It was before the dinner-time that Heraghty came in. It was more than an hour before dinner he came in; I suppose it was two hours but I am not sure. I didn't see him until he stepped into the house. He does not live on that side of the Mulroy at all. I was sitting with my hand on my eye and he said he would give me a drop of Doon Well water that he had for his mother, that she was losing her eyesight.* I gave him his meat, a drop of tea and a couple of eggs. I gave him that before my husband and son came in for their dinner, my husband and son 'Neece' McBride came in for dinner. I have another son, John; he wasn't working that day. Heraghty remained till my husband and son came in for dinner and he left when they were going back to work. My son John went with him. The bell surely rang that day as well as every other day. Heraghty said he had been coming from the Doon Well.[11]

Evidence of John McBride, of Turlaghan: I remember the day Lord Leitrim was murdered. I was not at work that day. I know Micky Heraghty. I saw him in the house of my mother on that day. I was not in when he came in. As far as I can tell you, I went into the house about an hour and a half before dinner. He was in the house when I went in. He was in the room when I went in. I think it was stirabout he had, and me and him had tea together. I saw him taking eggs. Micky Heraghty said he was at the Doon Well. He did not say when he had gone there. He stayed in the house till the bell rung, the last bell to go back after dinner. I went out with him then, and over to the ferry-boat at Rawross. I went into the boat and I went across with him. I helped Charles McElhinny, the ferryman's father, to pull him across. When he

* Doon Well water was credited with curative properties (A. L. L.).

was across he was at the side of the bay that he lives on. Eddy
Mills spoke about the murder while Heraghty was with me. That
was at Mills's own house, beside the ferryman's house. Mills told
me to button on my coat and not take it off again, that there
would be no work; that they were killed in the wood, three of
them, he said. I had not heard before that of anybody being
killed. Mills said his lordship and the clerk and the driver had
been killed. I can't tell whether Heraghty said anything after
that. He didn't say anything to my knowing about the murder
going across. I don't remember Heraghty saying anything
about the murder; I don't remember Heraghty saying anything,
good, bad or indifferent, about the murder. I don't remember
saying anything about the murder myself. Charlie McElhinny
was saying he didn't believe it yet. I eat eggs, of course; I eat two
eggs.[12]

Evidence of Daniel Gallagher, of Rossgull: I remember the day of
Lord Leitrim's murder. I remember seeing John McBride
crossing the ferry that day. Micky Heraghty was with him. I was
in the boat going across. We crossed about three o'clock. About
two minutes before we got into the boat I heard it said that this
case happened. I heard them saying his lordship was killed, also
two more. Heraghty was beside me when that was said. I don't
know who mentioned it first. Heraghty did not say anything
when it was first spoken of. When I was at the quay I heard
Heraghty saying that he was at Doon Well for water for his
mother. I was at Doon Well myself. To go the nearest road to
Doon Well from where the ferry starts I would say is about
eleven miles. I couldn't say anything about the murder. Johnny
did not say anything about it. Old Charlie McElhinny was in the
boat; he didn't say anything about the murder. I did not hear
him say anything about the murder.[13]

Information of Edward Mills, of Manorvaughan: I heard of the
murder from Gerrard Graham, and soon after John McBride
and Michael Heraghty of Tulnerdoll came up to where I was
standing, on their way to the ferry. I told McBride of the
murder, but he, so far from believing me, called me a damned
liar. Michael Heraghty, who was with him, made no remark
whatever, but stood with his mouth shut and showed no
symptoms of surprise. I looked at him and did think it queer

that he had not made any remark. He had no bottle in his hand, none in his coat pocket, and none that I could see. I saw Gallagher, a man whom I had previously told of the murder, go to McElhinny's house, where he met Michael Heraghty and shook hands with him, and say: 'I was going down to your home'. Heraghty replied: 'I was going to your home.'[14]

After a number of remands, the McGrenahans and Michael Heraghty were returned for trial at the Summer Assizes at Lifford in July 1878, but the authorities failed to find the McGrenahans responsible for the killing, and they were released. Michael Heraghty was further remanded, and died of 'black fever' (typhus) in the Lifford Prison hospital on 12 October 1878.

His funeral, on 14 October, was one of the largest ever seen in the Fanad Peninsula. Crowds of mourners joined the cortège at various points on the way from Milford towards Tullyconnel, and at Rossnakill the procession halted so that all could be given green armbands. A large number of police were present and many officers on plain clothes duty mingled with the mourners as the hearse travelled to the graveyard. Some said that Heraghty had not died, that he had been smuggled out of gaol and made his way to America, and that the coffin was filled with clay.

A ballad was made on Heraghty's death, which has been recorded in several versions but has so far remained unprinted. Authorship of the ballad has been attributed to one Jerry Boyce, of Donegal town, without firm evidence. Some stanzas run:

You friends to truth and justice throughout green Erin's Isle,
I humbly crave attention and ask you for a while
With Christian zeal and ferverance to join this mournful wail
On the death of Michael Heraghty who died in Lifford Gaol.

For the murder of Lord Leitrim on a sunny April morn,
From house and home, from kith and kin he rashily (ruthlessly) was torn,
On a mere suspicion of the crime for which it was confessed
He was guiltless as a newborn babe upon its mother's breast . . .

And you, my friends, may well conclude, with firm conviction rest,

His care within those prison walls was nothing of the best.
He died of (typhoid) fever arising from a cold.
Such was the doctor's statement here in the press we're told.

Oh, what a glorious sight it was upon his funeral day
To see three thousand marching forth, robes all in rich array,
Of stalward sturdy brave young men who all green ribbons
    wore.
You would not their equals find around our shamrock shore.

Five hundred of our peasant girls this grand procession joined.
For glorious deeds our Irish girls are never left behind.
The part they played on Limerick walls two hundred years ago
They would repeat tomorrow if necessity forced them so . . .[15]

History is the account of what happened; also of what people
believe to have happened. The massive, and for the most part as
yet unindexed, archive of the Irish Folklore Collections in
University College, Dublin, contains a number of manuscript
interviews with ordinary people, relating to Lord Leitrim, his
character, and the circumstances of his assassination. A random
few are quoted here. Through these documents, the peasant
speaks.

In the days o' the shootin o' the landlords in Tipperary the leadin
characters o' the world were there. There was the gallant farmer
Hayes, there was Rory on the Hill, and I don't know did Rory darlin
live in them days. There was a song composed for Rory darlin, and I
only know the chorus of it:

'Rise up, Rory darling, for they're knocking at the door,
There is no room for us in Ireland and the place is ours no more.'

Well, that's all I have of that *drachtín*, but there was a poor fellow by
name Rory on the Hill and there was a landlord in Tipperary and
twas very hard to get him. He had a band o' soldiers as a guard, and
he'd never come outside his own door until the sun id be risin in the
heavens, and before he'd come out the guard o' soldiers id come on
the entrance of the door and stand on each side of the door. He'd
come along then and he'd stand in the middle o' the door.
  Well, there was lots cast among the great fellows to know who'd
do him, but there was wan fellow in the job and he had six children,
and when the lots were cast this poor fellow's name came out; and
Rory says: 'Put 'em back agin,' he says, 'and give him another
chance.' His name came out the second time, and Rory says to him:

'You have a wife and children,' he says. 'Go home and mind 'em. I'll go and do it.' So he was to get an accomplice then, to go and do it. And there was a bottle o' whiskey got, and his accomplice got a glass o' whiskey and he refused it. He said: 'The hand is steady,' he says. 'I'll go and do that job,' he says, 'myself.'

So he was asked then how would he do it. He said that he'd bring provisions that id do him for three days, and that he ought to come outside his own door inside three days anyway. 'The sun ought to come in the heavens, but as shure as twill come there and he'll stand at the door,' he says, 'I'll drop him.' So he went there and he was twenty-four hours waitin at the door when the door opened and the soldiers came out, and this big buck came and he stood in the centre o' the door, and as soon as he did, Rory dropped three bullets into him and left him there and went back into his own field. So when he went back into his own field he was goin home that night and he met a priest, that was the parish priest o' the place, and he says to him: 'Rory, you'd want to go to confession.' 'Well, there's another fellow above there, and as soon as I'll be after gettin him I'll gup to you, father.'

He was wan day in the field and there was a fellow came in talking to him, and he says: 'They'll be evictions over here tomorrow,' he says, 'and the landlord,' he says, 'is going to town today.' So Rory used to have a gun in the field, and he come along to the fence, and he see the lad comin and he shot him, and he stuck the gun in the fence after doin it. So the police and the soldiers then went searchin, and they found the gun in the fence, and theyre was a watch put over the gun then; the soldiers or police were watchin it. When he thought everything was after dyin out then he went for the gun, and Rory on the Hill was hanged on circumstantial evidence: He went along and he pulled out the gun and he was hanged over that. That's all I know about poor Rory.

(From Liam Ó Cuirrin, Dugarvan, Co. Wexford)[16]

Lord Leitrim was an English landlord who was sent over to Ireland to persecute the Irish. He used to go about from house to house, and if there were any of the daughters he took a fancy to, he had to get her. And if the people of the house wouldn't let the girl go, he would turn them out on the roadside.
Once upon a time, a woman had three daughters. The youngest was a very beautiful girl and her mother liked her the best of the three. One day, Lord Leitrim went into the house and said to the mother: 'I want this daughter of yours. Let her come with me.' And he pointed to the youngest daughter. The woman cried and wouldn't let her go, but Lord Leitrim brought her away with him.

A crowd of boys from the neighbourhood went to Lord Leitrim's castle. They climbed up a big tree at the front of the castle and watched. After some time, Lord Leitrim was going out to walk. The men in the tree fired a shot at Lord Leitrim, and killed him on the steps of his castle.

(From Mrs Halton (70), Kilnaleck, Co. Cavan, via her daughter Rosaleen, 1938)[17]

Lord Laytrim was a bad rascal. The people used to say that he was not the son of Lord Laytrim at all but the son of a tinker. The story is that there was a tinker's camp near Lough Rynn Castle the night that Lord Laytrim was born, and that a son was born to a tinker woman that same night, and the auld people say that the tinker's son was changed for the real son of Lord Laytrim. There was a song which said: "He was unlike his father, who was so good and kind'.

This Lord who was afterwards ambushed and killed in Donegal had many by-children or bastards. He had a very big nose and people used to say of a boy or girl that they were by-children of Lord Laytrim. For example they'd say: 'That's a daughter of Lord Laytrim, wouldn't you know the nose?'

(From an anonymous informant, Co. Longford, 1955)[18]

One hundred years ago, and even later still, it was customary among the gentry to have their children reared by a foster-mother. Young Clements, the eldest son of the (Second) Earl of Leitrim, when being fostered in the house of one of his father's tenants, died. The tenant was afraid to incur the anger of his landlord, so he bought a child from the McDonaghs, a band of travelling tinkers who came to Leitrim from Galway. The Earl never suspected that the man who was to be his heir was not his own son. Many old people accept the theory. Personally, I wouldn't venture to put it forward to a McDonagh.

(From James Gilheany (80), Clogher, Co. Roscommon[19]

In olden times Lord Leitrim was the landlord. He lived in Lough Rynn Castle occupied now by Colonel Clements. He used to go round lifting the rent in a carriage with six white horses. He was a very bad man and everybody was afraid of him, for if you had not the rent for him he would employ men and they would toss the house on you. If you had not the rent for him, if there was a nice girl in the family he would take her off in his carriage to work in his castle in payment for the rent. Some of the girls returned and some never returned. That was the reason he met with his death in Donegal, owing to taking away these girls.

(From Emma Wood, Crickeen, Carrowallen, 1938)[20]

Every nice girl he would see he would take them with him. And if he wouldn't get them he would put the fathers and mothers out of their homes. So he would take the girls to his own house and keep them as servants. He would have about ten nice girls in the house and he had no need for them. He said he would leave the Catholics as scarce as eagles on the hills.

(From an anonymous informant, Co. Donegal, 1938)[21]

The *old* Earl of Leitrim was one of the best landlords in Ireland, and I'll tell you why: because Phil Higgins, who lived in Killamaun where Micky Gildea now lives, built a mill, and one day the Earl was going to the Assizes at Carrick in his coach and Phil crossed him at the bridge and told him what he had done. The Earl said: 'A very good idea.' 'My Lord,' said Phil, 'I have no money to put works in it.' 'I'll complete it,' says the Earl. 'I have another request to make,' says Phil. 'There are two small tenants between me and the road, and if your Lordship would shift them, it would give me great liberty.' 'Level the mill, Higgins,' said his Lordship. 'Don't leave a stone on a stone or I'll shift you!' Shh, he was a great landlord. His son the murdered earl, when he became owner, he summoned all the tenants to the rent office and doubled the rents in the majority of cases. And when after putting rack rents on tenants, he'd always say: 'The weightier I load you, the tamer you'll pull.'

(From Owen McGann (75), Killamaun, Mohill, Co. Leitrim)[22]

He was a very hard pleased man and oftentimes when tenants came to pay their rent, if they were anything short he would fire shots over their heads and beat him severely.

(Anonymous informant, Co. Leitrim, 1938)[23]

When we were living in Co. Leitrim, I would be listening to them talking about the killing of Lord Leitrim. He had an estate between Garradice and Newtowngore. He evicted several families and there was nothing left on the whole side of a big hill but the walls of the cabins that they were evicted out of. There were gaps along the road leading into the evicted farms, and Lord Leitrim put gates on them. They were painted black, and they called them 'The black gates of Leitrim'.

(From Patrick Smith, Co. Cavan, September 1950)[24]

One day (the tenants) agreed they would kill him and get a better man in his place. They marched as far as his house and asked to see Lord Leitrim. They also told his wife to get out of the house, and to take anything that she wished to take but to leave her husband in the house. She told the men that she would take as much as she was able to carry in a sack she held in her hand. When she returned to the house, she put her husband into the sack and left the house. The soldiers, little dreaming what she had in the bag, went into the spacious building to seek for the man. They then discovered what had happened, and they put the hounds to scent their track. After a few days, when they were nearly dead, they found him in the north of Ireland.

(From James Fox (71), Ballyboy, Manorhamilton, Co. Leitrim, May 18, 1938)[25]

At the time Lord Leitrim was killed in Donegal, his footman warned him at Lough Rynn Castle, previous to his going to Donegal, saying that Rory of the Hill or his men might meet him on his journey. The warning he got only enraged him, and he proceeded on his journey with a full bodyguard of his servants and agents and bailiffs, to carry out evictions. It appears some of his chosen bodyguard was in the private pay of Rory of the Hill, because one of the horses accompanying his entourage was driven lame before leaving from Lough Rynn Castle by the blacksmith that shod him. On the journey to Donegal this horse and caravan were not able to keep up with Lord Leitrim's coach.

(From an unnamed informant, Co. Leitrim, 1938)[26]

Lord Leitrim left from Lough Rynn, Mohill, on All Fools' Day '82, with his bums, sheriff and bailiffs to evict his tenants in Donegal who were not able to pay their rent. He was met on the way before he arrived by two gallant heroes. They call them Rorys. When they found him coming, their hearts jumped with glee. They gave three cheers for tenants' right, Home Rule and liberty. First they fired shots killing his horses. Then they fired on Lord Leitrim, but they were not able to kill him for he was dressed in armour. They had to haul him from his coach and kill him with their guns. Maxims, his driver, was shot dead too. He was shot dead; cried for mercy but got none. They answered him: 'No, no, for when you lie with dogs you'll surely rise with fleas!' So they threw him in a pool in Donegal and crossed the lake in a boat. It was the delight of Donegal to hear of his fate.

(From Mrs J. Kiernan, Augharan, Carrigallen, Co. Leitrim, 1938)[27]

The day he was killed he was going to evict about twelve families in Donegal. One of his horses was shod the day before. The blacksmith quicked him. This horse was going to bring the ammunition. The next day the horse struck lame when he had gone a few miles of the road. When he struck lame, Lord Leitrim was in a rage and would not wait for the ammunition. They were called on to halt when they were about half a mile from the ammunition. They did not halt, and one of the horses was shot. Three men were left in ambush to shoot Lord Leitrim. They fired at him and he only smiled. Then they saw he had a coat of armour, and they beat in his skull with the ends of their guns. A man named Makim ran back the road to tell the men with the ammunition not to come or they would be killed. When he told them he dropped dead on the road with fright.

(From Pat Kennedy (75), Milltron, Carrigallen, Co. Leitrim)[28]

Clements was his name. Even the Phoenix Park in Dublin belonged to him. The people of Leitrim made many unsuccessful attempts to take away his life, and the people of Donegal, equally enraged, ended his life by strategem. Evidently he was aware of his unpopularity, and he invariably had the shoes of his horse turned backwards so as to deceive his pursuers. He was usually protected by a coat of armour and accompanied by four footmen when driving in his coach or riding. His Donegal pursuers, aware of this fact, killed one of the horses, murdered the four footmen, then attacked Lord Leitrim who was then incapable of defending himself. His death was encompassed by shooting him through the head or mouth, his own gun being found in his mouth after his death. It was believed that on the morning of his last day on earth a woman in Donegal gave the sign of his approach by spreading a white sheet on a certain bush.

(From school, Cara Droma Ruise, Kiltoghert, Co. Leitrim)[29]

One day his horse lost a shoe and he had to come to Milford to appoint a new clerk because the old one had drowned himself. Before he left he had to get his horse shod in a little village near Mulroy called Carrigart . . . When the blacksmith shod the horse he drove a nail crooked and made the horse lame.

After this, Lord Leitrim left for Milford. The horse was getting lamer and lamer so that it could hardly walk. When Lord Leitrim came to Cratlagh Wood, a boatload of men from Fannet were waiting for him, so as he came near the Sounding Drum the men had guns and fired at him. His horseman, Charlie Buchanan, was shot dead, and Lord Leitrim could have escaped, but with great anger he came back with a stick to fight the men. When he came back the men battered him with the butt of the gun until they killed him.

Daddy was in a house where he saw the gun which shot Lord Leitrim. When they were showing the gun to another man, Daddy happened to see it. When the people saw him, they were sorry they showed the gun.

(From Irish Diver, Milford, Co. Donegal, *ca.* 1938)[30]

The morning he was killed in Donegal, when Kincaid the valet brought in the shaving water to his bedroom, he asked him not to go on the journey that day, as he was dreaming strange dreams the night before. But Lord Leitrim answered, so the song says:

> Sure, of Rory or the devil I never was afraid.
> I'd drive single or in tandem from Lough Rynn to Donegal.
> Make them sign to my agreements, bog tenants one and all . . .

After some distance out, the horse pulling the policeman got a nail in his hoof and couldn't go any further. At a bend in the road near a lake, a shot rang out and hit the driver and killed him instantly. Leitrim couldn't come down off the car without turning round, as he was lame and walked with a halt. When he turned round to come down, he had to grip both sides of the seat. Then his assailant jumped on to the seat beside him and killed him with a blow of a gun on the base of the skull.

Makim the agent died from shock, and the only one to escape was Kincaid the valet. . . . It is said that there was a fistful of red hair in Leitrim's hands after his death.

(From the son of John Gray, Mohill, Co. Leitrim, who
heard it from his father in 1898 or 99)[31]

Two Fanad men lay in watch for his coming. All of a sudden they fired three shots. They did not kill him out, so they finished him with the fourth shot. The both men that killed him fled by boat across Mulroy Bay. Unfortunately, one of the men was captured and taken prisoner. Some of his friends got in touch with the gaol wardens. They planned that he had taken ill and died, which was not true. They realized their danger, and coffined a skeleton instead, and buried it. The Fanad man fled to America afterwards.

(From Bernie Coyle, Letterkenny, Co. Donegal, *ca.* 1938)[32]

An old man who suffered under Lord Leitrim was coming to town. He met a priest, who told him Lord Leitrim was shot. 'Well, your reverence,' says he, 'I am very sorry to hear that.' 'That's very charitable of you,' says the priest, 'as you certainly had no cause to love him.' 'It's not that, father,' said he, 'but he'll be putting notions in the devil's head he'd never think of.'

(From Seamus Wilson, Manorhamilton, Co. Leitrim, 14 January 1938)[33]

He was coming to put a new clerk in his office because the old one was drowned. A crowd of people from Fannet who knew he was coming came over in a boat and waited for him at the wood now known as the Sounding Drum. As they were coming through the wood the people of Fannet shot at Lord Leitrim but missed him and shot Charlie Buchanan dead. The horse ran on about a hundred yards, and Lord Leitrim could have escaped, only that he was so angry that he got out and ran back to fight them with a stick. They couldn't load their gun in time, so they took the stump of the gun and battered him to death.

Lord Leitrim's butler was coming behind him in a car, but he was about two miles behind him. His horse was supposed to have been made lame because that morning, when the butler – whose name was Kincaid – was getting his horse in the forge, there was an unusually large crowd, and when they heard of his coming with the earl, they were supposed to have put nails in the horse and to make him lame. They did this because all the rifles were in the butler's car . . . The late Cardinal Logue's father was the driver of Kincaid's car.

(From Robert Hazlett (86), Milford, Co. Donegal, *ca.* 1938)[34]

The horses that drew Lord Leitrim's corpse from the place he was shot to Milford, the hooves fell off them.

When he was entering Cratlagh Wood his horse was shot. Then three men ran out of the bushes and shot the driver. They then pulled Lord Leitrim down off his car and tried to shoot him, but they couldn't because he had a steel coat and helmet on him. One of the men fired two shots down his throat. They took him then and smothered him in the water-table. Leitrim caught the man by the moustache and tore it off his face.

There was a man by the name of Heraghty who shot Lord Leitrim. He was taken to Lifford Gaol and was kept there. A friend of his was a priest. He passed a bill in Parliament to get him out of gaol. They got him out and sent him on a ship to America. They said he died in Lifford Gaol with faiver. They took him down in a coffin to Massmount and buried it. There were up to ten hundred people, boys and girls, at the funeral. He was not in the coffin at all.

(From an unnamed informant, Donegal, 1938)[35]

On this April morning, he was on his way to Leitrim on business. He quite well understood his unpopularity and consequently never travelled without an escort. On this particular morning the horses of the escort were owned by a man in Carrigart, the father of the great Cardinal Logue. This man got information that an attempt was to be made on Lord Leitrim's life on his way to Milford, where his offices were. He therefore drove nails in the horse's hoofs the night before, so that the horses carrying the escort couldn't keep pace with the carriage of the landlord. Those who planned and carried out the murder were three young men of Fanad named Herrity, McElwee and (blank in original). A little hawthorn bush beside a gate marks the spot where the actual murder took place.

Two horses were sent out from Milford to bring the corpses into Milford. One of the horses which brought the corpse of Lord Leitrim to Milford dropped dead after reaching Milford.

The story is told that a policeman from the barracks in Milford was on his way to Fanad one morning to arrest McElwee on the strength of information received from a Protestant man named Doak, who was a personal friend of Lord Leitrim and often assisted him in his eviction plans. The police called in to a public house in Fanad to have a drink before arresting McElwee. He had a few drinks in order to firm up his nerves. The barman remarked to the policeman that the murderers of Lord Leitrim were still at large. 'Yes,' answered the policeman sarcastically, 'but before many more minutes they will be behind iron bars.' He reached for his drink, let over the drink in one gulp, and walked towards the door. But before he reached there, he dropped dead. The body was brought to Milford, and the death caused much speculation in the district.

Herrity's trial was being postponed from court to court for lack of conclusive evidence to convict him. Many were working for his escape and several of the warders conspired to help him escape. They arranged it thus: Herrity was given some drug which, although harmless, caused Herrity to have a very high temperature. Herrity feigned sickness and it was soon rumoured that Herrity was dangerously ill in gaol. The startling news was spread that Herrity had died. The 'body' was brought home with great scenes of sorrow to his native Fanad, and the actual 'burial' took place. Crocodile tears were shed in plenty and the whole countryside sympathized with the stricken relatives who played their part excellently in the great camouflage. Herrity, who, needless to say, was very much alive, had little difficulty with the help of willing friends to make good his escape to America and there rejoined his two friends.

It is said that not a blade of grass ever grew on the spot where Leitrim's head fell.

(From Barney Boyce, Milford, Co. Donegal, *ca.* 1938)[36]

Colonel Clements, better known as Lord Leitrim. Perhaps the king of all the landlords for tyranny and cruelty. It was on his way, as the song relates, to hyrdle down the cabins in his demesne that this cruel monster was laid low. The news of his death was no doubt hailed with joy by his tenants and the whole Catholic people of Ireland as well as Donegal and Leitrim, was hailed with joy. The whole place was alive with bonfires.

> (From John Farell, Drumhass, Annaghmore, Mohill,
> Co. Leitrim, *ca.* 16 September 1938)[37]

It seems that three men were directly concerned with the ambush – Nial Shiels of Doaghmore, Michael McElwee of Ballywhoriskey, and Michael Heraghty of Tullyconnell. Nial Shiels was a tailor, and when he was teaching his son the trade, he often spoke of the events of the assassination. From these accounts, the son – Neil Shiels – pieced together the story, which was printed in a pamphlet, *The Fanad Patriots*, published in Letterkenny, Co. Donegal, about 1958.

On the night of April 1st at 10 p.m., Michael McElwee came to the Shiels home to make arrangements. Both left Doaghmore at 11.30, and picked up Heraghty on the way. All three were armed with muzzleloading guns charged with heavy slugs.

They went to a part of Muineag locally called the Bog, took a boat and crossed to the Rossgill side, where they changed boats. They arrived at Cratlagh Wood about 7 a.m., and took positions on the shore side of the road to await Lord Leitrim. A stroller passed, and the others, suspecting he may have noticed something suspicious, sent Heraghty to shadow him. Heraghty left his gun behind.

Shortly after Heraghty's departure, a car with Lord Leitrim, Buchanan (driver) and Makim (Court Clerk), arrived. McElwee opened fire and mortally wounded the driver. Makim next fell; both died on the roadside. Lord Leitrim was fired on but the car had proceeded some fifty yards, and he seemed uninjured. McElwee and Leitrim got to hand-grips. Lord Leitrim, though over seventy, seemed to be getting the better of McElwee. Shiels picked up Heraghty's gun, and with a blow on the head left Lord Leitrim lifeless on the roadside, the impact shattering the stock of the gun. The stock was left behind.

The men took to sea and arrived at the Hawk's Nest, a short distance below Milford Quay on the Fanad side. They proceeded over Ranny Hill above Kerrykeel, round the base of Knockalla, and finally arrived at Dan Sweeney's of Dargan, where Shiels was unemployed as a travelling tailor. McElwee continued through Kindrum Hill, Ballyhiernan, and arrived home in Ballywhoriskey. He died soon after of the black fever (typhus).* Heraghty, hearing of the death of Leitrim in Milford, went towards Doon Well, and from

---

* In fact he died in 1880 (A.L.L.)

thence returned through Cranford, passing Leitrim's castle on his way to Mulroy Ferry, where he crossed and arrived home. Shortly after, he was arrested and lodged in Lifford Jail, accused of being the owner of the gun found at the scene of the shooting. He died while awaiting trial. Shiels continued in his profession, never arrested, and died in 1921.[38]

In 1960, a memorial cross was erected at Kindrum, Co. Donegal, to the men who ambushed Lord Leitrim. It has this inscription in Irish and English: 'Erected to the memory of the three Fanad patriots, Nial Shiels, Doaghmore; Michael Heraghty, Tullyconnell; Michael McElwee, Ballywhoriskey; who by their heroism in Cratlagh Wood on the morning of April 2nd 1878 ended the Tyranny of Landlordism.'

A tailpiece to illustrate the verdancy of the historical memory in Ireland. The folklorist Tom Munnelly writes in a private letter to me (21 June 1978): 'My own first encounter with Lord Leitrim was when I used to attend the Fiddlers' Club in Church Street where he lies buried. Two middle-aged musicians, a fiddler and a flute player, used to make a point of going into the graveyard and urinating on the spot nearest to his vault, which is in the church of St Michan. This they did every week on their way home from the Club. Need I add that they are both Leitrim men?'

NOTES

1 The recording is deposited in the BBC's Archive of Folk and National Music Recordings. The prefix 'S' implies 'Not to be broadcast'.

2 From *The Freeman's Journal* (Dublin), Thursday, 11 April 1878, p. 3.

3 *The Fanad Patriots*, Compiled by a local committee. Letterkenny, Co. Donegal. Printed by McKinney & O'Callaghan, Main Street, n.d., p. 23, (The record of Court Proceedings were made available by the Boyce family of Drumniagh, Portsalon.)

4 ibid., p. 34.

5 p. 27.

6 p. 32.

7 p. 36.

8 p. 41.

9 p. 43

10 p. 46.

11 p. 49.

12 p. 49.

13 p. 50.
14 p. 51.

The following references prefixed IFC come from the manuscript volumes of the Irish Folklore Collections in the Irish Folklore Department, University College, Dublin (formerly The Irish Folklore Commission). An 'S' prefix indicates the *MSS na Scol* collection. I owe the sight of these documents to the generosity of Dr D. K. Wilgus, of the University of California at Los Angeles. They are reproduced here by permission of the Head of the Department of Irish Folklore, University College, Dublin.

15 IFC vol. 619, pp. 208–12, from Bhrigid Bean Ui Cearr, Co. Meath, March 29, 1939.
16 IFC Vol. 184, pp. 50–4.
17 IFC S994, pp. 277–8.
18 IFC Vol. 1457, p. 425.
19 IFC S225, p. 168.
20 IFC S229, p. 42.
21 IFC S1090, p. 482.
22 IFC S215, pp. 289–90.
23 IFC Vol. 512, p. 562.
24 IFC Vol. 1197.
25 IFC S197, pp. 23–4. A traditional motif, in this case transferred from a legend concerning Sir Frederick Hamilton, landlord of Manorhamilton in the seventeenth century.
26 IFC Vol. 512, p. 564.
27 IFC S226, pp. 83–4.
28 IFC S229, p. 390.
29 IFC S209, pp. 202–3.
30 IFC S1087, pp. 73–5.
31 IFC S237, pp. 16, 20–1.
32 IFC S1083, pp. 64–5.
33 IFC S195, pp. 277–8.
34 IFC S1087, pp. 68–70.
35 IFC S1090, pp. 480–3.
36 IFC S1081, pp. 29–30.
37 IFC S222, p. 577.
38 *The Fanad Patriots*, p. 53.

BERNARD SHAW
AND THE NEW SPIRIT

ARNOLD KETTLE

It has seemed to me for some time that much Marxist or left-wing assessment of the work of Bernard Shaw has been less than satisfactory. It is true that Shaw was in many respects a vulnerable figure. Both in his life and his art he offered a great many hostages to fortune, and fortune – in the form of the deepening crisis of capitalist society through which he lived so long – wasn't slow to take advantage of the situation. Yet when one has totted up the errors and the sillinesses, the false hunches and the jokes that fell flat or rebounded against him, what remains is greatly impressive and, like so much good writing, not easily predictable. It is not hard to see in a general way how he emerges out of the stresses and contradictions of his time; yet it is no easier to 'explain' him than it would have been to foresee those others he so much admired: Mozart and Wagner, Dickens and Ibsen. And perhaps what one most wants to say of him is that it is in the end to that company that he belongs.

What follows cannot of course be in the nature of a reassessment of Shaw's work. That would need far more than a short essay. All I can hope to do is to suggest certain approaches and perspectives that might make possible a more full and satisfactory estimate.

Caudwell in his essay on Shaw in *Studies in a Dying Culture* strikes a note I would want to query.

> Faced with proletarianisation, he clung to the bourgeois class. In the same way, faced with the problem of ideological proletarianisation in his reading of Marx, he resisted it, and adhered to Fabianism, with its bourgeois traditions and its social responsibility . . .

Well, yes, one sees what he means all right. And it isn't untrue. But is it really what most matters, what most needs to be said? Isn't there perhaps even something rather dangerously Platonic in the approach, a setting up of ideal standards, embodied in the word proletarianisation, and an insistence on judging not only a man's life but also his work against that ideal standard. One hesitates to use that argument with Caudwell who did himself make precisely that effort – and at the cost of his life – which he accuses Shaw of shirking. Yet the suspicion remains that, in concentrating so single-mindedly on what Shaw *wasn't* or on what he might have been, Caudwell runs the risk of missing what he was, what he brought to the movement he always tried, with whatever foibles and failures, to serve. To stress too much the role of Shaw as misleader is unsatisfactory not because the charges that can be made against him may not have truth in them, but because it becomes so easy, in the process, to miss what is truly original, the contribution no one else did or could make.

It is interesting to recall that Caudwell's criticism, which rather too readily equates Shaw's weaknesses with his Fabianism, is not in some ways so very different from that of Shaw's own Fabian friend and colleague Beatrice Webb. She too was shocked by what seemed to her Shaw's frivolity or irresponsibility, feeling that he sold the pass for the sake of effect or applause or some sort of bourgeois approval. In 1905, the day after taking the (Tory) Prime Minister to see *Major Barbara* at the Royal Court, she wrote in her diary:

> I doubt the popular success of the play: it is hell tossed on the stage – with no hope of heaven. G.B.S. is gambling with ideas and emotions in a way that distresses slow-minded prigs like Sidney and me . . . But the stupid public will stand a good deal from one who is acclaimed as an unrivalled wit by the great ones of the world . . .

I think that what both Caudwell and Beatrice Webb underestimated is the liberating effect of good art and, in particular, the complexity of the way that effect can work. It is true that the 'moral' of *Major Barbara seems* to be that the capitalist realist Undershaft holds all the cards. But the deeper burden of the play is that power can never be effectively challenged by idealism and Shaw's ability to open up *that* question for his audience is in the long run worth a score of easier moral victories to comfort the converted.

A more recent assessment of Shaw from the left – by Raymond Williams – seems to me representative of what a great many people nowadays think about Shaw:

> Shaw's dynamic as a dramatist is surely weakening, and it seems impossible that it can, as a major force, survive the period of which

he was a victim. Respect for his ability to laugh at a great deal of persistent nonsense will certainly endure; and respect for his great wit and for his skilful forensic and burlesque . . . but the emotional inadequacy of his plays denies him major status. He withered the tangible life of experience in the pursuit of a fantasy of pure intelligence and pure force.

It is a formidable dismissal and all the more so because it stresses Shaw's role as 'victim', isolated and frustrated by the socio-historical situation of his time and especially by the weaknesses of the British Labour movement and the strength of British bourgeois philistinism. But, again, it seems to me to go somehow wrong and to grant Shaw too little. And in this respect it is in striking contrast with the views of Shaw's most persistent defender among twentieth-century dramatists: Bertolt Brecht.

Brecht did not idealise Shaw. But he recognised him generously as one of the writers with whom he had special affinities. When he was working on his *Life of Galileo* his mind would go back to Shaw's *Saint Joan*, another twentieth-century chronicle-play set in the past and one he had watched from behind the scenes in the course of production in the twenties, when Max Reinhardt directed it in Berlin and Elisabeth Bergner was Joan. Brecht saw Shaw's Epilogue, in which Joan reappears, so to speak, both in and outside history, as his attempt to achieve the sort of 'distancing' or 'objectivising' effect that Brecht called *Verfremdung* and regarded as so important to his own drama. He was not satisfied with Shaw's solution and when, in East Berlin after the war, he himself worked on a Joan play for the Berliner Ensemble (an adaptation of a radio play by Anna Seghers entitled *The Trial of Joan of Arc at Rouen* 1431) he produced his own solution by writing a final scene for the play, placed squarely in France in 1436, by which he avoided the mystical element in Shaw's Epilogue. I mention the point merely to establish that Brecht's relationship to Shaw isn't just of the 'literary-history' sort, or my own hunch.

I think it can be fruitful to look at Shaw in the light of Brecht's subsequent achievement because the tendency has been to see Shaw's work too much as a failure to establish a socialist drama and insufficiently as a creative move in that direction. This tendency, I'd suggest, is what leads to Raymond Williams's dismissal which I have quoted, and it seems to me to inform also much of what is by far the most serious and rewarding Marxist study of Shaw – Alick West's *A Good Man Fallen among Fabians*.

To achieve the perspective I am proposing – a perspective more revelatory of what is truly valuable (and progressive) in his drama – it is necessary to see Shaw historically, not only in relation to the socialist movement of his time but also in relation to the development of modern European drama.

My hypothesis is that there are two very great modern European dramatists, dominant in the sense we can now see Shakespeare to have dominated the drama of his time and after. These are Ibsen and Brecht. They are great not simply in themselves, measured in terms of the quality of their individual output, but in terms of their centrality to their times and, consequently, the depth of their influence, which will outlast superficial movements of taste and fashion.

Ibsen, starting from an unlikely base in Scandinavia and a slightly more promising German tradition, wrought a fully serious drama out of the most basic human dilemmas and developments of mid-nineteenth-century bourgeois Europe. If one calls it a bourgeois drama, that is not because most of the characters belong to the middle-class nor because Ibsen is uncritical of bourgeois society and its values; but rather because it is a drama that operates and makes its effect within a structure of feeling and – to a large extent – ideological assumption that is at bottom bourgeois. Ibsen's people are stripped – before us and each other and themselves – of layer after layer of ideological comfort and illusion and falsity; but scarcely a hint of an alternative way of living emerges: as with Wagner, the redemptive vision of the love of a good woman is sometimes offered, but it in no serious way resolves the contradictions that have been revealed with that remorseless technique for the uncovering of ghosts that Ibsen perfected. As with Shakespeare and Brecht, Ibsen brings a world out into the open. Yet 'open' is not really quite the word one wants, for his art – even in *Peer Gynt*, the most 'open' of his plays – is much less open than theirs, much more caught up in the obsessions and neuroses it portrays, with a certain ingrowing overintensity against which Brecht himself was consciously in reaction in *his* sustained attempt to open up the world for twentieth-century men and women.

Between Ibsen and Brecht the best of the dramatists –

Chekhov, Strindberg, Synge, O'Casey, even Pirandello – all contributed to the opening up of Ibsenite drama. Of all these the most original, the most brilliant and the hardest to characterise, is Bernard Shaw. His plays are remarkably unlike anyone else's, so that in seeing him historically, as one must, one is in no danger of undermining his idiosyncrasy. And since he saw himself historically, never for an instant considering his art timeless or spaceless, there is no excuse for our not doing so.

Unlike Brecht, who frequently used Ibsen's middle-period plays as examples of the sort of drama he mistrusted and sought to avoid, Shaw looked on Ibsen as a liberator and presented him as such to the public, especially in *The Quintessence of Ibsenism*, first published in 1891, but later revised in 1913 after Ibsen's death. *The Quintessence*, everyone agrees, tells us more about Shaw than about Ibsen. It makes Ibsen's plays seem more didactic and self-consciously 'progressive' than they are and exaggerates those elements which it suited Shaw's own purposes to stress in his determination to *épater le bourgeois*. Shaw seized on Ibsen because his plays, unlike almost all contemporary drama, struck him as truly serious. He represented, Shaw said, that 'new spirit' which alone could grapple with the needs of the time.

The 'new spirit' is not altogether easy to define. Shaw associated it explicitly with Mozart and Wagner, Chekhov and Tolstoy, Samuel Butler and the later Dickens: figures whose highest common factor of novelty doesn't spring spontaneously to mind. Put negatively, the new spirit was what George Eliot and Matthew Arnold hadn't got. Its absence struck him particularly in the work of Henry James, one of whose plays he described in the nineties in the following terms:

'Mr Henry James' intellectual fastidiousness remains untouched by the resurgent energy and wilfulness of the new spirit. It takes us back to the exhausted atmosphere of George Eliot, Huxley and Tyndall, instead of thrusting us forward into the invigorating strife raised by Wagner and Ibsen.

This gives us an important clue if we link the mention of George Eliot, Huxley and Tyndall with another statement of Shaw's, made in connection with his discovery of the supreme importance of the 'economic base'. This time he is describing (to his biographer Archibald Henderson) his experience of

listening in 1882 to a speech of Henry George and suddenly
seeing his own intellectual development in a new light.

> It flashed on me for the first time that 'the conflict between religion
> and science', . . . the overthrow of the Bible, the higher education of
> women, Mill on Liberty, and all the storm that raged round Darwin,
> Tyndall, Huxley, Spencer and the rest, on which I had brought
> myself up intellectually, was a mere middle-class business. Suppose
> it could have produced a nation of Matthew Arnolds and George
> Eliots – you may well shudder . . .

This explicit linking of the intellectual forces he had come to
reject with 'a mere middle-class business' seems to me very
important. Shaw never committed himself to a Marxist position
and kept up a running battle against Marxian economics; but
reading *Capital* was a decisive event in his intellectual
development and, even before that, he had clearly been
influenced by the sort of approach we have come to call Marxist.
That description of so much serious Victorian thinking as a
'mere middle-class business' indicates what it was that attracted
him about the creative artists in whom he recognised a 'new
spirit'. Wagner, Tolstoy, the later Dickens, Ibsen had all broken
through to forms of art which couldn't justly be subsumed
within the category 'a mere middle-class business'. Their work
expressed and stimulated an 'invigorating strife' which their
more class-bound *confrères* sought to muffle or cover up. The art
imbued with the 'new spirit' had the effect of opening up the
nature and problems of bourgeois society in a manner which
those whose work could be described as a mere middle-class
business were without the resources to achieve.

What linked the purveyors of the 'new spirit' was not a shared
philosophy in the more formal sense of the word. Nor was it
something easily covered by even a loose use of the word
'ideology'. It was, rather, the ability to 'open up' through their
art the world into which they had been born. What *The Magic
Flute*, *Little Dorrit*, *The Ring of the Nibelung*, *Peer Gynt*, *Anna
Karenina*, *The Cherry Orchard* and *Heartbreak House* have in
common isn't at all easy to define. Marxists have tended to use
the word 'realism' – indicating that good art uncovers reality –
and perhaps there is no better word: yet one can't help feeling
that it's a word with as many snags as advantages, implying
either too much or too little and tending to play down the

importance of artistic form. If I stress the phrase 'opening up' it is to try to suggest that an important part of the achievement of those in whom Bernard Shaw recognised the new spirit was their reaching out for *forms* that liberated themselves and their audience or readers from a certain kind of emotional relationship towards art which generates its reduction into a mere middle-class business.

Shaw picked out two aspects of Ibsen's plays which particularly appealed to him. One he called 'realism', which he associated with an extension of subject-matter – the serious treatment of people (servants, workers, 'common people') and situations which remained on the fringes of ruling-class art; the other he called 'discussion' – and he claimed that the introduction of this analytical element into his plays was Ibsen's most significant technical innovation. Shaw probably exaggerated the 'discussion' element in Ibsen (the sort of thing that occurs in the last act of *A Doll's House* when Nora insists on *analysing* her marriage); but if he did so it was, from his point of view, in a good cause; for what he was urging was the need for a drama that made the audience think as well as feel and forced them to re-examine cherished emotional attitudes and assumptions. His remark that 'the question which makes the (Ibsen) play interesting is which is the villain and which the hero?' indicates what attracted him to Ibsen and also the extent to which he was himself rejecting the Aristotelian view of drama with its emphasis on some kind of 'identification' of the audience with the progress of the hero.

Yet, for all his propaganda on behalf of Ibsen, Shaw always recognised that his own plays were quite different in kind from the Norwegian's: 'My own drama' he wrote (in 1904) 'is utterly unlike Ibsen in its stage methods and socialist view of human misery.' It is an important statement, not only because it should warn us against thinking of Shaw as a sort of Ibsen *manqué*, but also because of its linking of form with ideas. It was Shaw's *socialism* that made him want a new *form* of drama, not simply a drama which might have a propagandist usefulness, though he didn't despise that.

Shaw played up Ibsen and played down Shakespeare. Brecht did the opposite. Shaw, despite the important distinction between himself and Ibsen I have just emphasised, saw Ibsen primarily as a liberating force. Brecht, operating nearly half a century later (though he died only six years after Shaw) and in a very different socio-historical situation, had to reject Ibsenite drama. This was not, of course, because he didn't *appreciate* Ibsen or recognise his greatness, but because – a committed Marxist in a sense Shaw never was – he felt himself able to develop a dramatic theory far more thoroughgoing and radical than Shaw – caught up in the British situation – was able to contemplate. Through his rejection of the whole Aristotelian theory of drama, with its emphasis on ritual, catharsis and the special role of the hero, Brecht was able to evolve a new basis for the opening up of the drama as an integral part of the opening up of the social world. He saw Ibsenite drama as, for all its power and honesty, trapped in the categories of bourgeois ideology and dragging its audiences into a sort of complicity with the bourgeois attitudes it so relentlessly exposed. Shaw, as we've seen, to some extent took a similar line, emphasising his differences from as well as his debt to Ibsen: yet he was unable to develop for his own practice a theory as basically helpful as Brecht's 'epic theatre'.

It is not difficult for us, with our easier hindsight, to recognise that Shaw was tentatively but insistently feeling his way towards the kind of dramatic theory that was to serve Brecht. And it is not yet possible, in any case, to make a long-term assessment of the value of Brecht's theories (nor would he, with his insistence that the proof of the pudding is in the eating, want us to rush into one). Yet it seems to me useful to look at Shaw's practice in the light of Brecht's theory and I suspect that some of the current underestimation of Shaw's writing comes from a failure to see the two outstanding socialist dramatists of the twentieth century sufficiently in relation to one another.

When Raymond Williams writes (in the passage quoted above) of the 'emotional inadequacy' of Shaw's plays he seems to me to be expecting a Shaw play to be essentially *like* an Ibsen play in structure and mode of operation. That is to say, he seems to assume that the shape and structure of the play is governed by the shape and structure of the emotional situation which the dramatist is concerned to convey, so that the experience of the audience involves a high measure of 'identification' with the movement of the situation which is evoked on the stage. Now, I would not wish to argue that Shaw never works in this way: the endings of *Candida* and *Saint Joan* are instances and they are examples of Shaw at his most vulnerable. But I see them as somewhat exceptional: not in the sense that there are necessarily more good bits than bad ones in a Shaw play, but in the sense that they lead us away from his most basic originality.

That originality, I would suggest, lies most centrally in his concern about ideology and in his discovery of a dramatic structure – based on wit – which frames that concern in a creative way. The concern with ideology I have already touched on, his determination to create a drama that was more than a mere middle-class business. Shaw's plays are about power: it is his obsession, and an obsession which marks him out from the bulk of nineteenth-century British writers who run away from questions of power as from the plague and accept a bourgeois view of politics as a sort of professional technology. That is why it is misleading to describe his plays as 'drama of ideas'. What he is interested in, above all, is the power of *ideology* – that is to say, collections of ideas, attitudes, feelings and prejudices linked together by their relationship to certain general needs and aims, the needs and aims of certain people at a certain time. The coherence of an ideology lies, in practice, in the part it plays in serving the needs of a class. The very conception of an ideology rests on the recognition that ideas are themselves not 'pure' but gain their hold over men's minds through the importance they acquire as *forces* serving or preventing the realisation of felt and discovered needs. This Shaw came to understand, as a sort of revelation, in the eighteen-eighties. It took him a decade to discover how to incorporate his knowledge in a style. But a style is precisely what differentiates a play like *Mrs Warren's Profession* (in the nineties) from the bourgeois drama of the day. Because its subject is prostitution it took thirty years for the curtain to rise on a public performace of *Mrs Warren's Profession*, but when it goes up, the curtain (an ordinary west-end curtain in a west-end theatre, as middle-class as you like) goes up on an ordinary west-end theatrical scene and the people on the stage seem to be just like the people Pinero or Henry Arthur Jones or Tom Robertson or Wilde (at least before *The Importance of Being Earnest*) put there. But when they begin to talk you discover they are not the same people at all: or, rather, the same sort of people revealed in quite a new way and therefore different people. It is Shaw's style that has transformed them and that style is by no means a matter of tricks or technique or 'literary' qualities. The style is the ability to convey the power of ideology in the shaping of a human situation.

When Raymond Williams writes that despite our respect for his great wit we have to recognise the emotional inadequacy of Shaw's plays I think he is underestimating the part wit plays in Shaw's dramatic art. Wit, in a play like *Major Barbara*, is not an embellishment which improves the play, it is the motive-force which informs its very structure and movement. There is a moment in the second act of that play, set in the Salvation Army shelter in the East End, when Barbara introduces her father, the capitalist arms-manufacturer Undershaft, to the poor man Peter Shirley who has been forced, to his humiliation, to accept help from the Army. The following exchange takes place.

> BARBARA   . . . By the way, papa, what is your religion? in case I have to introduce you again.
> UNDERSHAFT   My religion? Well, my dear, I am a Millionaire. That is my religion.
> BARBARA   Then I'm afraid you and Mr Shirley won't be able to comfort one another after all. You're not a Millionaire, are you, Peter?
> SHIRLEY   No; and proud of it.
> UNDERSHAFT (*gravely*)   Poverty, my friend, is not a thing to be proud of.
> SHIRLEY (*angrily*)   Who made your millions for you? Me and my like. What's kep' us poor? Keepin' you rich. I wouldn't have your conscience, not for all your income.
> UNDERSHAFT   I wouldn't have your income, not for all your conscience, Mr Shirley.

What is involved here is not a dramatic situation embellished by a prettily-turned exchange *of dialogue*. The wit is basic to the whole enterprise and informs its very nature including the conception and presentation of character. The perception that a society in which one has to choose between conscience and income is intolerable is precisely what Shaw's play is about: not about the love-affair (if that's the word for it) between Barbara and Cusins or the family problem of who is to inherit the Undershaft millions. What I am driving at is that the dialectical wit which everyone recognises as a feature of Shaw's plays is the very basis of his dramatic method and the structural principle on which the plays are built. This is why people who expect Ibsen-type plays often complain that Shaw's 'fizzle-out', fail to achieve the sort of emotional climax the audience, imbued with Ibsen/Aristotelian anticipations of how a play should work, expects. If the endings of Shaw's plays are often arbitrary and almost incidental it is because the resolution of the situations – the interplay of forces – he has evoked remains for the future to work out: the air-raid in *Heartbreak House*, for example, brings the play to an end but is in no sense emotionally 'inevitable': it has no cathartic effect on the audience and the producer who tries to impose such an effect is wasting his time.

Running through a good deal of criticism of Shaw as a dramatist lies the complaint that, for all his talent, he is not truly serious: he spoils his good mind. There is, of course, plenty of justification for such criticism in the sense that the plays are very uneven with far too many bad jokes and irritating idiosyncrasies which time has not been kind to. But basically, I believe, the complaint is a disastrous one, sweeping aside Shaw's triumphs along with his failures. Again, Brecht can help put the perspective right. Writing in 1926 when he was in his twenties and Shaw was seventy, he said:

> Shaw has applied a great part of his talent to intimidating people to a point when it would be an impertinence for them to prostrate themselves before him . . .
>
> It will have been observed that Shaw is a terrorist. Shaw's brand of terror is an extraordinary one, and he uses an extraordinary weapon, that of humour . . .
>
> Shaw's terrorism consists in this: that he claims a right for every man to act in all circumstances with decency, logic and humour, and sees it as his duty to do so even when it creates opposition. He knows just how much courage is needed to laugh at what is amusing, and how much seriousness to pick it out. And like all people who have a definite purpose he knows that there is nothing more time-wasting and distracting than a particular kind of seriousness which is popular in literature and nowhere else . . .

Brecht was not, of course, so naive as to use the word terrorist blindly. He knew very well that terrorism in the revolutionary movement implies attitudes characteristic of the petty bourgeoisie rather than the working class and he wouldn't have disagreed with Caudwell's (or Lenin's) analysis of Shaw's political position. The word terrorist does indeed indicate one of Shaw's artistic weaknesses: just as the political terrorist easily becomes bomb-happy, the intellectual one tends to be idea-happy and Shaw could seldom resist a bright idea, even when it disrupted his own deeper purposes. But Brecht's remarks do much more than put a finger on one of Shaw's weaknesses: they also indicate his strength.

Behind what Brecht has to say about Shaw lie his own experiences of and reaction against a 'particular kind of seriousness', the German kind which found its expression not just in the heaviness of so much Romantic art but in a technique of obfuscation to which Marx in particular brought his special attention. Brecht's description of Shaw as a 'terrorist' is extraordinarily apt, especially when the word is linked with an emphasis on his humour or (as I would prefer to call it) wit. That image of Shaw the terrorist upsetting an applecart containing bourgeois concepts of what is and what isn't serious seems to me very much to the point, not only because it characterises Shaw's role in a plausible way but because it forces us to think about the whole concept of seriousness.

One of the most helpful ways of looking at much 'Modernist' literature of the early twentieth century is, I think, to recognise its role as puncturing or undermining the *sort* of seriousness, the sort of consciousness and therefore the sort of art which nineteenth-century capitalist society all the time tended to generate and encourage. Shaw and the modernist writers of his time had little sympathy for one another (T. S. Eliot said that Shaw as a poet was stillborn) but I think it may be fruitful to stress what Shaw and Brecht and the modernists had in common: an assault on the *forms* of bourgeois realism.

THE CONTRIBUTORS

MAURICE CORNFORTH, Marxist philosopher and lecturer, is the author of *The Open Philosophy and the Open Society*.

MARGOT HEINEMANN, Fellow and College lecturer in English at New Hall College, Cambridge, is the author of a forthcoming study of Thomas Middleton.

CHRISTOPHER HILL, retired Professor of History and Master of Balliol College, Oxford, is the author of, most recently, *The World Turned Upside Down* and *Milton and the English Revolution*.

ERIC HOBSBAWM, Professor of Economic and Social History at Birkbeck College, London, is the author of *The Age of Revolution* and *The Age of Capital*.

ARNOLD KETTLE, Professor of Literature at the Open University, is the author of *An Introduction to the English Novel*.

VICTOR KIERNAN, retired Professor of History at the University of Edinburgh, is the author of *Lords of Human Kind* and *Marxism and Imperialism*.

A. L. LLOYD, writer and broadcaster, is the author of *Folk Song in England* and *Come all ye bold miners*.

JACK LINDSAY, writer and critic, is the author of recent studies of William Morris, Gustave Courbet and William Blake.

EDGELL RICKWORD, poet and critic, was joint editor of *The Calendar of Modern Letters* and of *Left Review*.

JOHN SAVILLE, Professor of Economic and Social History at the University of Hull, is joint editor of the *Dictionary of Labour Biography* and the author of studies of Ernest Jones and Robert Owen.

WILLIE THOMPSON, Senior Lecturer in History at Glasgow College of Technology, is the editor of the *Scottish Marxist*.

NAME INDEX

Names have been omitted if they are marginal to the essay in which they appear and do not relate to wider contexts. Italic numbers refer to the pages of essays on the individual listed.